The Realities of Faith is a book about the changing status of the Christian faith in Western culture and the reorientation of its role as it confronts the forces of world revolution. The work had its beginning in the author's journey to India and Burma to deliver the Barrows Lectures.

In keeping with the purpose of the Lectureship, Professor Meland's initial intention was to bring to the peoples of the East a fresh glimpse of the thinking of the West bearing upon Christian faith and its witness to the modern age. The book became more than a set of lectures, however, for the author kept seeing new dimensions of the problems of faith and culture as he reflected upon his encounter with people of other faiths, and as he settled back in the grooves of Western culture.

Underlying the whole discussion are such questions as: Has Christianity run its course? Have we entered upon a post-Christian era? What bearing will science and the resurgence of non-Christian peoples have upon the witness to Christian faith? The author recognizes the widespread secularization of life in the West and the rise of secular forces in Eastern culture. At the same time he notes a decisive shift in the imagery of thought stemming from developments in modern science. As a result, Professor Meland says, modern man is awakening to dimensions of his existence which radically alter his attitude toward ultimate questions. Furthermore, he argues, explosive human energies are being released in modern societies, reasserting the claims of basic human needs at all levels of culture. The times call man back to something elemental and real.

Divinity School, University of Chicago. He was formerly Professor of Religion and Philosophy and Head of the Department, Central College, Fayette Missouri, and Associate Professor
Head of the Department, Pomon
fornia. He has been an editor of
Religion since 1946. He is the aut
of books, including *Faith and Cul.*
Education and the Human Spirit.

The Realities of Faith

The Realities of Faith

THE REVOLUTION
IN
CULTURAL FORMS

BERNARD EUGENE MELAND

The University of Chicago

53327

New York
OXFORD UNIVERSITY PRESS
1962

© Copyright 1962 by Oxford University Press, Inc.
Library of Congress Catalogue Card Number: 62-9826
Printed in the United States of America

To Margaret

Preface

All about us there is talk to the effect that Christianity has run its course; that, in fact, we have already entered upon a post-Christian era. The upsurge of nationalistic forces and non-Christian faiths among cultures of the East that have recently shaken off the bonds of Western control has given warning that Christian missions, as this has been commonly understood during the past century, has come to an end. What persists under this guise is in the nature of an interim holding operation, pending the maturing of indigenous Christian organizations capable of independent support and initiative. This turn of events in itself, however, should not be interpreted to mean the dissolution of Christian faith in Asia. If anything, there is promise of its achieving a more authentic witness within the cultures themselves. Nevertheless, something decisive is occurring in the over-all structure of missions altering the status and influence of Christianity abroad. And this is having consequences that impel reappraisal of the relevance of the Christian witness both at home and abroad.

The threat to the Christian ethos appears to be even more serious in developments within Western culture, in the form of a growing secular tide. Communism is only one expression of it. At the moment it represents the most formidable, self-conscious, and concerted attack upon the Christian ethos. Throughout Western culture, however, there are widespread manifestations of a growing secular temper ranging from an outspoken disavowal of Christian belief and imagery, in the interest of pursuing a more sharpened, scientific understanding of evolving man, to a crass indifference to all sensibilities of the spirit. Even within the churches, according to young ministers who are serving in them, there is appearing a cynical lethargy among people of the congregations who, as one young man put it, blandly dare the minister to evoke in them, if he can, a response to the Christian gospel. The much heralded upsurge of faith in this country, like the nationalistic renaissance of religions in the Far East, tends to obscure this movement of the human spirit away from the sensibilities of faith. And mass revivals tend only to consolidate the illusion that the Christian ethos is intact.

How real is this dissolution of faith? What is its meaning to Western culture and to people of other cultures who are inextricably bound up with this heritage of faith? These questions bear close scrutiny; for something of our destiny as people of faith and as citizens of a civilization now under threat are bound up with them. In this work I have addressed myself to various problems (out of which such questions arise) and have tried to find a responsible answer to them.

What impresses me about the present period of our history is the complexity and ambiguity of the forces that sustain and mold our way of living. Science and industry, for example, are reshaping the destinies of millions upon millions of people around the world, and in large measure are the benefactors of the human race. Yet out of these constructive labors are issuing also modes of interest and ways of living which radically impair and even dissipate the sensibilities and styles of living in the cultures to which they are bringing aid. Again, religious faiths the world over bear the burden of nurturing the human spirit in the deeper motivation of a heritage that looks toward an ultimate destiny and toward an ultimate measure of truth and justice in the ways of men. Yet, in culture after culture, one finds massive evidence to the effect that the religions have become but apologists for nationalistic zeal and ambition with little or no sense of responsibility for exercising prophetic judgment upon these ambitions, or of pointing beyond restrictive ends.

The malady that strikes at the vitals of modern civilization is a human introversion that leaves men unresponsive, if not insensitive, to realities beyond our own human formulations. The intensity of effort in the face of crises arising in rapid sequence leaves little room or incentive for self-criticism. Hence the points of view to which partisan groups cling tenaciously and the vested interests each cherishes drive human thought farther and farther from the realities that basically affect and mold our situations.

The role of Christian faith is not to decide between differences, but to bring the judgment of an ultimate measure to bear upon all differences motivated by the restrictive vision of self-interest and partisan ambition. What has limited our capacity for Christian criticism and Christian judgment has been the loss of distance between what is zealously sought within cultural objectives and what is apprehended in the witness of faith. The blurring of these two dimensions of experience, causing them to coalesce in some instances, has left us without clear directives, except as we have fashioned them for purposes at hand. And this has provided us with only expedient measures.

One of the underlying arguments of this book is that this loss of distance in modern culture, and, with it, the loss of a sense of judgment upon these expedient measures, has followed from a conception of man and of man's powers, formed in response to the scientific outlook dating from the seventeenth century. In a word, the mechanization of nature gave rise to an idealization of man and of the human equation. In this idealization of man, realism concerning the nature of our human existence went out of our mode of thinking and living; and, with it, a responsiveness to saving realities that are not of man's making.

The corrective of this misconception of man, I have argued, is not the abandonment of science, but a fuller acceptance of the new vision to which the sciences themselves have come, and, a recognition of the release which this vision brings from the circumscribed world-view of an earlier period of our history. For since the turn of the present century, the image of the world, and of man's powers to understand its reality, has been undergoing continual change as a result of radically new developments in modern physics following the discovery of radiation and the formulation of relativity and quantum-mechanical theories.

The dispatch with which modern physicists came to terms with this new image of nature, and set to work to alter their method and mode of experimentation, attests not only to their flexibility and adaptability in meeting new situations but to their humility of mind as well. They had much to lose professionally and personally in abandoning what, for the scientific world as well as for Western culture generally in the nineteenth century, had become a fixed view of nature. Scientists who placed vested interests and professional comfort above the call of inquiry found reasons to remain within the accepted Newtonian world-view. In that way lecture notes remained intact; procedures long established could be continued with passable results as long as one veered away from the frontiers of research. An orthodoxy of scientific knowledge was thus made possible, skeptical or even intolerant of the new vision of science. Yet the story of modern nuclear physics with its dramatic innovations in atomic energy and space research, presaging inter-planetary exploration and travel, make clear that the courage and independence of pioneer effort prevailed in the sciences. And the new age of power, along with an expanding universe, is the telling fruit of their labors. One theologian in our day has observed that the one area of human endeavor in which this modern period of history has achieved stature is that of modern science. One can say this without eulogizing all that the sciences have wrought.

Although most of our modern society has received, and is accepting, the technical benefits and conveniences afforded by the sciences, relatively few people of our generation give evidence of participating in the processes of thought and in the understanding of human existence which underlie these scientific contributions. The subtlety of the issues in some of their aspects and the unsettling effect of moving from a static and fixed point of reference to a dynamic and relative one may well explain the general indifference to these matters. One is less able to understand the lag among cultural disciplines where the study of man and the nature of our existence is more consciously in focus, and where presumably a more sharpened effort to probe these matters might be expected. It is true that the technical inquiry of the sciences has assumed a stance so alien to the extant common-sense view of things, and the precision of scientific procedures in certain specialized areas is of such a heightened nature that this part of it is available only to the highly trained mind in each special field. Yet the shift in orientation by which new vistas of experience may be opened up to one, and the changed imagery of thought, made imperative by scientific discovery, can be appropriated, studied, and assimilated even by one who is only moderately conversant with the sciences. The concern to do so becomes especially important in those areas of thought and experience which have become moribund or which are, in large measure, frustrated in dealing with contemporary problems mainly through a fixation within an historic scientific imagery that is no longer tenable. We see instances of this in several areas of our cultural life, but nowhere has it became more evident than in the religious thought of our day. Ironically enough, the frustration is more marked among liberal thinkers in religion, for it is they who are more directly concerned with the issues of culture upon which scientific thought and its imagery bear. And in many instances it is this historic scientific imagery that obstructs rather than illumines these issues.

There is need for a frank facing of the demands and possibilities which the new imagery of thought in the sciences places upon us, especially as this bears upon religious thought. What makes it particularly urgent that religious thinkers give heed to this new vision of science is the contribution that it makes to our understanding of man's capacity to deal with ultimate issues. The theory of relativity alone radically modifies our various approaches to many basic questions, including our understanding of the cultural forms in which the realities of faith are grasped and interpreted.

There are realities being pointed to in the witness of Christian faith which are indispensable to our present cultural experience and to our ultimate meaning. Much that we have sought to live by is an inheritance from a generation given to idealization as an escape from mechanistic theories of nature; this has actually served to create barriers to belief in these realities. The current revolution in the cultural forms of thought and experience, particularly in the sciences, but also in world events opens up new vistas of the human condition. It thereby enables us to penetrate the façade of idealization and to take hold once again of the realities that are available to us in our heritage of faith.

This claim will appear strange, if not absurd, to many of our generation for whom the innovations of science today have brought about growing uncertainty, not only as to the realities of faith, but concerning the very meaning of man's existence, if not man's survival. In this work I try to come to terms with these antinomies that plague all serious and conscientious thought about our human condition in the face of what seems to portend only our dissolution. After analyzing some of the innovations in cultural forms, and the theological implications of the new imagery of thought as these have been developing in recent years, I venture to reformulate the vision of Christian faith within the modern idiom and to indicate its present importance as a potential directive of Western life and culture and as a distinctive contribution of our Western experience to the spiritual life of mankind.

Some of the chapters in this book were written in preparation for giving the Barrows Lectures in India and Burma. Most of them, however, were written afterwards and convey reflections upon that experience. Thus while the problems with which I deal are ones with which we within Western experience are familiar, I am led to view them in the setting of world revolution, and to point up aspects of these problems that are appearing in cultures beyond the West.

B.E.M.

Wildewood,
Pilgrim, Michigan
Summer 1961

Acknowledgments

This book had its beginning in an opportunity to travel to India and Burma to give the Barrows Lectures, the purpose of which was to bring to the people of the East a glimpse of the thinking of the West concerning Christian faith and its witness to the modern age. The book has grown beyond the bounds of the lectures, yet in Parts II and III it contains the essence of what was prepared for that occasion. I wish to take this occasion to express appreciation to the Barrows Committee of the University of Chicago for the opportunity which was provided me in being appointed the Barrows Lecturer, and to my colleagues, Dean Jerald C. Brauer and Professor Pierce Beaver, for their part in preparing the way for this undertaking. I am grateful also to Dr. S. D. Malaiperuman, Chairman of the Barrows Committee in India; to Dr. G. P. Charles, Professor Hla Bu, and the Burma Christian Council, who sponsored my lectures in Rangoon, Burma. My thanks go to Mr. and Mrs. Norman Ford of Calcutta, to Dr. and Mrs. M. H. Harrison of the United Theological College in Bangalore; to Dr. and Mrs. G. S. Sahai of Leonard College, Jabalpur, and to Mr. and Mrs. Addison Eastman, formerly Dean of Judson Chapel at Rangoon University, for their hospitality and many kindnesses to Mrs. Meland and me during our stay in their homes while these lectures were being given.

I am indebted to many other friends in India who gave support and encouragement to my efforts during these arduous and rewarding months, but I wish to mention especially Dr. and Mrs. C. E. Abraham of Serampore College as well as faculty friends and students at Serampore, where I was privileged to lecture for a term.

To the many individuals in India and Burma, among them Hindu, Buddhist, and Moslem scholars who took time to open my eyes to the wonders and perplexities of their land and people, I am deeply grateful. No experience was more rewarding than the hours of conversation I was privileged to have with them.

I am indebted to Professor Daniel Day Williams of Union Theological Seminary, New York, who read the manuscript in its initial form and offered many helpful suggestions. I wish to express thanks also to Minerva Bell, Rehova Arthur, and Gloria Valentine for their efforts beyond the call of duty in getting the manuscript ready for presentation.

Finally, I wish to acknowledge my indebtedness to my students at the University of Chicago who read and discussed every chapter of the manuscript with me. The stimulus of their questions and criticisms has enabled me to see issues as well as implications in what I have written which otherwise might have escaped me.

Chapter IV and parts of Chapter XV originally appeared in *The Journal of Religion;* and portions of Chapters XI and XII appeared in *Encounter.* I wish to thank the publishers of these journals for permission to reprint this material.

I am indebted also to the following publishers for permission to quote from books published by them, acknowledgment of which in each instance appears in a footnote reference: Doubleday & Company, Inc., Harcourt, Brace & World, Inc., Harper & Brothers, Indiana University Press, The Macmillan Company, W. W. Norton & Company, Inc., Oxford University Press, Charles Scribner's Sons, Society for the Promotion of Christian Knowledge, S.C.M. Press, Ltd., The University of Chicago Press, and Yale University Press. I wish to thank the following for permission to quote from works copyrighted by them: National Council of the Churches of Christ, Lucian Price, Robert E. Mathews, and Michael Polanyi.

B.E.M.

Contents

PART THREE

THE WITNESS OF FAITH

Part One

THE REVOLUTION IN CULTURAL FORMS

I World Revolution and Christian Faith

When the controlled release of nuclear energy became a reality in 1945, it was as if chaos of such magnitude broke upon the world as to bring to a close the drama of history which, up to that time, had presented modern civilization. The chaos was primordial in its impact. It seemed to thrust us back momentarily into another period of cosmic history as planetary forces, both destructive and creative in their release of power, took the stage. Man was the initiator of this cosmic event; yet he stood aghast before the miracle of his brains and hands, for he knew that through it realities had broken in upon him which would revolutionize his life if they did not first destroy it.

The shift from one source of power to another in human history has always been marked by radical innovations in man's way of life. The harnessing of water power released both man and beast from much labor and opened the way for extending travel and for illuminating the world. The utilization of steam extended these dimensions of man's life, making possible railroads and factories and accelerating industrialization. Electric power brought increased freedom and a better distribution of energy, facilitating the rise of vast enterprises in every phase of industry. But the releasing of nuclear energy was more than just a change to a new source of power. It was an event of catastrophic proportions, prescient of changes both ominous and alluring: on the one hand, envisaging the possibility of an end to our planetary life; and, on the other hand, impelling imagination and human effort to

3

extend man's reach into outer space. This was innovation on a radically new scale.

Though the release of nuclear energy, with the consequent increase in power, has been the most dramatic source of innovation in modern history, it has not, however, been the only source. Between 1947 and the present day no less than twenty declarations of independence have been heard around the world, releasing people from age-old structures of life and from alien powers, and releasing in them more vital human energies which, too, have been at once creative and destructive. Nationalistic zeal among newly created governments has become a mounting reservoir of internal power, matching the release of cosmic energy in its persistent effects altering the shape and way of modern life.

Civilization, as fashioned in East and West, has thus been confronted with two mighty mediums of innovation: the threat and promise of atomic power, and the explosive assertion of the force of human communities seeking independence and the possibility of self-determination.

To the man of faith our period of history presents a Janus face. On the one side it is erupting with radical innovations in human sensibilities and expectations, a result of scientific achievement and cultural revolution; on the other side, its very imagery of thought, a reassertion of the significance of concrete realities and the complexity of meaning attending them, is in the process of providing man with insight into the nature of human existence which may enable him to recover sensibilities previously lost. These innovations are world-wide; hence the revolution in human sensibilities takes on meaning for all cultures and for all forms of religious faith. In this sense revolution today means world revolution. However much local incidents and grievances within any single culture, giving rise to revolt, may issue from a sequence of specific historical events, the break with past precedents and authorities, or the renascence of past loyalties along with new commitments, such a revolt partakes of an historical *élan* that appears to be expressive of a state of mind that is currently pervasive. East and West are linked together in a common travail of soul and body despite their tensions and misunderstandings. And they confront a common problem of survival even as they struggle, with and against one another, to wrest from the turmoil of conflict and co-operation some clues to what beliefs can give meaning to the will to survive. Hardly any aspect of our lives is immune from this sense of common involvement. Hunger in any part of the world looms as a possible threat to our well-being and as a responsibility to which we must give attention. So it is with the problem of population, with the problems of health and education, with the production and the distribution of goods, and with the yearning for human dignity and self-determination.

Or, think how the issue between science and religion has broadened in recent years, linking it inextricably with the issues of world revolution. For more than three hundred years this issue has been a preoccupation of Western minds. With science and industry now playing a major role in the cultural revolutions in modern Asia, the issue is assuming world-wide proportions and significance. This has occurred to a marked degree already, as is evidenced by the concern being shown by educators and religious leaders in various countries of Asia, where the impact of the sciences in the schools and of the demands of industrialization upon village and city life is presenting acute problems. Furthermore, the very turn that cultural development in the East is taking, restricting or excluding the operations of Christian missions at the very time the countries are importing scientific and industrial aid, has the effect of replacing Christian forces abroad with a new kind of Western emissary. This could be looked upon as a renewed spreading of what Arnold Toynbee has called "the leaven of secularization" which began at the close of the seventeenth century and "spread progressively from one stratum of the Western society to another till it had permeated the whole mass," culminating in "the discrediting of the West's Christian heritage,"[1] and the elevation of a technical civilization that has only tenuous connections, at best, with the Christian heritage and ethos.

The issue here is by no means as clear as this characterization might suggest; for while the effects of science and technology on the ethos of any culture can be iconoclastic, stripping it of its cherished traditions and characteristics, its motives are generally charitable, being bent on relieving human suffering, improving conditions of livelihood, and increasing productivity. Consequently its results in this regard are beneficial. In fact, it could be argued that it was missionary zeal itself that initiated the importation of science and technology into Eastern countries, by employing a ministry of the medical missionary, and the technical guidance of scientific farming, along with its program of evangelism. One can point to instances in India where village reclamation begun under missionary auspices was instrumental in awakening local governments to their responsibility in these spheres. And several of these projects now have the support of the national government or have become an integral part of the series of five-year plans looking toward economic renewal. This would seem to argue that it is not science and technology as independent, secular spheres of Western culture that have entered everyday life in Asia and replaced Christian missions; it is the scientific and technical aspects of these missions that have assumed strategic importance in the national programs of reclamation in Asian countries in a way that no other aspect of missionary effort has done.

Nevertheless, science and technology as they now operate abroad go far beyond these initial, pioneer attempts under Christian auspices, both in scope and intensity of experimentation. The agencies with Western support and

[1] Arnold Toynbee, *An Historian's Approach to Religion*. Oxford University Press, 1956.

6

direction have become industrial and educational foundations, working with representatives of Western governments and local political or educational activities. Thus the marginal technological and medical phase of missionary activity has been widely supplemented, and in a way replaced, by a more intensive and concerted effort under political and educational auspices to lift the level of livelihood in Asian countries. What was once considered to be but a secondary aspect of Christian missions has soared into a formidable, independent sphere of technical guidance in all phases of Eastern civilization. What is thus arising in Asia as a nascent technological civilization begins to take on the semblance of Western secularization. And in this sense it is of a piece with what has transpired in the West in the last few centuries.

Again, when one looks at the larger political scene in Asia one detects the emerging pattern of common involvement in the cultural revolutions themselves. The American Revolution of 1775 and the French Revolution of 1789 provide a kind of watershed in Western history, dividing the modern era of cultural sensibilities from its classical past in setting the negotiable rights of individual man over against the absolute claims of a monarchical order of law and authority. The Russian Revolution which followed in 1917 can be said to have been an extension of the pattern of revolt which had formed in Western Europe a century and a half earlier. But by this time, what had broken forth in the eighteenth century as a political response to the romantic rediscovery of the individual now assumed the realism of calculated economic and social reform, looking toward the elevation of proletarian man and, eventually, the well-being and common status of communal man. Meantime a full-bodied literature in modern idealism had emerged in Western Europe, declaring "the vocation of man" to be the fulfillment of the human equation against all competing odds, whether they be the repressive measures of social organization and

7

political tyranny, or the impersonal forces of nature. The Russian intellectuals of the twentieth century who fashioned this instrument of revolt were the heirs of two centuries of European probing into social and philosophical issues altering the status of modern man. We hardly need to be told that ideas have consequences. But their consequences will vary according to the circumstances in which they take root and come to flower. The contrast between the histories of social reform in Western democracies and in Communist republics will in large measure document this judgment. For historically their theoretical bases have much in common, rooting in a movement of life that looked to the idealization of man. Strange as it may seem one must include Marxism as one of the rebellious heirs and stepchildren of the Idealistic movement, despite the fact that, in basic notions, it is an inversion of the idealistic turn of mind. For while it is true that Marx sought to locate the creative force of destiny in the historical process as a dialectical materialism, the premise upon which this inversion was possible and from which its formative imagery proceeded was Absolute Idealism. The idealizing process persisted in Marxism, with a utopian society envisaged as an inevitable outcome of the fateful class conflict within the historical process. The critique of bourgeois man in Marx should not blind one to the persisting idealistic strain in the Marxist conception of proletarian man. The same illusions which are found in Romantic Idealism concerning elemental man, and later universal man, appear in the Marxist classless society. I do not mean to obscure the important differences that arise here with regard to the nature of persons. The primacy of the person established in modern idealism is rudely dissolved in the Marxist idealization of the classless society and in the fateful class conflict which must precede this historical outcome. In the Marxist analysis the person as a unique individuation of the human spirit with a distinctive destiny, and with rights and opportunities appropriate

8

to that spiritual destiny, tends to be set aside as an obstacle and a possible threat to the communal goal. Thus the radical and important differences in the different conceptions of man. But one may acknowledge this important distinction without setting aside the judgment that Idealism and Marxism share illusions in common concerning the nature of human existence. And as a consequence both contribute to an idealization of the human equation.

What is commonly overlooked is that cultural revolutions in the East reflect a direct line of inheritance from the three major revolutions of the West. The historical lineage between the People's Movement in China under Sun Yat-sen and the Russian Revolution is, of course, well known.[2] But a study of the Indian revolt and its struggle for independence will reveal a direct acquaintance with ideas and strategies of the American Revolution and with specific instances of political rebellion in American history. We have Gandhi's own admission, for example, of the influence of Henry Thoreau's essay, "Civil Disobedience" on his own thinking in formulating the technique of civil disobedience, which he used so effectively against British rule throughout the Indian Revolution. And few historical and political documents, we are told, were studied more closely by Indian nationalists during their initial period of revolt than those pertaining to the American War of Independence.[3] As Henry Wriston has said, "Read aright, our Declaration of Independence makes us kin to all the new nations which have escaped from the status of wards and attained the stature of independence."[4]

The current revolution in cultural forms, which has become world-wide in its consequences and influence, is thus not an outcome wholly of recent events, nor merely

[2] Cf. Harley Farnsworth MacNair, *China in Revolution*. University of Chicago Press, 1931, pp. 72ff.

[3] Cf. Lawrence K. Rosinger, *India and the United States*. Macmillan, 1950, pp. 9ff.

[4] Henry M. Wriston, "The Age of Revolution," *Foreign Affairs*. Vol. 39, No. 4, July 1961, p. 536.

an eruption of local politics of the East; it is a situation that has been forming throughout the modern period out of the subtle interplay of historical forces. At times the connections between East and West in these developments have been tenuous and incidental; at other times they have been substantial and significant. Earlier developments reveal a dominance of Western influence upon Eastern institutions and thought, and a consequent subservience of Eastern modes of reform and change to Western experience. Today a basic factor in world revolution in the Far East is the casting out, or the withdrawal, of Western control in the East and Middle East, and the consequent resurgence of nationalistic forces in these cultures. Ironically enough this is accompanied by a widespread Westernization of Eastern cultures at another stage, though on Eastern terms, through industrialization and the acceleration of scientific and technological education. The all-out effort among Asiatic nations to achieve industrialization in a remarkably short period of time, and to extend the use and influence of the sciences throughout their societies (reaching even to village schools in some instances), is creating a substantial secular tide in these countries. This has become particularly noticeable in India, Burma, Japan, and China. At present this secular influence is especially evident in literature and in the arts as well as in education and business. Here a swift transformation of the cultural ethos consonant with scientific advance in a technological civilization is anticipated and encouraged. This secular tide is expressive of the new mind that is forming, accompanying and to some degree countering the resurgence of the traditional religious faiths, except where the religions themselves are assimilating scientific influence in their fashion.

We should note here that the term "Secularism" tends to be understood in two ways among Indian intellectuals and leaders. On the one hand, it has been taken to imply cultural freedom from the oppressive restraints of established religions, providing some measure of detachment and enabling discerning Indians to assume a critical stance in relation to traditional mores. Among certain Indian groups this very detachment from the so-called spirituality of Indian culture has resulted in social criticism and resistance to such religious restraints which block social change. Some would argue that this attitude has been an important factor in bringing about recent social reforms on a national scale and in opening the way for a more inclusive, cosmopolitan culture. On the other hand, Secularism takes on an ominous import for sensitive Indians when it is identified with the kind of social change which industrialism and an undue emphasis upon science in the schools are bringing to city and village life alike. Some educators and civic leaders give evidence of a growing anxiety about this shift in the quality and feeling of Indian life. These two ways of viewing Secularism are quite obviously two attitudes toward the same phenomenon, and they reflect a responsiveness or reaction to different aspects of its impact upon Indian life.

I have noticed that when Western observers report on what is happening in the Far East they generally dwell upon the resurgence of Asiatic religions to illustrate the awakening of nationalistic forces, as if nationalism in the East meant a reassertion of their traditional mores. The impression I got from seven months abroad was more complex than that. Nationalistic zeal was certainly evident in religion, particularly Hinduism and Buddhism, in the areas I visited; but nationalistic tendencies restraining, reforming, and even countering these faiths in their traditional guise were even more evident. One could make a case for saying that it is not the traditional faiths that are taking the initiative or being given the prominent role in this nationalistic resurgence. Rather, it is the liberalizing and reforming movements within them. In India, for example, Neo-Hinduism is clearly to the fore in the national renaissance, attempting on the one hand to bring

Hinduism into accord with new cultural objectives, and on the other hand attempting to correlate these secularizing forces with traditional values. Radhakrishnan, known chiefly in the West for his philosophical writings on Hinduism,[5] is now vice-president of India. In this role he has become a kind of minister of culture, encouraging the renaissance of Indian art and literature, and at the same time assimilating these creative activities, along with other current social forces, to the advancement of Neo-Hinduism. Under Radhakrishnan Neo-Hinduism seeks to keep abreast of all modern developments, culturally, educationally, and religiously. He seems bent on channeling the cultural revolution in India in the direction of a revived, yet revised Hinduism. This means not only impressing the ethos of Hinduism upon this awakened Indian life but reforming the Hindu ethic and reformulating Hindu philosophy to accord with world enlightenment, particularly as they bear upon scientific and industrial developments now in process within India.

I found university people, especially philosophers and political scientists in centers like Banaras, Santiniketan, and Calcutta, vigorously supporting this Neo-Hindu movement, not so much as an effort to stem the secularizing influences as to absorb them, or to channel them into cultural paths consonant with Indian values. From a reading of Indian literary reviews and journals, however, one would get the impression that a trans-Hindu mind is also forming. Although not allied with Communist forces, it is expressive of a nonreligious humanism, or transreligious humanism, which appears to be in rapport with Communist values in the way that social liberal movements in the West during the 'twenties and 'thirties espoused the Marxist cause without becoming politically involved in Communism. Yet even here Radhakrishnan

5 Radhakrishnan's principal works include: *Indian Philosophy, The Hindu View of Life, The Philosophy of the Upanishads, East and West in Religion,* and *An Idealist View of Life.*

appears to want to assimilate both the Indian Communist mind and this new humanism to Neo-Hinduism. Speaking before a Congress of Art and Literature in Calcutta in the fall of 1957, he observed that Marxism refuses to set any deity above man. Then, as if to point up its affinity with the Hindu heritage, he added, "Hinduism also has traditionally opposed any effort to put anything between man and divinity."

From some rather brief observations in Burma I would judge that similar crosscurrents of nationalistic revival and a sophisticated cosmopolitanism are being interwoven to form a complex, cultural attitude toward events both at home and abroad. The difference is that Burmese Theravada Buddhism does not seem to aspire to the same kind of integrating role of absorbing these countercurrents, that one finds Neo-Hinduism assuming in India. Instead, Buddhism has bent every effort locally toward becoming the state religion of Burma. Pronouncements of the prime minister in 1960 would indicate that this goal has now been achieved.

The resurgence of Asiatic religions in their more traditional aspect in Southeast Asia takes the form both of a revival of Hinduism and Buddhism in the various villages and towns, and of an awakening within these faiths to possibilities of a world-wide mission. Perhaps "revival" is not the most accurate word to use in speaking of the resurgence of these traditional faiths. It would be more precise to say that these religions in the villages and towns have become more assertive, more aggressive. This takes a variety of forms, ranging from mere nuisance acts, such as blaring forth Hindu ceremonial tunes on a loud-speaker to the disturbance of their Christian neighbors, to overt acts of violence against Christian groups. It may be fair to say that Hindus in India feel that they have the tacit support of the local governments and thus are privileged to "lord it over" other faiths, particularly over Christians, precisely in the way Christians in India during British rule, according to reports by Indian Christians themselves, took on an air of being a part of the religion of privilege. The national government, through legislation and frequent public utterances by the prime minister, tries to support and even to emphasize the freedom of all religions; but the precedent has been established for favoring the "in-group," however much the freedom of all faiths may be publicized.

It is interesting to note that, simultaneously with the curbing of Christian missions in the Far East, religions of the East are looking forward to world expansion. This is especially true of Buddhism which appears to be preparing for extensive missionary effort. Such preparation takes the form both of studying literature on Western Christianity, and of revising Buddhist literature, setting its stories of the Buddha in a context familiar to the Christian mind. A group of Indian Christians, who had recently been in touch with a Buddhist community, reported that this Buddhist group was at work editing the life of the Buddha to accord with stages in the life of Jesus. Thus in recounting the life of Buddha they were including an account of the miraculous birth of the Buddha, a story of Buddha among the doctors, discourses by the Sea and on the Mount, and, of all things, an Ascension story. More sophisticated efforts among Buddhists looking toward world expansion are also to be found. These take the form of stressing the rational and scientific temper of Buddhist thought, thereby demonstrating its relevance to a scientific age. Sober and scholarly activities concerned with the study of texts and their reinterpretation are also being projected. This has assumed impressive proportions in the Theravada Buddhism of Southeast Asia, particularly in Rangoon, Burma. I shall have more to say about this aspect of the religious resurgence in Asia in the final chapter, where I discuss encounters between Christian and non-Christian peoples.

The resurgence of Asiatic faiths is an impressive phenomenon and should not be treated lightly in gauging the present temper of events in Asia. I found discerning Hindus on university faculties in India, however, insisting that the revival of Hinduism was not to be taken as anything more than a symptom of nationalistic zeal. They were unwilling to attribute any spiritual or ethical significance to its renaissance. One might accept this judgment and still acknowledge the latent power of these faiths to affect the cultural and political destiny of Eastern society. As I have already indicated, I am not ready to call these activities the most significant symptoms of an awakening East. The significance of countercurrents within these cultures, protesting against any religious reading of events, is not to be underestimated. If, as is often suggested, the religious forces of Asian society present a formidable resistance to Communist aggression within these cultures, the secular fringe represents a substantial and growing segment of Asian society, ready to assimilate much of what Communism represents in its antireligious attitude to its own assertive efforts in creating a transreligious culture. This is why the so-called spiritual resistance to Communism, which some observers see in an awakened Buddhism and Hinduism, may not be as real or as formidable as it may first appear.

Communism in the East, however, seems to have become less important as a spiritual movement in recent years, compared with its status in this respect a generation or more ago. Its significance has in large measure narrowed to one economic solution to Asia's poverty and its attending human ills. And if this solution is ever made convincing beyond the borders of China it may well assume a spiritual potency as well, which could be difficult to counter either politically or religiously.

World revolution in the East, however, means more than these numerous crosscurrents of national awakening. It implies a reversal of a mind-set that has suppressed much of the native heritage for generations. Through the

15

release of nationalistic pride and feeling an appreciation for things Indian or Burmese, as the case may be, has been reappearing. This has evoked a zest for creative effort, reasserting motifs of native art and music long obscured under Western influence; stressing native classical literature along with current writing; and even reviving educational methods appropriate to the native culture, as in Visva-Bharati University at Santiniketan. Nowhere is this concern to reactivate native motifs more articulate in India than among Indian Christians. Their insistence that Indian music should replace Western hymns in the churches; that employing Indian forms of thought to express Christian teaching should be encouraged in theological schools, if not to displace, certainly to supplement the prevalent interest in Barth and Kierkegaard; that Dravidian architecture is to be considered worthy for a Christian house of worship, all indicate a state of mind that both reaffirms native values and resists the perpetuation of Western influences which obscure or overtly oppose native motifs and forms. This recovery of the native culture among Indian Christians I shall discuss more fully later.

Alongside of this phase of the cultural renaissance, however, there is the constantly increasing importation of technical education and guidance for industrial purposes. This, together with the spread of the sciences in the schools, as already observed, is injecting into the cultural life a degree of Westernization that far exceeds earlier forms of Western influence. And, it is bound to become more pervasive as industrialization proceeds. In the long run the shaping of these influences could be decisive, as it has been in the West, in lifting to dominance the secularizing forces that attend such enterprises. Discerning Indians know this and deplore what it portends for Indian culture.

World revolution means, too, an economic upheaval of vast proportions abroad, carrying with it cultural implications that as yet can hardly be anticipated within specific societies. The obvious form it takes at the moment is a blatant and noisy contest between democratic capitalism and Communism, with neutral aspirations and experiments timorously venturing in between. One thing became clear to me from listening to Asian talk, and from reading between the lines whenever they expressed resistance to Western ways: that is, this open conflict between the two world economies has complicated the cultural issue between East and West almost beyond resolution. For this has compelled the West to declare allegiance to our capitalistic economy with its individual enterprise and simultaneously to praise democracy and freedom. In the West we have historically thought of these three phases of our culture as belonging together and have often equated them with each other. In the East, however, the historical experience of many of these cultures has led them to associate the capitalistic economy of the West with imperialistic rule and enslavement, not with democracy and freedom. And present national upheavals have generally meant the eradication of capitalistic governments which, to these people, symbolized the denial of freedom and the obstruction to democratic relationships in their societies. Thus the economic solution we offer as an alternative to Communism is at the outset an obstacle of huge and menacing proportions. The historical experience of these people can offer them no other judgment. The fact that one after another of these communities has expressed or indicated resistance to Communism as being patently alien to its own heritage for other reasons leaves them with a vacuous and uncertain choice of neutralism, which in plain language means, "A curse on both your houses!"

And yet there are sensibilities implicit in our pretensions to democracy and to Christianity which do not escape these people of the East, and which are consonant with much that they find in their own spiritual heritage. Through a glass darkly they see us as fellow human beings. And they do this despite the historical experience which brands Western people as their exploiters and their deceivers. Thus the term "Western," implying European and American alike, tends to connote to many Asians ambiguous cultural and human values, merging these democratic and Christian sensibilities with a vivid and resentful memory of the imperialism and enslavement which the Western economy, moving eastward, imposed upon them.

If Westerners, mindful of the democratic zeal in the West to be done with imperialistic ambition and its exploitation, are justified in resenting this Eastern stereotype linking the West with imperialism, Easterners may be excused, for a time at least, for continuing to hold this stereotype, considering the indelible imprint of historical events upon any structure of experience. A resolution of this apparent impasse lies in the hope that the new image which the West has begun to form of itself can be made convincing to the Asian peoples, and that this newer image of Western democracy will continue to become a firmer reality among Western people and nations as well.

These developments in the East, curbing or casting out overt Western intervention in its cultural life, have brought about radical changes in the role of Christian missions abroad and in the relation of Western Christianity to the life of Christian institutions in Asia. One point that needs to be kept in mind is that the continuance of the Christian religion in Eastern lands is not necessarily challenged by the termination of Western authority and influence in Asian churches. What is occurring is a transfer of authority and property from Western auspices to indigenous Christian groups. Thus what continues as a liaison personnel between Western and Eastern Christianity is quite consciously and overtly a body of co-workers serving in a transitional period to complete the transfer of Western holdings and leadership to the indigenous churches and to help launch nationalist Christian leaders upon their new responsibilities.

In these transitional efforts one sees evidence of a deep-seated loyalty (even affection) between Eastern and Western Christians and of smoldering resentments among native Christians (long suppressed or sublimated) which now break out into the open to reassert the claims of the native culture. This was brought to my attention rather dramatically on one occasion. I was talking with a young Indian instructor in a theological school who had grown up in a mission compound in North India. He had since graduated from a university and a theological college in India and had spent a year abroad studying in an American theological seminary. In addition to his work in the theological college he was active in guiding the work of evangelism in the villages of the region. "We are no longer aware of ourselves as just Christians," this young man said. "We are Indians as well." Not being familiar with what was behind this statement at the moment I was not prepared for the intensity with which he made it. But he went on to inform me about the Christian missions in India and of the impact they had made upon him. The gist of his remarks was to the effect that the mission compound had been a world to itself. To enter into its community had been tantamount to being uprooted from the culture into which one had been born. One took on the ways of the compound and learned to suspect whatever was native to Indian culture. The Hindu faith and its practices were the chief adversaries, but one learned that everything in Indian society had been tainted or even more seriously infected by Hindu influence. He was, of course, speaking out of his own early experience. "We have moved out of the compound," he continued; "or rather, the compound has been removed from us. We are now in competition with the full range of alternative ideas and social forces of our culture, as members of the Indian community. We have to know our way around."

The feelings of resentment here were unmistakable;

but I also sensed something even more human and native underneath these feelings in this young man's outreach toward the wider, Indian community. It was an inner release of himself as an Indian. There seemed to be evidence of a new birth in the look on his face as he spoke, giving sparkle and determination to his words. I saw this same look of zest and determination in the faces of other young Indian theologians and clergy with whom I spoke. Everywhere the story was the same, though it appeared in various versions. Before national independence Christianity in India had been a hothouse growth. And they who came into its community had shared the artificiality of being housed under a protective covering and nurtured by specially prepared formulas imported from distributors abroad. They had been kept aloof from the Indian mind and its cultural responsibilities because these things had been regarded alien to the Christian gospel. I am paraphrasing here words that were spoken to me by several young Indian Christians. Indian Christians of this bent of mind are not numerous, but they are in strategic posts where their influence is being felt. And it may very well be that they are in such posts precisely because they provide the Indian churches with a cutting edge at the point of contact where this is needed.

The impression grew on me as I moved about India that a sizable portion of Indian Christians, especially among the young people, is in the process of reclaiming the native cultural heritage and of becoming self-conscious Indians along with the rest of their countrymen. Among some of the older churchmen this state of mind had matured into ardent conviction. It was they who were urging their fellow churchmen to put aside their fear of syncretism and to take the Indian culture more seriously as a medium through which to express their Christian faith. This emphasis has been having its effects within the churches, not only in encouraging the use of native art forms in worship and in church building, as we have noted, but also in adapting the Christian message to the demands of the new situation.

The Indianizing of Christianity, as this process of accommodation is called by Indian churchmen, takes a variety of forms. In some quarters it assumes the form of a forthright avowal of syncretism. This emphatic stand has had its advocates for many years, even before national independence had been attained in India. One of the most winsome and widely known spokesmen for this point of view is A. J. Appasamy, a bishop of the Church of South India in Coimbatore, who for more than three decades has been urging a more serious integration of Christian preaching and worship within Indian culture.[6] The essence of Bishop Appasamy's concern is stated in these words written in 1942:

It is my object in writing this book to study afresh the life and teaching of Jesus as they are recorded in the Gospels and to explain them in relation to the spiritual heritage of India.

What is known as Christian Theology is an exposition of the teaching of Christ by Christian thinkers of the West who brought to their task their own natural aptitudes and the peculiarities of their own philosophy and culture. In the early Christian Church, to mention but one instance, Greek Philosophy was studied by many Christians and in understanding the mind of Christ they used the ideas of Greek Philosophy with which they were familiar. This was inevitable. Every man understands Christ in the light of his own experience and culture. So long as this experience and culture are in harmony with the mind of Christ, this method of knowledge is quite legitimate. When we become the followers of Christ we need not empty ourselves of all our national and cultural peculiarities, nor need we absorb Christian doctrines which are connected

[6] The works of Bishop Appasamy include: *Christianity as Bhakti Marga,* Macmillan, 1927; Madras, 1930; *What is Moksha?* Christian Literature Society, 1931 (published in England under the title *The Johannine Doctrine of Life),* S.P.C.K., 1934; *Temple Bells,* Y.M.C.A. Publishing House, 1928; *Christ in the Indian Church* and *The Gospel and India's Heritage,* S.P.C.K., 1942.

more with Greek or other systems of Philosophy than with the mind of Christ. An effort must be made to separate genuine Christian experience from the doctrines which the Christian theologians have expounded, and to state this same experience in terms which could be easily grasped by the Indian mind.[7]

He then follows with these revealing words:

I have used throughout the book many Hindu words such as *Moksha, Karma, Jnana, Bhakti, Saguna* and *Dharma.* Any careful student of Hindu Literature will know that these words are frequently used in India but do not always have the same meaning. They are used in different books with quite different meanings. Unless we know who wrote a particular book, when he wrote it, and to what sect he belonged, we cannot understand their correct meaning in that book. Christians in India can use these old religious words putting into them a distinctively Christian meaning; it will be quite different from the meaning which they have in their Hindu contexts. But by the use of the old religious terms we show that we are thinking out the same problems, experiencing the same difficulties, dealing with the same facts as our people did, though not always coming to the same conclusions. In this way we convince ourselves and others that Christianity is not a foreign religion which has come from some other country and which does not meet our national needs.[8]

Other Indian Christians who have contributed substantially to this effort are V. Chakkarai, a Christian lawyer and politician; [9] Dr. Eddy Asirvatham, an economist, whose book *Christianity in the Indian Crucible* presents a vivid account of the new situation affecting Christianity in India since Indian independence in 1947; and Professor Rajappan D. Immanuel, of Leonard Theological College

[7] *The Gospel and India's Heritage*, pp. 20-21.
[8] *Ibid.* p. 21.
[9] His writings include: *Jesus the Avatar,* Christian Literature Society, 1932, and *The Cross and Indian Thought,* Christian Literature Society, 1933.

in Jabalpur.[10] A vigorous spokesman for syncretism among the younger clergy of the Church of South India is Bishop D. Chellappa of Madras, whose address before the synod meeting of the Church of South India in 1958 was a ringing challenge to his fellow churchmen to give serious attention to adjusting their sights as Christians to the fact that they are also Indians. Bishop Chellappa's words are so crisp and pointed, and so expressive of the intensity with which the younger clergy feel the urgency of this effort among Indian Christians that I cannot resist quoting some excerpts from his address.

Concerning the theology of Indian churches:

We are so afraid of the danger of syncretism—a very real danger since the advent of Basic Education—that we hesitate to assist in the coming into being of a theology that is at once Indian and Christian. The pioneer attempts made about a generation ago by scholars like Dr. Appasamy still remain pioneer attempts. Our theological students are better versed in Kierkegaard and Barth and the Existentialists.

As to church architecture:

If there has been a difference since 1947, it is probably for the worse, especially where decisions have rested with Indian Christians, as these native Christian gentlemen are often more British and American than the British and the Americans themselves.

Bishop Chellappa then recounted a story to drive home his point of the absurdity of the Christian purism that resists native art forms in Christian buildings:

Recently an Indian Revivalist went to conduct a Retreat at an Ashram, and he sniffed at the beautiful Dravidian Christian temple there, obviously Dravidian, yet looking natural in its setting, and yet equally obviously Christian, with a large cross surmounting the *gopuram* and devoid of idols and of all heathen symbolism. But all

[10] Cf. his *The Influence of Hinduism on Indian Christians.* Leonard Theological College, 1950.

23

that the Revivalist brother could do was to roundly accuse the brethren of trying to please the Hindus and not the Lord Jesus. To the poor, ignorant, misguided man, the style of architecture known as Gothic (which means "pagan") was apparently more Christian, because forsooth! it came from the West, from whence was imported his brand of Christianity, and particularly his Fundamentalism.

Complaining of the Indian churches' dependence upon Western music rather than responding to experiments in the use of Indian music and in Indian forms of worship, he went on:

The music in our Churches, too, continues to be Western and shabby. When I hear many town choirs and some village choirs, formerly Anglican, attempting to render Cathedral chants in a procrustean attempt to fit Tamil words into tunes which were never meant for them, I am reminded of the famous saying of Dr. Johnson, in another context; "Sir, it is like a dog standing on its hind-legs; it is not done well, but you are surprised it is done at all!"

Then, in the spirit of a lament, while making no pretense of obscuring his resentment:

Our people are naturally reverent, but the unimaginative Protestant Missionary has well nigh destroyed their innate *bhakti* by teaching them to pray, not standing, or prostrating, or kneeling, but sitting, even sprawling—not in silence, but always jabbering—and by dispersing immediately after the last "Amen," without so much as a "Thank You" to God. Such pernicious and irreverent habits have helped to develop pride in a people, naturally humble, and made the Almighty unduly familiar to them, not as One who is both Transcendent and Immanent, or as One who is Love, yet is of purer eyes than to behold iniquity.

Among other Indian Christians, the problem of coming to terms with Indian culture within the Christian Church is not a matter of emulating its art forms and philosophies, but of confronting serious problems that exist between Hinduism and Christianity.[11] This means studying Hinduism and its role in Indian culture with a thoroughness that is new among Indian Christians. Ultimately the intention is to engage their Hindu countrymen in serious conversation on basic matters of faith and culture, though it is conceded that Indian Christians may not be ready for such an encounter for some time. A serious effort in this direction is being made by Dr. V. C. Samuels, who, before joining the theological faculty of Serampore College, was engaged in a long-range research project exploring this problem. A similar effort has been under way at Bangalore College, where for several years Professors Paul Devananden and M. M. Thomas have been the moving spirits.[12] These theologians are convinced that a more basic study of the new situation in which Christianity is to pursue its tasks in modern India is necessary before a clear judgment of its responsibilities in relation to other Indian faiths and to Indian culture generally can be made.

A more direct approach to the problem of confronting Indian culture among Indian Christians is being voiced by some of the younger theologians. They see the matter, not as involving syncretism or even interchange as a self-conscious effort but as being a prophetic responsibility of Christians to consider social and cultural problems, now emerging in modern India, within the perspective of the Christian gospel. In one theological college where the faculty has made this problem something of a live issue over a considerable period of time, I detected a readiness among theological students to engage their contemporaries in an open discussion on issues that were then before

[11] A significant effort in this vein is Surjit Singh, *Preface to Personality: Christology in Relation to Radhakrishnan's Philosophy.* The Christian Literature Society for India, 1952. Cf. also his recent publication, *Christology and Personality.* Westminster Press, 1961.

[12] The journal *Religion and Society,* edited by Devananden and Thomas, carries articles covering the work of their Christian Institute for the Study of Religion and Society.

the nation as well as on other cultural problems in which all of them, Hindu and Christian alike, as modern Indians would have a concern. As one of the young Indians put it, "Our Christian witness would declare itself in the very way in which we address ourselves to these questions." This approach to the problem will have the effect of relating Christian thinking and preaching to the contemporary cultural scene in India, thus integrating Christian and Indian thought and feeling by relating them to a common focus of interest. Whatever syncretism or interchange follows from such a confrontation, these young men argue, will be incidental to the main task of carrying on a responsible prophetic ministry within Indian society.

All three forms of Indianizing Christianity represent something of an about-face from the emphasis of Christian missions as it was conceived and practiced during the era of the mission compound, when becoming Christian virtually meant the withdrawal from Indian culture and the relinquishment of native habits and customs.

One should not assume that these efforts to relate Christianity to Indian culture are representative of Christianity in Asia as a whole, or even within India itself. Much of its witness continues in the mood and pattern of the compound as a cult withdrawn from the cultural life about it, and apprehension about the threat which the revived vitality of non-Christian religions, more integral to the cultural heritage, presents to the Christian community. This is true among many younger Indian Christian leaders as well as among the more experienced ones. For example, I found among many theological students a decided reticence, if not apprehension, about what the Christian encounter with Hinduism could mean for them. Many of them seemed to welcome the fact that they would be sent to the villages following graduation, where, they assumed, such direct confrontation with the more aggressive Hindu or Buddhist minds might not arise, and where day-to-day relationships with their Indian countrymen might not present a serious problem. Their reticence seemed to arise from a sense of uneasiness in the presence of non-Christian Indians of their own age and experience, rather than from any firm conviction about the issues which should or might arise in such an encounter.

As I listened to one discussion after another bearing upon these problems, I could not get away from the feeling that in this critical situation, so explosive, yet promising, the absence of a sense of direction or of any clear directives concerning such engagements was a bit frightening. My sympathies were with the more audacious ones who were looking to their responsible role as Christians in the new life of modern India; yet I understood, too, how the other young men felt who preferred to seek out more remote areas for preaching the gospel, presumably under less disturbing and less menacing circumstances. The irony of it all is, of course, that concentration on village reclamation as part of India's five-year plans is bringing the same new cultural forces to bear upon these remote areas as well. So these young men will soon find that there is no hiding place there either.

The action of the National Congress of India, granting freedom of worship to all faiths, gives assurance of a sort to Christian groups, as has been said. Yet where Christians have remained remote from the affairs of the community, allowing tensions between themselves and Hindus to become acute, no amount of official insistence upon freedom in worship can guarantee immunity from this ever-present threat. Thus the insecurity persists, and tensions rise to subside with or without incidents, despite all that the national government might do, or that discerning and temperate-minded Hindus and Christians might devise to alleviate or to change this situation.

The insecurity which Indian Christians feel toward Hindus, and possibly other of their countrymen, however, stems from different sources of uncertainty. To some extent it comes from a deep-seated uneasiness about their ability to compete culturally or intellectually with their non-Christian contemporaries. I found evidence of this uneasiness among some of the theological students of whom I have spoken. Such apprehensiveness is understandable in view of the Indian Christian's own awareness of the paucity of his acquaintance with historical as well as contemporary aspects of Indian life and culture. His Hindu contemporaries, on the other hand, have been reared from childhood on the native lore which underlies the motifs of its historical art forms, its social structure, its philosophy, and its literature. Even when the Indian Christian is psychologically ready to assume his role as an Indian nationalist, or to take its problems seriously, he cannot do so on even terms with his Hindu countrymen. Hindus are aware of this, too; and the more brash among them are quite ready to call attention to it. They often use the fact that Christian teaching and preaching were first addressed to outcast communities as a basis for claiming that Indian Christians are, in large measure, from the illiterate masses of Indian society and thus without any claim upon or knowledge of India's cultural past. This is a half-truth; but it has enough basis in fact to make it intimidating to many Indian Christians. One soon discovers, however, that the number of Indian Christians who have come from Hindu families of social standing, or who attained eminence under British rule, is sizable. And the proportion of Indian Christians who have been educated in Indian colleges and universities, and then gone on to Cambridge or Oxford, and more recently to American universities, to receive advanced degrees, is impressive. This in itself is not a true measure of their worth, or of their claim for recognition as participants in the new India; nevertheless, it is an observation to be put over against any assumption that would underestimate the intellectual quality or cultural force of the Indian Christian.

The continuance and consolidation of Christian communities in Asian cultures under arrangements congenial to nationalist governments is itself something of an achievement in the face of iconoclastic developments which have attended cultural revolution in these areas. Yet no amount of integration and acceptance of Christianity as an indigenous faith can obscure the fact that, in these cultures, Christians are a minority. Being a member of a minority faith in modern India and Burma under present conditions is a different matter from having minority status under British rule. In the latter instance the prestige of being identified with the government in power added luster to every act and representation, even though feelings to the contrary prevailed underneath. Under present nationalist powers, even when they aim toward a democratic policy of recognizing all faiths, or of being neutral toward each, the pressure of majority religions to attain special status is strong. And in these cultures the religion most representative of the national heritage and customs tends to assume the character of a state religion, even when it is not officially acknowledged to be so. In time it may make its case, as Buddhism did in Burma in 1960. Thus at best Christianity pursues an uneasy course in Asia with only its claims to its indigenous character, together with the esteem in which many of its representatives are held, to support it against being overridden by the pressure of events.

The pressures which Christianity is experiencing from the revival of Hinduism and Buddhism may prove to be relatively minor compared with the growing threat of secularization in Southeast Asia as the impact of industrialization and scientific influence continues. As contrasted with Western experience, India and Burma up to now have known little of the corroding effects of this secular temper and outlook upon religious faith, or upon cultural institutions. One hears much of the "spiritual" character of Indian culture until the reiteration of this theme palls on the discriminating Western consciousness.

For much that parades itself here as "spirituality" can better be described as intellectual arrogance at one level, or indolence at another, justifying the neglect of honest labor and of applied energy, which are so sorely needed to counter human degradation and poverty. But after Western irritation on this point has spent itself, the fact remains that a heritage of sensibility favorable to the pursuit of religion, art, and the life of the mind does exist in this culture. Not only has this depth of sensitivity in Indian life elevated the contemplative and appreciate concerns of the human spirit, but it has perhaps contributed more to providing a receptive state of mind for much that Christianity has had to offer than is commonly recognized. The readiness with which Hindus have received and honored the person of Jesus, even when they have resisted what they called "Churchanity," subtly suggests the nature and degree of this receptivity. It is grounded in a sensibility that instinctively responds to the lone teacher, the *Sadhu,* who persistently and patiently pursues the light of truth regardless of cost or sacrifice to himself. But, this sensibility becomes amplified at a level of reflective life to embrace the ideals of sensitivity and gentleness as controlling ideas in abstract and inclusive ways, in common practices and sensibilities, and in disciplines in daily life which will generate and nurture this spiritual capacity.

There is much in Indian life that perverts and betrays these sensitivities of the spirit; but take away this deep undertow of spirituality from its culture, where the firmer moral and ethical restraints are already lacking, and one would find a situation strangely impervious to the appeals of religious faith.

Christianity in India, along with other religious faiths, has fed upon this cultural sensibility, so marked in Indian life. Cultural anthropologists commonly speak of India as a "religious culture," by which they usually mean that its mores and customs root in and continue to draw nurture from the religious cult and its heritage. Various religious traditions, as the anthropologist will point out, contribute to and participate in this caldron of custom; and the differences between them are what add complexity to this fabric of faith. Thus one who chooses to study Indian society, cultural anthropologists have said, will be led to center his attention upon Indian religions; for religion is the heart of the matter.[13] To be sure, anthropologists, in speaking this way, to a large extent have in mind the external, observable evidence in custom and practice which he can examine and study; nevertheless, he is pointing to this inner core of sensibility and its dominance in shaping the ethos of its life.

Whether this sensitivity to the spiritual dimension of existence which anthropologists relate directly to religious cults—is an attribute of the heritage of faith that has grown up with the culture, or of an *élan* peculiar to the particular history and human formation which has shaped both religion and culture in India, is a question that remains unanswered. Many ingredients combine to give it character and direction. Consciously cultivated habits may not always be the most primal or decisive directives. Something in the opportunities afforded by time and place, and the trends that follow, elicits in a people spontaneous and vital responses which in turn become cherished, sought after, and re-enacted as a tradition of life. What then emerges as an organized existence or a social organization will tend to provide institutional practices and regulations favorable to such experiences and satisfactions. Religion, art, politics, and philosophical reflection all participate in the shaping of this *élan,* once it has become manifest in a people. But to what extent the total orbit of sensibilities can be identified with any one aspect of the social organization, or traceable to its influence and shaping, becomes less and less obvious the more one ponders the matter. Something more primal than these, pos-

[13] I am indebted to my colleague, Professor Milton Singer, Director of South Asian Studies in the University of Chicago, for this observation.

sibly in the structure of life which has evolved, possibly in the release of energies of grace that can be received by such a structure, enters profoundly into the situation to provide historical occasions for cults and institutions to take form, for ideas to break forth, for ways of living to emerge and to perpetuate themselves.

In any case it does become clear that nurture and the cherishing of sensibilities, along with the satisfactions they bring, are indispensable to the continuance of this qualitative attainment in a culture. For while that something in opportunity of time and place may persist, to break forth on repeated occasions, it can also be blurred and obscured by interests and efforts imposed from without, unless these, too, can be assimilated within the prevailing orbit of sensibilities. What is rich in qualitative attainment as heritage and depth in the structure of experience may go unnoted and thus unreceived by the symbolizing process of an individual as it shapes the individual consciousness. The reception of stimulus is itself the final act of selectivity by which individual man orders his way of living. He may respond to many other facets of his environment and of the persisting structure of experience that underlies his way of living. But response can mean negation and rejection as well. The act of rejection will have its own effects upon the temper and range of individual experience, acting as a habitual closing of doors to what appears to confront him. What is received, on the other hand, becomes a fund of internal meaning upon which the appreciative consciousness feeds and is nourished, by which taste and psychical yearnings are elicited, and in terms of which qualitative judgments are made in every act of self-expression or self-assertion.

The historical phenomenon of apprehension toward change and innovation will be better appreciated when this process of assimilating the qualitative experiences of a culture is understood. They who have pressed toward conserving such values have generally been highly cultivated in the experiences of them. And conversely, persons bent on innovation have often been indifferent to values accruing through tradition and thus have found them expendable. But there is a pathology of the conservative mind, tending to obscure the qualitative attainments of experience, and to elevate in their place the instruments of conservation. Thus tradition tends to be extolled for its own sake, and change is resisted as a matter of course.

The truth is, values are not retained in a culture simply through acts of conservation. For they then tend to become objects of appreciation or of resentment. In either case they are devoid of function and purpose, and thus lose vitality as a cultural force. They may be formalized and celebrated, but often this becomes a form of interment. To persist as live ingredients of the structure of experience, such values must be assimilated into the creative advance toward new forms, even new dimensions of meaning. This is what Whitehead undoubtedly meant to imply when he said that the past lives on only as an ingredient of the present. As an ingredient of the present it contributes depth and qualitative appeal to every instance of innovation. Innovation that assimilates and transmits inherited and recognizable values, even as it re-creates them through experimentation with new forms and perceptual experience, not only is thereby made durable, but is enabled to speak with more authority and power than is generally possible where bare innovation has occurred. We appear to be more familiar with this general principle in the realm of art and music than in the realm of ideas or of thought. At least we give recognition to its application more readily in those two spheres. Thus we recognize that Beethoven has power of expression and durability beyond most Romanticist composers of his period; and possibly that Richard Strauss and Sibelius, or even Stravinsky, are able to employ tonal dissonance with greater range of appeal and invention than much modern

33

music that dissociates itself more radically from the tradition of employing melody.

Now in this respect, the role of science and industry in the shaping of mores and human values in any culture is a fascinating but disturbing one. No one may say that science lacks a sense of tradition. Its very procedure of exploration and discovery is based upon a sequence of interrelated discoveries and decisions. It has its eruptions and periods of radical departure from historical precedent; nevertheless, its total history reveals a web of interacting theories and findings.

What is different about scientific method and scientific sensibilities is its ardent commitment to future attainment and its readiness to risk all else in the pursuit of its goal. Modern science, it has been said, is interested only in the truth of a considered fact, and it pursues this end unflinchingly and with a disregard for all inhibitions. The one qualification that is needed to make this assertion true is that scientific inquiry from the time of Galileo onward has confined itself to an exploration of a restricted area of phenomena, stressing principally motion and force; this greatly reduces the range of truth and fact that is relevant to its enterprise and all but ignores the problem of value. One may not say that it disregards value altogether, for insofar as the function and the determination of physical facts enter into the determination of value, science utilizes qualitative experience, but in its own fashion. Nevertheless, its role relative to the historical experience of cultural values has generally been constrictive rather than formative. It dispels more than it creates in this area of qualitative meaning.

The cultural significance of science as a human enterprise, apart from what it contributes to human well-being, lies in the vigor of its dedication to creative advance. It is the precursor of cultural change, relentlessly attentive to the expanding frontier of knowledge and experience. But again, such knowledge as it seeks, and such experience as it prizes, constitutes only a portion, an aspect of the organon of existence. While the materials it handles are concrete, physical realities of a given place of existence, the knowledge that it seeks about these materials is abstract and statistical, distilling from these concrete realities a generality of meaning. This has strategic and functional importance for many aspects of every culture; a culture that has been without a scientific generality of meaning suffers serious forms of deprivation. But a culture that has acquiesced wholly to the scientific vision and its form of meaning will accentuate material well-being, on the one hand, and overvalue abstract and statistical meaning to the disregard of concrete experiences and values on the other. Both these habits of mind tend to depersonalize existence and to undervalue unique and individual events of joy and satisfaction. A whole range of appreciative experiences and explorative ventures that can be revelatory, both deepening and broadening man's powers of apprehension and understanding but without general or statistical import, remain unknown, and thus nonexistent, for a culture limited to the vision of the sciences. It is for this reason that such a culture is sorely in need of the ministries of art and religion. But the disturbing fact is that the pursuit of science and the emulation of science tend to become so absorbing and complete that they command the full allegiance of a people's energy and attention. Scientists themselves are more ready to recognize and acknowledge this concern than others who slavishly accept and acquiesce in their findings; hence they are often more attentive to the problems that science can create than their admirers.

The role of industry in civilization has been similar to that of science in certain respects. That is, it has of necessity been committed to the forward march of mankind. Industry follows and thrives upon invention and the obsolescence it brings. Thus it promotes both as occurrences integral to its way of life. In this respect industry is the most radically modernizing force in any culture. But again, this applies solely to the physical realities of a culture. In the realm of ideas and moral or religious restraints, the industrial community, insofar as it is attentive to this aspect of culture, tends to be conservative to the point of obstructing the changing of values in society.

As the provider of things essential to the culture's physical existence, industry, like science, tends to accentuate material well-being above every other interest. Again, anyone who has observed what can happen to a culture where the continual support of industrial genius and enterprise has been lacking cannot speak disdainfully of the contribution which this concern with material well-being makes to a society. Yet the demands of industrialization are costly, not only in what it imposes as a way of life in any community, but in what it progressively crowds out of existence when a full commitment to its demands is given by a people. Industry imposes its own form of generality and statistical measure upon a community, countering the concrete, individualized, and revelatory mode of experience. Its methods are mass production and advertising (mass media). Its scale of production and demand for return on investment depend on both these modes of operation. That which is capable of being produced in quantities, and which appeals on a mass scale, dominates the market and determines the quality of goods available. Quantity thus intrudes as an arbiter of quality. Thus industry in its own way imposes the impersonal measure, with its generality of meaning, upon society to determine social taste and a way of existence.

In the sense in which we have been speaking, one must say that both science and industry contribute to the secularization of existence in any culture in which their processes become dominant or controlling. The meaning of secularization, as I am using the term in this context, can best be defined as a pathology in taste and judgment following from a truncation of experience where attention and concern are restricted to the abstract generalities of physical realities. A looser way of stating it, and perhaps a more recognizable way, would be to say that secularization is a relinquishment of the spiritual dimension of existence. I have tried to fix upon the specific character of the pathology rather than to indicate what is negated by the pathology. There are actual consequences that proceed from this preoccupation with abstract generalities of physical realities, altering the way we see things and evaluate them. The statistical measure and mass media provide an outlook upon experience which determines the kind of significance that is cherished and desired. Herein lies the distortion of experience and whatever meets us in experience. There is a positive form of pathology involved in this truncation of experience, therefore, as well as that which issues from a negation of the concrete meanings which open up the spiritual dimension of our existence.

It will be noted, however, that I speak of a pathology that issues from a preoccupation with the generalized concerns of science and industry. I am not making a broadside indictment of science and industry as such. There is, of course, venerable precedent for doing just that. We have our own instance of it in the agrarian movement among southern writers.[14] Mahatma Gandhi, however, was the most eminent and dedicated advocate of this view in our generation. And there was Tolstoy before him. Gandhi decried the building of railways and the erection of power industries.[15] His devotion to craft industries and to the self-sufficiency of villages based upon this mode of livelihood appealed to many of his countrymen, and

---

[14] Cf. Allen Tate, *I'll Take My Stand,* Harper, 1930; John Crowe Ransom, *God Without Thunder,* Harcourt, Brace, 1930; Herbert Agar and Allen Tate, *Who Owns America?* Houghton Mifflin, 1936; Donald Davidson, *The Attack on Leviathan.* University of North Carolina Press, 1936.

[15] Cf. Mahatma Gandhi, *Sermon on the Sea.* Universal Publishing Co., 1924.

37

swayed some of the leaders whom he gathered about him. His successor, Jawaharlal Nehru, however, is of a different turn of mind. Bent upon seeing India emerge as a world power, capable of taking her part in the world of nations, he has given his energies to persuading his countrymen to take a different course. Thus, in 1947, when India was given independence, with Nehru as prime minister, India set out upon a serious program of industrialization with the launching of its first five-year plan.

The shadow of secularization, in the definitive sense of the term, thus looms on the Indian horizon, possibly for the first time in its history, as it does in other cultures of Asia. India has yet to experience the full momentum of this way of thinking and existing. She is hardly beyond the late-nineteenth-century stage of Western experience in certain respects, though with the availability of advanced types of machinery and the technical guidance from societies already highly industrialized, her rate of progress can be expected to exceed that experienced earlier by the West. Already one detects issues arising in the literature of India reminiscent of problems that were to the fore in European and American experience in the 1920's. One can see that a scientific humanism is incubating which will undoubtedly gather momentum as the influence of the sciences spread. Similarly, one can say that the Neo-Hindu movement in the universities and in other intellectual centers in the major cities of India breathes an air of conciliation and reconception strikingly similar to the liberal movement of the West when the constructive efforts of an enlightened Christianity sought to come to terms with the scientific mentality and the emerging modern consciousness. One should not assume that these issues and problems are altogether new to Indian intellectuals. For a generation or more, at least since the turn of the century, when Rabindranath Tagore began his dream of universal man, Indian students and scholars have been in touch with Western learning and with the cultural problems issuing from the West's own encounter with a scientific discovery and industrialization. If a Gandhi, and a Tagore, could receive all that the West could give and still remain a confirmed Indian, and Hindu, in culture and faith, there were others like Nehru who found the scientific mentality more to their liking.

But attention to a problem that is remote from immediate experiences and pressing responsibilities can be only a theoretical adjustment of vision. Thus being informed in a Western outlook that had no immediate application to urgent problems of the East contributed at best to a sense of world awareness and enlightenment that could become doctrinaire without any possibility of verification.

The events of recent history have materially changed all this. The teaching of the sciences in the schools has become an actuality. The training of technicians and the developing of first-rate scientists are becoming increasingly urgent. The tempo of life, responding to the demands and scale of production and the new facilities of travel, is being accelerated. As technical vocations in industries make their demands, young men and their families move to the cities, breaking up the tradition of filial life in Hinduism, and tensions within families begin to mount. Everywhere changes are required to meet the new demands of successive five-year plans. In this kind of culture in ferment the issue of modernity is made real. Tradition and its cherished values are clearly at bay.

The one person, apart from the prime minister himself, who has become a kind of symbol of Indian adjustment to this new situation, and a weather vane of current developments, is the vice president of India, Radhakrishnan, who, as we have said, is the moving spirit of the Neo-Hindu movement in modern India. Radhakrishnan stands between the two tendencies just noted. He is a confirmed modernist in his sympathies and outlook and a zealous participant in the nationalist movement of modern India. Yet his speeches and writings clearly evidence a concern to hold to the historical faith of his culture and to channel currents, moving toward secularization, in a direction that will compel the new nationalists to take account of India's historical values. This means reinterpreting the historical faith to agree with the modern idiom. It is much too early to know whether or not this program of assimilation and reconception can succeed; but much may be determined by its venture, affecting the issue of India's faith and culture. And what happens here may well decide the fate, not only of Hinduism, but of all religious faiths within Indian culture.

II Secularization and the
Christian Ethos

The revolutionary changes in the cultures of the East, cur-
tailing and, in some instances, precluding the spread of
Christianity in Asia, have given rise to speculation about
the future of the Christian religion in these lands. Doubtless what prompts some of this speculation, especially
among Western Christians, is the misgiving about the
possibility of indigenous Christian groups coping success-
fully on their own with rival religious faiths in the new
nationalist situations that have arisen. There is also concern that cultural assimilation and accommodation will go
on to such an extent in Asian churches, as Christian
groups in the various cultures seek to overcome the bias
of Westernization, that the real thrust of the Christian
ethos will be lost to them. What is often overlooked when
these fears are expressed is that cultural accommodation
among Eastern Christians is occurring simultaneously
with ardent participation in the world community
of churches. There is no intention among these indigenous Christians of letting the church lapse into local,
isolated establishments, or simply into national religious
communities. There are, in fact, no more active and dedicated members of the World Council of Churches than
the Christian leaders who represent Asian churches. Nor
is there any serious tendency among them to let anti-
Western feeling curtail or compromise their participation
in the world community of Christians. For the Asian
Christian does not equate the concept of world community with Westernism. And insofar as he thinks about his

participation in the ecumenical church, he conceives of himself as transcending the provincialism of both East and West.

The Asian Christian, of course, is experiencing the zest and excitement of a new opportunity as he confronts the responsibilities of independence, both as a churchman and as a participant in the nation's renaissance. This may impel him to idealize his situation beyond its actualities. But if to Western eyes the withdrawal or dismissal of Western leadership from Christian churches in Asia portends the end of the Christian era in these lands, to the Eastern Christian, alive to the immediate tasks that are upon him, it is more like a new day dawning in which his own native experience as a Christian is about to come into its own. To be sure, as we indicated at the close of the preceding chapter, the Asian Christian, like his Hindu, Moslem, and Buddhist countrymen, has yet to experience the full impact of secularizing forces as they gather momentum in these cultures. A more revealing test of his confidence in this reorientation of Christian faith will come when this situation is upon him.

I

Secularization as we have known it in the West is relatively new in the East. This means in effect that the formative myths of these cultures persist to a considerable extent, with sufficient power and persuasion to inform not only the sensibilities and intellectual reflection of most of the people but the processes of state and the social structure as well. This is not true in every instance, but it is true to a remarkable degree in many of these cultures. There have been radical breaches in the cultural fabric, resulting from the intrusion of modern currents of thought, as when the Chinese philosopher Hu Shih countered the Confucian tradition in China with the philosophy of pragmatism,[1] in what was to become a major

[1] Hu Shih, *The Chinese Renaissance*. University of Chicago Press, 1934.

literary movement of reform. The present situation in Communist China is, of course, a deviation of radical proportions, affecting at least the processes of state, and progressively much more. In Japan the influx of Western ideas has had a continuous transformative effect upon its institutions and manner of life. And the all-out effort of the government of occupation, following World War II, to modernize the structure of government and to modify its laws accordingly has had telling effects in changing the tone and general appearance of Japanese life. Yet the quality of sentiments and feelings in many areas of Japan have remained remarkably attuned to the primal notions of its inherited culture. In India the integrity of primal notions has remained even more intact. Only within the past decade, with the concerted effort on the part of the National Congress, and under spirited protest from regional communities, have marked changes come about, countering the formative influences of the past. One does not detect in any of these cultures, until very recent times, anything comparable to the schism that occurred in Western experience at the beginning of the modern period with the rise of the scientific movement and the beginning of the industrial era. At this time the primal ethos of the West was confronted with a formidable current of counter-formative notions. Some would interpret the break with past mores at this juncture of our history as being so decisive and radical as to have initiated a new ethos, and possibly a new mythos as well. A careful scrutiny of the controlling ideas and intuitions in our cultural history since that time, however, even where the sciences have been in dominance, will not, in my judgment, bear this out. On this point I may be taking issue with Arnold Toynbee's generalization upon the events of this period,[2] though we may be assessing different aspects of their development. Certainly a break with the classical Christian struc-

[2] See quotations pp. 5 and 6.

ture of life more radical and far-reaching in effect occurred in the era of Enlightenment and scientific discovery than that which followed from the renascence and reform culminating in the events of the sixteenth century, yet not to the extent of effecting the dissolution of the Christian ethos.

I use the term "Christian ethos" here in the sense of the Judaic-Christian and Hellenistic complex of human sensibilities, for it is this fabric of valuations that has been formative in Western culture in designating the spiritual stature of Western man. Other historical cultures have employed a different complex of sensibilities with a different nexus of religious ideologies to give rationale and dramatic force to their expression. But for Western man the nurturing matrix of his civilizing influences and spiritual vision has been the Christian ethos, understood as this complex of sensibilities.

When one speaks of Western culture being dominantly Christian one is speaking descriptively rather than normatively. One is not saying necessarily that the West consciously practices the Christian ideal, or that it exemplifies Christian virtues. Rather, one is saying that the mode of existence, the bent of mind, and the direction of man's outreach in Western society, hence the motifs in his art forms as well as his fundamental notions in thought have been shaped under the pressure and lure of the Christian mythos. By mythos one means the pattern of meaning and valuations which has been imaginatively projected through drama and metaphor expressing the perceptive truths discerned in the historical experience of a people. The related term "ethos" implies "the character, sentiment, or disposition of a community or people" or "the spirit which actuates manners and customs," to employ a dictionary definition. Every culture exemplifies some historical pattern of meaning issuing from a cluster of basic perceptions and ideas. This perhaps is more readily recognized in looking at cultures other than our own. For ex-

44

ample, when one calls up such terms as "transmigration," "karma," "caste," "dharma," one is made aware that he is designating the essential themes of the Hindu view of life. Or when one mentions the fourfold truth of suffering, the eightfold path of release from suffering, and nirvana one is aware that he is describing the foundations of the Buddhist way of life. Christianity has its own cluster of perceptions and apprehensions which has been formative of its tradition and, in varying degrees, of the culture in which Christian faith has been dominant.

A full account of the evolving cultural experience of the West would reveal the Bible to be the primary document of Western culture. By this one means that the primary intuitions and perceptions which have gone into the shaping of the human psyche in this geographical area first appeared here in public and communicable form. Furthermore, the Bible has been the visible carrier of these persistent perceptions of our racial experience, at times serving simply as a repository when cultural upheaval has momentarily turned society aside from its nurture. At other times it has been a working document of the most immediate and contemporary kind, fortifying reform groups within Judaic-Christian history, or simply providing staying power for those who are capable of receiving its nurture.

Once one has been awakened to the realities of any culture from the perspective of a cultural anthropologist, one is led to see that the Bible, and its tradition, has a priority in our cultural experience which no other document shares; it cannot be dissolved or denied without serious loss and possibly radical dissolution of the controlling sensibilities of our common life.

What is basic here is not simply the pictorial imagery and poetry in which Biblical literature abounds. This, to be sure, has been remarkably retained and reproduced throughout the artistic and literary development of the West, from early Christian monuments and illuminated manuscripts to the stained-glass windows of Gothic cathedrals, and from the writings of the anti-Nicene Fathers, Augustine, and Dante, to the work of Shakespeare, Milton, and T. S. Eliot. These artistic forms and imaginative portrayals are persistent reflections of a distinctive thrust of the human spirit which is basic to this Western ethos. Contained in these imaginative accounts are clusters of ideas, like the Covenant, the redemptive acts in history, and the Creation story. The Biblical account of Creation, interestingly enough, does not precede the Biblical accounts of Redemption, but follows from it as a generalization upon these acts. These stories have become so commonplace, if not hackneyed, through reiteration and unimaginative exposition, that they have lost much of their lure and excitement. Yet they are the seminal perceptions of the race. They grasp what is primordial in our psychical experience and project into the vast unfolding drama of Western history their metaphorical imagery and their direction of imagination and rationale.

So much unfolds from these primal notions that we should be too long delayed in trying even to enumerate representative strands of experience and motifs, but a selective account of basic themes can be indicated. The root metaphor of this mythos, arising out of a Judaic reflection upon history, is the Covenant relationship—the notion that God comes to man in a personal encounter and establishes a relationship with his people, binding them together in a mutual pact of obligation and responsiveness. It is a relationship correlating faithfulness and freedom. These two facets provide the interplay between God and man in the Judaic-Christian understanding of the human situation, and contribute to the complexity of human nature which is found in the Christian doctrine of man. For the relationship defines man as being really free as an individual person, yet responsible to God and to other men. Herein lies the possibility of sin as meaning a violation of the pact of the Covenant through man's irresponsible assertion of his freedom and his consequent unfaithfulness. The breaking of the Covenant does not imply a breaking away from the relationship, but a breaking of the bond of trust, thus turning the relationship into a bond of judgment. This estranged situation is regarded as the source of man's sense of alienation. In the Christian mythos, only the act of divine forgiveness and its reception by repentant man can restore the relationship to one of trust and to a condition of freedom and faithfulness. Christian theology has given this root metaphor ontological status and meaning in formulating the doctrine of the *Imago Dei* (the image of God in man). But the relationship remains one of interplay between faithfulness and freedom. There is no automatic transfer of divinity to human nature. Man is really human. And the distinction between humanity and divinity is judiciously observed. This relationship is personal, implying freedom, decision, and responsibility in human acts. All these elements enter into the Christian understanding of man to give it its distinctive quality of concern and its historical assessment of the human situation.

The root meaning of this metaphor has reappeared, or at least has been presupposed, in various Western formulations. In an abstract context it informs the issue between the One and the Many, impelling Western Christian formulations of this issue to take account of the personal dimension of deity. At a more practical level, the Covenant is probably the root of this ever-present notion in Western experience that the individual person has a specific significance and destiny. This notion of individual significance has been expressed in various ways, ranging from a concern with the redemption of the individual to an emphasis upon the primacy of the person in the ethical sense. In exaggerated form it has become an ardent individualism. But the root metaphor presents individual men and women as being related to one another through God in a personal bond of community, thus giving meaning to the individual, even as it gives dignity and status as a free being. The idea of individual identity and reality, underlying our insistence upon individual freedom, also has its beginning here. I have argued in my *Faith and Culture* that the metaphor of the Covenant is probably basic to our understanding of the notion of relationship as this is employed in various contexts, countering automatic or mechanical causation. This concern with personal relationship is often attributed to a passion for freedom, stemming from more recent periods of Western history such as the Renaissance or even the period of the Enlightenment. But the notion of freedom in relationship has a deeper history than these explanations imply. And its primal ground is the metaphor of the Covenant. The Covenant, I would argue, is formative of our understanding of justice, and possibly of much that occurred in the Christian reinterpretation and adaptation of Roman law.

In a similar way such themes as the redemptive experience, forgiveness, and creation can be expounded as formative notions in our cultural pattern of life. The theme of personal identity and destiny, for example, to which we referred earlier, issues explicitly from the Redemption story in the New Testament. Here Christianity goes beyond the Hebraic myth in lifting up the person of Jesus Christ as the New Creation, offering a new dimension of life and hope to man as a release from his own involvement in sin and alienation. Thus the Cross and the Resurrection become symbols of the Christian mythos as distinctive of Christian culture as transmigration and karma are distinctive of Hindu culture. These terms point up peculiarities of Western sensibility and hope which set its people apart from non-Western peoples.

To point out the various ways in which these two symbols, the Cross and the Resurrection, have become expressive of the higher sensibilities of Western people would take a considerable amount of time. In juxtaposition they represent a correlation of the realities of evil in existence with the idealities of an ultimate faith in God. Together these two themes provide the clue to what is distinctive in our Western Christian conception of goodness, which implies an attitude of abandon toward the cost of relationships and its corollary, an investment of self, with confidence in the ultimate resolution of the crises that may follow from such a course, issuing in possible death and momentary defeat.

The theme of cultural optimism, which issued so readily into a doctrine of progress under the influence of evolutionary thinking in the nineteenth century, can be said to be a thin and partially secularized version of this redemptive theme. It has seized upon the idea of an ultimately confident resolution of current perplexities without taking account of the Cross. Thus history itself, or the sheer passage of time, is seen to be the answer to all problems as they move through their historical cycles. But whether this theme appears in its primal form as a correlation of the realistic and ideal elements of experience, or in its idealized version as cultural optimism, its "world-affirming" outlook, as contrasted with the "world-denying" outlook of Eastern cultures, to use Albert Schweitzer's words, is unmistakable. Strictly speaking, of course, the redemptive theme is world-affirming in the sense that history is seen as being under the judgment of God and thus redeemable through the resources of grace.

Closely allied with the redemptive theme and implicit in it is the motif of forgiveness. Here again one sees the imagery of personal decision and judgment taking precedence over unrelenting fate and mechanistic causation. The ultimate determination is not impersonal causation, but a working of grace. I am not meaning here to interpret the Christian doctrine of forgiveness, but to give some hint of the primal notion underlying the doctrine and the sensibility that issues from it to qualify the cultural outlook. In its classical formulation, the doctrine of

49

forgiveness has sought to integrate law and forgiveness.[3] To one outside the Christian ethos, however, this notion as doctrine or as sensibility appears to be indifferent to causal factors and their consequences, or fails to take them seriously and thus generates or encourages an irresponsible attitude toward them. It must be acknowledged that the cultural derivative of this notion has often degenerated into a sentimental attitude of expecting not to be held responsible for one's acts or decisions. "Somehow something will be done in my behalf to forestall the consequences!" This turn of mind is of a piece with the mood of cultural optimism, counting on everything working out all right. The force of the original intuition is lost in these perversions, for the sense of judgment is cancelled out, and with it, the cleansing and purgative effect of receiving the judgment of a good not one's own.

Underlying all these motifs, or perhaps we should say root metaphors of the Christian experience, Covenant, Redemption, Forgiveness, Cross, and Resurrection, is what the Swedish theologians Nygren[4] and Aulen[5] have designated the leitmotif of Christian faith, namely, agape, or love, by which is meant the impartial self-giving of God toward his creatures, and the inexhaustible source of grace which this assures. This notion, too, has had a history of transmutation, ranging from belief in the grace and judgment of a righteous God to a sanguine trust in providential care. When one studies the theological history of this motif of divine love underlying human existence, one is made aware of its grandeur and subtlety of thought. What it seeks to accomplish is an understanding of the correlation of holiness and goodness, of majesty and graciousness in the divine nature. When taken out of

---

[3] See Paul Tillich's discussion of this problem in *Love, Power, and Justice.* Oxford University Press, 1954.

[4] Anders Nygren, *Agape and Eros.* S. P. C. K., 1932.

[5] A. Aulen, *The Faith of the Christian Church.* Muhlenberg Press, 1948. A helpful account of this school of thought is Nels Ferre's *Swedish Contributions to Modern Theology.* S. P. C. K., 1932.

its specifically theological context, however, this motif tends to generate an air of familiarity and repose in the face of an ultimate destiny. The stark creature-feeling of earlier peoples, or the grim sense of destiny which characterizes many of the cultures of the East, stand in sharp contrast to the cultural outlook of the West where this transmutation has occurred. It may not be too much to say, in fact, that the sense of the holy in correlation with ultimate goodness is difficult to come by in the Christian West. To be sure, it appears in various expressions of Christian theology as a reaction against the sentimentalizing of relations with the Deity; [6] but the cultural outlook itself has been remarkably consistent, except for occasional interruptions of dissenting rebels, in maintaining an air of confidence and self-assurance in relation to whatever forms the backdrop and final ending of the human drama. This again has ranged from a full commitment to an overseeing Providence to an aggressive "self-reliance," in which the powers of nature and the ultimate turns of destiny are assumed to be in tune with human nature, or to be answerable to the will and designs of man. All three forms of cosmic familiarity, Christian piety, the philosophy of Immanence, and Humanism, have had the effect of releasing Western man from a preoccupation with the tragic sense of life.

What gives to modern Existentialism its dramatic quality in the present situation, and for many, a sense of realism, is its firm rebuff to all sanguine interpretations of human existence. Born of despair in the modern mood, and a lineal descendant of such historic rebels as Schopenhauer, Kierkegaard, and Nietzsche, it seeks to lay bare the tragic discrepancy between man's wishful or innocent participation in life and the realities that intrude to contradict his affirmations. Yet even here something of the

---

[6] Cf. Calvin's stress upon adoration and the sovereignty of God; Jonathan Edward's theme of austerity; and Rudolf Otto's numinous idea of the holy.

motif of familiarity escapes from his lips as he affirms his own humanity. All else is lost to him, every support fails him, nothing remains but his own authentic selfhood which he must now affirm and thus win for it its true reality. By contrast with an earlier Christian piety, or even with earlier forms of Humanism, Existentialism is a grim gospel. But compared with other cultural resolutions of the plight of man, notably those held in the East, it is almost heroic.

A comparison of the primal motifs of the Christian ethos with these cultural derivatives reveals how the process of cultural accommodation has tended to deprive them of stature and structural balance. This is not uncommon in the history of religions, for the dissemination of any gospel or teaching has generally met with compromise. And while reforms within religions have often been motivated by a responsible and enlightened concern to correct existing defects, zeal and a reactionary temper of mind have served again and again to mar balance of judgment. Thus sectarian developments have occurred, fragmenting or trivializing basic themes of the faith, or reinterpreting them to accord with momentary sentiments or feelings. It is rare that any schismatic group by itself, once it has made absolute a single theme and excluded others, succeeds in recovering either the logic or the dramatic unity of its primal notions. The genius of the contemporary ecumenical movement in Christianity is in its effort to reorient the Christian witness within Protestant churches toward its central affirmation, belief in Jesus Christ, thus putting the accent on its unifying center as a judgment upon its divisiveness and fragmentation. But while this restores a central point of focus, eliciting from each participating member a reach beyond its own particularized orbit, it does not enable any one group, or all of them together, to repossess the historical dynamics of faith to which this central focus points. This can be won or repossessed only if the central point of focus in Jesus Christ is seen to be not just a rallying point for contemporary Christian loyalty and dedication, but a summit point leading back into a drama of history and a cultural witness of faith, ultimately illumining man's life in God. These several strands form a logic of faith, or as we have said, a dramatic unity of themes expressive of its total structure of meaning.

Three types of theological inquiry have arisen in modern Protestantism, directed toward accomplishing this recovery of structure in the Christian witness. One is the motif research of the Lund school of Swedish theologians which seeks to single out and to clarify the essential themes of the Christian faith.[7] A second is the Trinitarian Scheme of Karl Barth which undertakes a reconception of the classical structure of Christian faith through a repossession of the kerygma and an elaboration of its meaning within the Trinitarian formula.[8] A third employs a current ontological system of meanings either symbolically or analogically for reconstructing the logic of faith. Paul Tillich's Systematic Theology exemplifies the symbolic method within this form of inquiry.[9] Process theologians have sought to employ the basic notions of the philosophy of organism analogically to give ontological vision and direction to reconstructing the themes of Christian faith.[10]

[7] G. Aulen, *Christus Victor*, S.P.C.K., 1931; *The Faith of the Christian Church*, Muhlenberg Press, 1948; Anders Nygren, *Agape and Eros*, Macmillan, 1932-39; *Commentary on Romans*, Muhlenberg Press, 1949. See also Nels Ferre, *Swedish Contributions to Modern Theology*. Harper, 1939.

[8] Karl Barth, *Die Kirchliche Dogmatik*. Vols. I-IV. C. Kaiser, 1932-1959. English translation, *Church Dogmatics*, Vols. I-III, Pt. 4, Scribners, 1936-1961. Emil Brunner and Reinhold Niebuhr also try to adhere to an exposition of an explicitly Biblical faith, yet with a more attentive ear to apologetic concerns. Cf. Emil Brunner, *Man in Revolt*, Westminster Press, 1947; *The Mediator*, Westminster Press, 1947; and his recent works in *Dogmatics*. Also Reinhold Niebuhr, *The Nature and Destiny of Man*. 1941-43.

[9] Paul Tillich, *Systematic Theology*, Vols. I and II. Vol. III in Preparation.

[10] William Temple, *Nature, Man, and God*, Macmillan, 1935; *Christus Veritas*. Macmillan, 1954. Lionel Spencer Thornton, *The Incarnate Lord*, Longmans, Green & Co., 1928; *The Common Life in the Body*

What may not be fully understood by those who are occupied chiefly with the practical concerns of faith is that theologians, in pursuing this effort, are not simply trying to make faith intelligible, or to give it intellectual respectability. They are concerned basically with restoring to the witness of faith the stature which its historical structure had attained, but which had been lost to the church and to society through cultural accommodation, sentimentalization, and the attrition that normally comes to it through secularization. To some extent this very act of reinterpreting the faith within a current idiom partakes of cultural accommodation; but, in being systematic, with full attention to the total unity of the historical witness, such a theological reinterpretation is able to avoid many of the distortions and fragmentations that befall incidental acts of accommodation where more immediate and occasional concerns are to the fore.

Now a question that will have been forming in the minds of many as they read these pages, recounting the themes of the Western Christian mythos, is: What relevance does this metaphorical heritage have to the serious thought and action of the contemporary man? I shall not go into the whole problem of the claims of tradition upon any society. In this context I am concerned to point out the bearing of this deeply laid, historical shaping of the sensibilities and the imaginative capacity of any people, and to suggest that it persists long after individuals within

of Christ, Dacre Press, 1950; Revelation and the Modern World, Dacre Press, 1950; The Dominion of Christ, Dacre Press, 1952; Christ and the Church. Dacre Press, 1956. Cf. also Norman Pittenger, Rethinking the Christian Message, Seabury Press, 1956 and The Word Incarnate, Nisbet, 1959; Daniel Day Williams, God's Grace and Man's Hope. Harper, 1950. My Faith and Culture, Oxford University Press, 1953, is an effort to establish the basis by which a post-liberal theology within this perspective might present the basic structure of Christian faith, and the present work continues that effort. A recent statement on theological method, contributing further to this effort, is Schubert Ogden's Christ Without Myth. Harper, 1961.

a culture have consciously disavowed it, or sought to counter its shaping within that culture. Thus it is a reality in existence of the most efficacious sort, despite all that sophisticated processes of criticism and reflection might do to dispel it. I am also concerned to say that a culture disavows this historical shaping at great risk to its own character and operation, and possibly at the cost of courting dissolution of significant fibers in the fabric of its cultural experience which become manifest through the sensibilities, yearnings, and disposition of a people, and that form their character. Qualitative attainment in any people is a long and arduous process, requiring the interplay of many dimensions of a culture's historical experience. As I tried to indicate earlier, such attainment is not solely the work of the past; nor is it retained simply by clinging to the past. It is a mystery of creative interchange between inherited and immediately available resources and opportunities in the present. The depth of experience in the present is retained or sustained only as this creative interchange occurs. The doctrinaire resistance to change as well as a ruthless commitment to bare innovation are the two modes of impoverishment that threaten every period of a culture's history; but they become acute and menacing in periods of cultural revolution. These opposing extremes in themselves, however, are not to be deprecated. For purposes of initiating decisive action, either to bring a cutting edge to bear upon issues or to provide a firm resistance at any given time in history, they may be important. These extremes arise as significant emphases within history in response to events, precisely out of this kind of spirited attack upon issues as they emerge. Nevertheless, in acknowledging their role and purpose, we may not overlook the casualties they tend to impose upon a society when they persist as doctrinaire states of mind, indifferent to the fresh demands of historical occasions.

The art of retaining a cultural heritage through transmutation and adaptation to historical changes is a great art which is difficult to practice. The remarkable thing is that the successful practice of this art occurs with unfailing regularity in culture after culture, though not without great anguish and cost in the expenditure of energy, and often life, both on the part of those who resist historical change, and those who press for the claims of innovation.

II

Alongside this effort in modern thought to retain or to repossess the primal meanings of the Christian ethos, there is a counter effort at work in Western culture to dissociate contemporary ethical and religious thinking from this primordial ground. On the surface it would seem that this effort clearly represents a secularizing of religious and ethical thought. Scholars who undertake to extricate such motivation from its historical heritage openly speak of giving up all reference, say to Christian terms. What is overlooked here is that all thought occurs within a matrix of cultural meaning, the nature of which is not necessarily altered by a shift in terms. The elimination of a theological vocabulary may not extricate one from the ethos out of which the theological vocabulary has emerged. For this reason people who speak most zealously about "being done with Christian terms" are often deeply involved with concepts, sensibilities of thought, or even structures of meaning, which are but veiled or transmuted forms of these primal notions.

Mircea Eliade has observed that

Nonreligious man has been formed by opposing his predecessor, by attempting to "empty" himself of all religion and all transhuman meaning. He recognizes himself in proportion as he "frees" and "purifies" himself from the "superstitions" of his ancestors. In other words, profane man cannot help preserving some vestiges of the behavior of religious man, though they are emptied of religious meaning. Do what he will, he is an inheritor. He cannot utterly abolish his past, since he is himself the product of the past. He forms himself by a series of denials and refusals, but he continues to be haunted by the realities that he has refused and denied. To acquire a world of his own, he has desacralized the world in which his ancestors lived; but to do so he has been obliged to adopt the opposite of an earlier type of behavior, and that behavior is still emotionally present to him, in one form or another, ready to be reactualized in his deepest being.[11]

There is much in the history of modern Western thought and in current thinking that conforms to this pattern of inversion: attaining release from a religious orientation by defining itself against that which is rejected. But for one who is attentive to the cultural matrices of thought and experience, such inversion never gets outside of the formative notions and the texture of meaning it imparts. It merely dissociates itself from certain historical formulations of these notions and then proceeds to reformulate their meaning in new terms.

There can be little doubt that much of the ethical idealism and humanism that has developed in the West since the seventeenth century is a truncation of the Christian ethos. One might be tempted to say, in the language of the day, that it is a "demythologizing" of this ethos. But this would not be accurate; for "demythologizing" implies a retention of the depth and mystery of the event, or insight in transposing it to a more familiar and acceptable discourse within the modern idiom. The motive back of much current ethical and humanistic thinking, on the contrary, continues the effort of the rationalists of the Enlightenment period, namely, of stripping these notions down to "fighting weight," which is to bend them to an

[11] Mircea Eliade, *The Sacred and the Profane,* Trans. from the French by W. R. Trask. Harcourt Brace, 1959; Harper Torchbook, 1961, p. 204.

occasion. The concern here is commendable; yet there is a sacrifice of proportion and judgment that follows from a disregard of the total structure of meaning being employed; one is often betrayed into mistaking zeal and decisiveness for righteousness and truth. Nevertheless, one errs, in my judgment, when one points to this current of thought and effort as secularization; for much of the zeal for righteousness and truth is retained in it. In fact, one must say it is accentuated and sharply focused to achieve specific ends within the culture.

We would do well at this point to look at this phenomenon of secularization as it has been identified and understood in Western thought. A simple, but relatively superficial, way of understanding secularization is to think of it as being the opposite of the term "sacred" and then to identify the sacred with classical Christian doctrine. Whatever deviates from the accepted system of Christian doctrine and the authoritative system that sanctions it may then be designated secular. I call this view superficial because it leaves uncalculated the subtle influx and penetration of all primal religious notions into the cultural discourse, and thus assumes that meanings can be captured and controlled by an authoritative system in the way that people who use meanings are controlled. But it is also arbitrary. It establishes its own systematic discourse as the norm of sacred meaning, and on this basis all thought which diverges from its center, whether religious or not, is said to partake of secularization.

Another familiar way of speaking of secularism in our Western discourse is to identify it with everything that has happened in Western society through the influence of the sciences. The challenging of classical Christianity, this view holds, did not become serious in Western society until the coming of modern science. Intimations of its seriousness had been given by the work of Copernicus and Galileo, and by the zealous efforts of Francis Bacon; but the movement of dissolution, it is said, begins in full force with the seventeenth century. Arnold Toynbee has expressed this view aptly, saying:

> The opening of the seventeenth century had found the Western Christian Wars of Religion in full swing and Western Christian fanaticism still at its height. Before the close of the same century, Religion had been replaced by Technology, applying the findings of Experimental Science, as the paramount interest and pursuit of the leading spirits in the Western Society. When the century closed, this revolutionary change in the Western attitude and ethos was, no doubt, still confined to a minority. Yet it is remarkable that even a minority should have moved so far in so short a time, and, still more, that they should have set the rest of Society moving in their wake. In the course of the quarter of a millennium running from the beginning of the eighteenth century to A.D. 1956, the leaven of secularization and the zest for Technology had spread progressively from one stratum of the Western Society to another till they had permeated the whole mass.[12]

A close study of this seventeenth-century period will disclose that science was only one of the cultural forces contributing to the breakup of the Christian mythos and its influence as classical Christianity had formulated it. And in England science was a late-comer, not really asserting itself as an organized influence, as Canon Charles Raven has observed,[13] until the middle of the seventeenth century. Nevertheless, as other cultural causes subsided, the scientific view of nature and of human experience loomed more and more as the directing vision of a new ethos.

The issue has never been clear, however. For scientists in the main have not consciously contributed to the dissolution of Christian faith or its ethos. Individual scien-

[12] Arnold Toynbee, *An Historian's Approach to Religion.* Oxford University Press, 1956, p. 184.
[13] C. E. Raven, *Science, Religion and the Future.* Cambridge University Press, 1943.

tists such as Newton were as concerned with theological problems and their history as they were with science itself. Their own lives reveal a sensitivity and faithfulness to the Christian ethic as well as to worship. Similarly, liberal Christians, from the time of the Enlightenment through the nineteenth century, and after, have employed the findings of the sciences, even as they sought to come to terms with them, not to counter or to supersede Christian faith, but to illumine it within the idiom of modern culture and thus to transmit its teaching more readily to their fellow men who had also felt the persuasion of the sciences. It is for this reason that the liberal Christian has not been willing to equate science with secularism. The scientific understanding of man and his world, the liberal has insisted, is a dimension of experience which aids self-understanding. It enables man to develop a critical sense in dealing with factual matters, and encourages disciplined thought where the use of facts is relevant to knowledge. Insofar as we depend upon physical realities and upon an ability to employ them with intelligence and confidence, the liberal has argued, we are beholden to the sciences and to whatever measure of scientific learning we can assimilate. Science becomes a secularizing force in one's thinking, the liberal has contended, only when its understanding of physical realities is made to suffice for an interpretation of the whole of man's nature and destiny. One then relinquishes the responsibility to confront scientific insight with the claims of faith, or conversely, to confront the claims of faith with the facts of science.

The history of liberalism will reveal that liberal theologians have relinquished this responsibility at times when they have made one or more of the sciences the arbiter of theological judgment, thus replacing theological inquiry with an appeal to scientific method. But one should recognize that this is a deviation from what liberalism has intended, and is not to be taken as being expressive of its representative voice.

However, one will detect within liberal history the acceleration of a temper of mind that gradually despairs of holding the two sides of this dual allegiance together, or of attempting to confront the one with the other. This mood, in effect, began with Francis Bacon, despite his condescension to theology, and forms a rather consistent tradition of thought and inquiry through the nineteenth century, of which Thomas Huxley and Herbert Spencer may be taken to be representative thinkers. In our time the names of John Dewey, Bertrand Russell, and Julian Huxley are generally associated with this temper of mind. For the most part, this tradition of Western thought seeks to widen the orbit of scientific inquiry to include the sphere of human interests and problems which are defined as ethical and religious and which apply specifically to the social concerns of society. Thus one may not say that it is a restriction of concern to physical realities, or simply a lifting to dominance of the demand and measure of these realities. It represents rather a social transmutation of physical facts or an idealization of their meaning, such that the base of inquiry is seen to be science itself, though the theoretical analysis and interpretation is made to yield humanistic implications capable of informing man's ethical and social problems. When secularization is taken to mean departure from the orbit of Christian doctrine, the term applies readily to this scientific humanism. No doubt most scientific humanists would accept and welcome this judgment, for they have made it clear themselves that they wish to dissociate themselves from Christianity. But the difficulty with employing the terms secularization in this restricted way is that it then soon comes to mean simply non-Christian, and thus loses all significance as a descriptive term in relation to non-Christian cultures.

It would seem that Mircea Eliade has offered a helpful solution to this problem in his book, *The Sacred and the Profane,* where he treats the question in relation to the whole history of religions. Eliade writes:

Whatever the historical context in which he is placed, *Homo religiosus* always believes he is placed in an absolute reality, the sacred, which transcends this world but manifests itself in this world, thereby sanctifying it and making it real. He further believes that life has a sacred origin and that human existence realizes all of its potentialities in proportion as it is religious—that is, participates in reality. . . . By reactualizing sacred history, by imitating the divine behavior, man puts and keeps himself close to the gods—that is, in the real and the significant.[14]

Profane man, on the other hand, writes Eliade, "is the result of a desacralization of human existence." And:

The nonreligious man refuses transcendence, accepts the relativity of "reality," and may even come to doubt the meaning of existence. . . . Modern nonreligious man assumes a new existential situation; he regards himself solely as the subject and agent of history, and he refuses to appeal to transcendence. In other words, he accepts no model for humanity outside the human condition as it can be seen in the various historical situations. Man *makes himself,* and he only makes himself completely in proportion as he desacralizes himself and the world. The sacred is the prime obstacle to his freedom. He will become himself only when he is totally demysticized. He will not be truly free until he has killed the last god.[15]

This is indeed a clear and forthright demarcation between religious and nonreligious man, between the sacred and the profane; but does it really deal adequately with the question we are analyzing? It certainly characterizes the state of mind of the modern humanist of whom we have just been speaking—the one who has despaired of holding together the two sides of modern's man's dual allegiance. And perhaps none of the men we have mentioned would object to being called profane in Eliade's

14 Op. cit. p. 202.
15 Ibid. p. 203.

sense of that term. But does this answer the question we are asking about secularization in Western life? I think not altogether. For our problem of secularization is not simply a matter of conceiving the world within or without the transcendent vision. It is a question of being responsive to realities within experience which evoke in man a sense of his relation to something ultimate or significant, be it truth or goodness, or some dimension of value inherent in himself, which lights up his existence with meaning beyond the terms of physical realities. I would tentatively distinguish between the terms "secular" and "profane" as Eliade uses them. The profane, as he says, implies a conscious rejection of "the sacred space" and thus the profane defines a human attitude. The relation of the profane to the sacred, or to the religious dimension of existence, is an ambiguous one, as I have indicated, and as the earlier quotation from Eliade suggests.[16] Secularism, I would hold, is a condition that befalls a situation or a society. It implies the disregard of the religious or the ultimate dimension of existence, but this is a condition of judgment that takes hold of a community or a person; it is not consciously or purposely embraced. In this sense it is a pathology that settles in the human character, in the process of a society or in the mode of life of a community or culture.

In defining secularization as a pathology in the social process affecting taste and judgment, following from a truncation of human experience in which ideal and spiritual values are disregarded or denied to man, one is not so apt to interpret its meaning within a single point of view or philosophy. Instead one will see that it is a condition and response within human existence which disregards all intrinsic meaning as this applies to man, and thus deprives him of dignity and of a personal destiny. So defined, the term secularization can have meaning to

[16] See pp. 56-7 of this chapter.

63

Christian and non-Christian alike as a threat to man's spiritual life.

When secularism is understood in this way, it becomes apparent that few serious efforts to analyze or to interpret the human problem can be designated secular; for most of such efforts have been motivated by a concern to deal with man's plight as it relates to his intrinsic meaning, or to improve his destiny. The element of the sacred has entered into these calculations, if only in tenuous form, as a concern for the significance of human beings. Many scholars and churchmen will object to expanding the notion of the sacred to this extent, for it is more commonly applied to what is beyond man or other than man. But here I am concerned to do justice to the most minimum expression of ultimate worth as it appears in our human reckoning and in every concrete situation, so as not to ride roughshod over any serious and responsible theory about or perspective upon man in applying the term "secularization." The question as to the adequacy or inadequacy of any one interpretation of man and his destiny, or of one's understanding of the sacred, is quite another matter.

III

In this context, then, secularization is not an overt interpretation of man, but a condition that befalls him or his culture when the spiritual challenge to his sentient and psychical life is dissipated through trivial absorptions, or when it is set aside through exposure to processes of society which cancel out all consideration of the human being as a reality worthy in himself and answerable to an ultimate destiny.

What renders science and industry so vulnerable as purveyors of secularization in any culture is the impersonal and abstract character of the processes upon which they depend and which they employ. Living realities are reduced to pin points and to statistical equations. A vast array of graphs and figures forms the faceless portrait of statistical man. The mass effect, generalities writ large, are what survive and determine decisions.

Now we should not fail to recognize the beneficent strain of meaning that runs through this maze of abstractions and mass effort. What lifts the level of human well-being for each individual in a technological society is the accumulation of highly specialized knowledge and its application to human need. Science and industry contribute this to mankind! But we would be most sanguine and naïve if we were to assume that such knowledge and resources are put to service only to improve our human condition and to minister to human need.

In a technological society promotion and enterprise become a necessity, and the means at hand, often subtle and concealed, can be highly effective in directing and controlling public opinion or consumer judgment. In all of this man is a utility, a point on the chart, or a puppet to be manipulated for ulterior ends. Now it is both the overt use of these resources of abstract knowledge and data for dubious and for even corrupt ends, and their consequent effects upon the human psyche that contribute to the pathology we have called secularization. Both the dignity and the spiritual stature of the human spirit are at stake in this issue. Both the meaning and identity of man as man, and each man's own self-understanding and esteem, are involved here.

But even the good that is served by such technical skill and its resources contributes to decadence in a technological society. For an economy of abundance is put to it to remain fluid and productive. Hence consumption must keep pace with production. This endless circle of necessity accentuates the concern with marketable goods and the need for more and more of them in numerous varieties until, in Emerson's words, "things are in the saddle and ride mankind." Man's sense of need is elastic and can be made to respond to stimulation. There is literally no end

65

to which this concern with creature comfort or appetition and its ministries can be carried in a technological society. This, in fact, becomes all-absorbing because it is so basic to the survival of the structure of life that promotes it. Thus a structural necessity and a cultivated sense of need combine to lift a secondary theme of existence to a major preoccupation. Physical comfort and well-being become the all-important goals of man's life. Accordingly, man's sense of dependence upon trivial discriminations in every aspect of his physical well-being increases. The sheer expenditure of time and energy in satisfying these cultivated needs can be enormous. The days and the years will not suffice to encompass it. There is human degradation that results from poverty and from the lack of proper and adequate means to heal and nurture the body. There is also human degradation that follows from the pursuit of physical well-being when this is made the chief and all-absorbing end of life.

The problem of physical well-being has become so acute and central in the struggles of world revolution today that no one can simply dismiss this concern as being a symptom of secularization. Whatever pathologies may have occurred in our own exaggerated pursuit of this end, we cannot be oblivious of the fact that millions of human beings are denied their humanity for lack of a concern with well-being. Yet it gives one pause to realize that in transmitting our own cultural experience in scientific invention and industry to other cultures in need of bodily renewal, we may be transmitting the pathologies of this concern as well.

It is clear that decisions have been made within Eastern cultures to alter or to depart from traditional mores in their turning to industrialization and to science to combat existing problems of poverty and disease. The Asiatic, when he is expressing the traditional bent of mind of the East, as it has been shaped by Hindu and Buddhist teaching, looks upon all concern with human comfort, conven-

ience, or improvement of human conditions as materialistic. Compassion for those who suffer or who are in need
is one thing. This is a grace of the human spirit that can
be encouraged. Preoccupation with the removal of suffering and need by increasing man's economic abundance or
by eliminating bodily ills amounts to a physical solution
of the problem. Only the Buddhist has said explicitly that
existence is suffering, thus giving this condition ontological
status; but it could be said that the East generally, insofar
as it follows this traditional bent of mind, acknowledges
suffering to be the general condition of man. And this
becomes a major premise from which other deductions
are made. Suffering is in large measure conceived to be
the result of desire; in any case it is accentuated by desire.
Consequently, the elimination of desire or the limiting of
its effects would mean the elimination of suffering. This,
in their judgment, is the spiritual solution of the problem.
This presupposition and this solution have far-reaching
cultural implications insofar as they are consistently carried through, as one may observe in studying the history
of the cultures in which they have been controlling factors. The fact of the matter is, however, that Westernism
has had a more pervasive effect upon the East than is
generally acknowledged by Easterners themselves. And
this has countered the logic of the traditionally Eastern
bent of mind in shaping the social practices of various cultures of the East. Nevertheless, the rationale for turning
aside from any positive concern with human well-being in
the Western sense has persisted, and in its way has continued to be effective in certain regions of these cultures,
even as national measures of reform are being projected.

The West, as we have said, is looked upon in the East
as being materialistic. This applies not only to our preoccupation with economic abundance and with "things,"
but to our interpretation of the human problem. Our dependence upon physical comforts and conveniences is the
most evident sign of our materialism; but beneath this

habit and way of living is detected a prevailing concern for well-being which takes for granted that desire, interest, sensibility in matters of qualitative goods are legitimate and acceptable ends to pursue. Even the way we interpret "the pursuit of happiness" as a social and political goal appears to Eastern eyes to take on materialistic implications. Thus our solution to the human problem, assuming that we, too, start with a recognition of suffering and human need as basic conditions with which man must contend, takes the turn, not of eliminating human desire, or even of tempering it, but of altering the circumstances and the environment. The definition of the problem thus turns us inevitably to tasks addressed to the material conditions of existence.

Now as Westerners, we should not be too easily intimidated by this term "spiritual" as the Easterner often uses it, or by the judgment upon us by those who proclaim spirituality as a panacea for our ills. Spiritualism, when it is set sharply over against the concern with material goods, tends to exaggerate and to exploit the powers of the mind in the way that materialism exaggerates and exploits the demands of the body. Spiritualism and materialism are polar opposites only in the sense that each has pursued excessive measures in opposite directions. Each of them roots in a one-sided conception, or possibly a misconception, of the nature of man. If materialism finds justification for ignoring the things of the spirit, and accentuates the practical concerns of a culture out of all proportion to man's needs and his ultimate good, spiritualism can find justification for regarding the physical life of man unreal, and thus neglect these physical needs to the point of incurring human degradation in a culture. The issue between spiritualism and materialism, as it is commonly posed by Eastern critics of the West, is a fallacious one. Or perhaps we should say it poses the question of man's ultimate good in a way that actually obscures the reality of spirit and its claims upon our human dimension.

Not only can spiritualism and materialism alike become evils in their respective ways, bringing about human degradation; but each in its own way can have obstructive effects in blocking the way to an understanding of the realities basic to man's existence.

Our problem in the West, however, is our materialism, or the secularization of our ethos to the extent of absorbing us in a debilitating concern with the physical realities of existence. No amount of critical evaluation of other cultural traditions, or resentment toward dubious criticisms of our way of life, should keep us from facing this predicament in our culture. The problem has been radically heightened and made more acute by the startling innovations in technical and industrial processes, following from nuclear discoveries, automation, and space exploration. These innovations are radically altering people's perspective of themselves and of the world they must live in. The tensions of the cold war serve to intensify apprehensions associated with this new situation, and to focus events so exclusively around the concern for defense, or in terms of rivalry with Communist aims, that no clear perspective on what is really occurring, or possibly emerging in this nuclear age, seems possible. The one sharp intuition that intrudes itself as a haunting intimation of what is happening to us is the realization that mechanization is on the increase, and is accelerating at such a rate as to defy our imaginations to keep pace with what it portends for the future. With mechanization comes dependence upon technical knowledge and the skill of technicians, and eventually upon the humanlike operations of machines. The more massive and powerful machines become, the more deadly and ominous their threat to human life and safety appears when things go wrong, or even when things are going well; hence the more acute our sense of dependence upon the technical or the mechanical mind. Mechanization is the long arm of scientific invention and industrial "know-how" reaching further and further into our mode of existence. The prospect of what this can mean appears somewhat frightening to lay people when their uninformed and intimidated imaginations begin to play over these circumstances. Yet their apprehensions take on substance when one reads the announcement that Soviet Russia is creating a city of scientists that will be presided over by robot supervisors.

A question that comes to the fore, then, as one reflects upon the situation, is: Has the process of secularization, implicit in a technological civilization, progressed so far in the West that sensibilities inherent in the Christian ethos can be expected to become ineffectual, or cease to make any claim upon us as a people? There is really no ready answer to this question. If one is determined not to be discouraged by secularizing trends that appear to be mounting daily in force and effectiveness, one will find assurance in the awakened zeal of Christian inquiry and dedication as this becomes manifest in the upsurgence of faith that has been reaching mass proportions, as well as in the theological renaissance that has stirred modern Protestantism for more than three decades. The vigor of these activities might argue that a religious resurgence is as evident in our culture as in the cultures of the East where Hindus, Buddhists, and Moslems are astir with renewed vitality. In the present world context, of course, all religious resurgence partakes of the ambiguities of cultural ambitions which are now being sharply focused around nationalistic objectives. Every culture that I know anything about presents this kind of ambiguity. We have striking instances of it in our own country. These instances simply illustrate the fact that where religion assumes the proportions of mass power it will become a political force, either as a threat to national purposes, or as an ally of them. And if it can be employed to further political ends, there are usually agencies ready to employ it.

But this matter gets out of hand if we allow ourselves

to deal with it cynically or unsympathetically. Whether we are speaking of the rapport between religion and culture, or simply analyzing an upsurgence of faith within the culture, we need to see that issues here are never black and white nor are the motives clearly suspect or wholly above suspicion. The religious resurgence in America, for example, gives ample evidence of being a genuine struggle of soul to ransom our culture from the impoverishing effects of its own materialism and, at the intellectual level, to repossess a capacity for wonder and elemental faith of which our sophistications in scientism have stripped us. Furthermore this upsurgence of faith reflects a sober and genuine response of Western people to the upheaval in values and loyalties which has occurred in the civilized West within recent memory, as well as to the imminent threat of human destruction which this new power age imposes. No one plumbs the depths of this renascent spirit of faith, in this country or in cultures abroad, unless he senses this genuine mood of penitence and reappraisal which underlies the surface currents of reaction and their conservative tide.

Has secularization progressed so far in the West then as to make the Christian ethos ineffectual in its mode of life? To answer this question it is not enough to look to the status of the Christian church in Western culture, or to the persisting influence of Christian doctrine. An assessment of these influences would provide only a partial reading of resources that are relevant to the question. Other witnesses to this complex of sensibilities such as Judaism and the various humanistic expressions of nonconformities, including modern Existentialism, would need to be taken into account. For where Christianity in its formal expression in some churches appears to be lagging in its witness to this historical ethos, and even participating in the secularization of faith and culture, a prophetic witness is being heard outside the churches, actually serving to awaken contemporary thinking to the demands of this ethos. There can be little doubt but that the most incisive and penetrating portrayals of the human situation in our day, prompted by a despair with this technological civilization, have come from Existentialist writers such as Jaspers, Heidegger, Martin Buber, Berdyaev, Gabriel Marcel, and Albert Camus.[17] In most instances the Existentialist's anguish is Judaic-Christian, though his solution to the human situation may not be. In his painful awareness of the meaninglessness that has come into human living, of the absurdity that can stare out from the pathos of events, and in his clear delineation of the human cry that demands more than this civilized state of man can yield, the Existentialist voices a prophetic protest and awakens our sense of judgment, even though he may be without the authority to utter, "Thus saith the Lord!"

The Existentialist writer who perhaps has brought the most illumination to our generation in enabling us to see beyond the crisis and tragedy of our day has been the Jewish philosopher, Martin Buber.[18] His sensitive and searching writings have served to give a clearer vision to many who have pondered these issues, not only in what he has been able to lay bare of the lonely individual, but in what he has offered as insight into the way of relationship between human beings. The pen of the Russian philosopher, Nicolas Berdyaev, was relentless, especially in his earlier writings, protesting the mechanization of modern life, and man's acquiescence to his enslavement. In later works, *Slavery and Freedom,* and *Freedom and the Spirit,* Berdyaev offered a probing reconception of the life of the spirit. His *Destiny of Man* is a remarkably complete and many-sided exposition of the Christian conception of man, attentive to the creative and artistic ca-

[17] A helpful survey of this current of thought is F. H. Heinemann's *Existentialism and the Modern Predicament.* Harper, 1953.
[18] Martin Buber, *I and Thou* (originally published in Germany, 1923). English edition, T & T Clark, 1937; *Between Man and Man,* Kegan Paul, 1947; *Eclipse of God,* Harper, 1952; *To Hallow This Life,* Harper, 1958; *The Prophetic Faith.* Harper, 1960.

pacities of the human spirit as well as to man's moral problems. For a graphic portrayal of the character and plight of modern man, and a delineation of the source of his sense of meaninglessness, few modern writers have matched the skill and incisiveness of the late French Existentialist, Albert Camus, in such works as *The Rebel, The Plague,* and *The Fall.*

Christian theologians of our day, among whom there are also seminal and prophetic minds, are deeply indebted to these Existentialist writers as well as to the Existentialist stance in dealing with the human psyche. Some of the most acute analyses of the human problem in our day, from the point of view of Christian criticism of man, have been made possible because of this way of looking at the human situation. The writings of Reinhold Niebuhr and Paul Tillich come to mind as theological works that have been attentive to the Existentialist analysis of the human condition. If the stature and productivity of theological literature in our time give any clue to the temper of the current culture of the West, one could hardly say that a recession in the Christian ethos is in evidence. But this in itself is not decisive. The vitality of the Christian witness and of its creative expression are certainly pertinent, but the appeal of its instruction and insight in the culture as a whole could still be marginal.

We are confronted in this age by the most baffling, the most ominous, yet the most expectant, and conceivably the most tragic period of history for man. The demands upon us are of such magnitude that decision, so it appears, must be made by default or out of a mood of despair. The one decision we can make with dispatch and certainty is that indecision, even when ventured as a suspended judgment, will itself have decisive consequences for us. I am almost persuaded that the decision of some of our contemporaries "to be done with things Christian" in the interest of summoning the human consciousness to "a higher order of sensibility" shows more of a sense of responsibility in these

73

times than the lassitude of Christian people whose very indifference, both to the resources of their faith and to the issues at stake in the culture about them, presents a form of secularism within the churches that is virulent precisely because it is internal and often unsuspected. If anything in our culture might be indicative of the extent to which secularization has progressed in our society, even to the point of malignancy, this condition of languor with regard to the Christian witness in many of the churches could well be it.

I see only one alternative to the disavowal of Christian faith in this tragic period; that is, to become more self-consciously Christian within the enlightened demands of both faith and culture. This would imply becoming more fully apprised of the distinctive Christian witness among the world of faiths, sharpening its formulation, proclaiming its good news of faith and hope to an age of power, and sharing with one's contemporaries within this culture the sense of judgment and criticism upon our human acts which this vision of faith affords.

The decision to become self-consciously Christian and forthright in one's witness to Christian faith can be motivated, not simply by a passion of will, but by discernment which possibly only this generation of history could provide. For that discernment stems from circumstances within recent history, and from a revolution in our imagery of thought, which enables us to apprehend the realities of faith in their bearing upon these problems of culture with a freshness and vividness we have not known in Western culture since the modern period broke upon us. Ironically enough, it is the revolution within scientific thought itself that has released this new imagery of thought, making available tools of thought with which a reformulation of the depth and force of the Christian ethos can be made. It is to an exposition of this thesis that I now turn.

III *Faith and the Formative Imagery of Our Time*

We have described the present period of history as being Janus faced. On the one side, it is erupting with innovations so far-reaching in character as to alter radically our expectations and sensibilities as human beings; yet on the other side, these very changes in stance and procedure which the sciences have assumed have afforded us a new imagery of thought bearing upon every aspect of our life. This new imagery has the effect of lifting many of the barriers to belief in ultimate realities, barriers that have obscured our vision for generations.

As a result we have come into an era of theological inquiry that is literally burgeoning with fresh power and insight concerning the meaning of Christian faith. We are rid of some of the blinders that hampered several generations of Protestant theologians who labored under the domination of a confining imagery. We have broken free of much of the oppressive moralism that readily equated class or cultural sensibilities with the Kingdom of God. We have achieved some sense of realism regarding human nature, enabling us to see through the idealizations of human powers and ideals and to repossess with some degree of understanding the Christian criticism of man. We have become responsive to dimensions of our creaturehood and to intimations of depth in relationships which once again stab us awake to a sense of the holy and to the reality of spirit as a dimension of new freedom. We have come upon a vision of the wholeness of the Christian witness in our stumbling efforts to create an ecumenical church, which is itself new in Protestantism. This is by no means an assured good; but as a concrete step toward envisaging what we in fact are in our life in God, and as a model for living together with differences, it is probably of immeasurable importance to us.

As a direct consequence of these new facilities of thought, many of our generation have been enabled to be confronted by the reality of spirit as a dimension of human existence requiring a more realistic judgment of our limits as human beings. And in being confronted by this sense of our limits, we have, as it were, come upon new clues to our possibilities. All this I see as offering a new opportunity to interpret the force of the Christian drama of Redemption in a way that can be relevant and instructive to this age of power.

The witness of faith is above and beyond the arguments of men. I am not persuaded that anyone is led to confess that Jesus Christ is Lord because his reason tells him this is so. Nevertheless, I am persuaded that many a Christian, who in his heart of hearts has known this to be so, has suffered a deadly cleavage of mind and spirit because what he affirmed with all his heart could not be received as a vision of mind as well. And, conversely, what has been held as a presupposition of thought and experience has often proved to be a formidable barrier to belief in the life of the spirit. It is not only the "mind's allegiance to despair" that routs the act of faith; one's allegiance to a frame of meaning can also do so. For in its very formulation of fact and truth it may seal off the light of faith.

I

The thinking of any people or generation within a historical culture moves within a circumscribing imagery that both illumines the meaning of terms and limits the range of terms which can be used meaningfully. This is so because the creation of meaning occurs within an intelligible discourse which itself is organic, either to the living situation of a given period and place, or to experiences available within that situation. The vocabulary of a cultural group within a given period tends to form afresh around a certain set of experiences which have had decisive or dramatic consequences. In juxtaposition with these innovating terms, and somewhat related to them, one finds a cluster of words and phrases carrying into the period inherited meanings; these words and phrases simultaneously define and restrict the import of experiences which are being freshly described or reported. Thus first-century Christians, alive to the events centering around the Cross and the Resurrection, spoke in impassioned ways about recollections of these events and experiences—experiences that had been reported within their generation. Yet all of this was colored, too, by terms and phrases that recalled an earlier time and place, an earlier set of historical experiences: words such as "Messiah," "the Son of Man," and "the Suffering Servant." Past events and their terms, along with innovating experiences and the language they evoked, merged into a single discourse as a common witness. Similarly, Reformation voices rang out with the language of revolt and protest against abuses within the Church simultaneously with individual confessions of sin and the experience of forgiveness, bespeaking an imagery of an immediate encounter with the righteous God. "Direct access to the inward working of the Holy Spirit," as Calvin phrased it, opened up a wealth of imagery which had been virtually blotted out in medieval Christendom, except among the Piety groups, or except as it had been sublimated in the adoration of the Virgin Mary, who appears to have been the medieval counterpart of the Comforter. More of the medieval imagery of thought was retained in these impassioned declarations of Christian freedom than is often assumed; yet even more of an earlier imagery, recalling the vitality and zeal of that first eschatological community, was being repossessed and conveyed in this concern with "the direct access to the inward working of the Holy Spirit." Or again, the discovery of the individual person in the eighteenth century as a disclosure of the Infinite led to a fresh insistence upon individual freedom and liberation from social institutions as well as from the coercive control of nature, now viewed as a vast cosmic mechanism. But even as eighteenth-century language gave vent to resentment and resistance against current forms of oppression in its stress upon individuality, it echoed forms of thought which had been reactivated in a Platonic renaissance in an effort to retain a sense of ultimate unity amidst this buzzing confusion of immediate diversities. Out of the interplay of innovating experience with inherited and disinherited notions, there was evoked a mind-set in which freedom and determinism loomed as the defining antinomies.

We are in the process today of emerging from the shock of revolutionizing experiences out of which new metaphors, peculiar to our time, are forming; and we are on the brink of new ventures more radical in their degree of innovation than anything the human race has known in its history. For the range and character of experience itself is rapidly changing as the space in which these events and experiences occur expands beyond the scope of our imagination. Hence our imagery is in flux. Having already been jolted out of the formative notions of preatomic times, we are tentatively and hesitatingly groping our way in a discourse, the terms of which are but partially apprehended, and the directives only vaguely prescient of meaning.

Now it is generally true that innovating experiences create a break in established imageries, either by rendering certain notions obsolete and irrelevant, or by intruding swiftly and decisively a new fund of meanings expressive of these innovations. But there is an ordering of terms which seems to occur simultaneously with this inundation of fresh meaning. The structuring of language and discourse that follows such experience has the effect of establishing controlling ideas or concepts that seem to define the bounds of intelligible thought and discussion. Within the range of symbolism afforded by these ideas, this structuring of language tends to give a certain spread of meaning as well as a sense of direction to the course of intelligible inquiry. It is as if these controlling ideas formed a vast canopy over the minds of people within a given generation, or as if a low-hanging cloud enveloped them.

I do not wish to make the emergence of imagery appear too arbitrary, for no period of history is as singular or as consistent in the fashioning of its discourse as my words may seem to suggest. I am talking about the distinctive discourse of a period. In every such period an accumulative complex of inherited terms persists as a vocabulary within a vocabulary. Yet when dissociated from the core of events, or from earlier controlling ideas which once gave these terms general currency throughout the culture, such vocabularies take on a different character. Either they become cultic, formalized, even archaic; or they undergo a metamorphosis of meaning in the context of these newer formative notions. Thus every period has its live, efficacious discourse, expressing an imagery which is singularly meaningful in terms of insistent events, along with an accumulative complex of fragmented, formalized terms or new conceptions of them.

Now we may see from this analysis the dilemma into which religious discourse invariably falls. What gives relevance and contemporary insistence, in a word, intelligibility to its terms, may not assure it motivating power. That is to say, words bearing an ultimate reference tend to have motive power proportionate to their generality of accepted meaning. When they are given explicit meaning to accord with a specific frame of meaning which is currently expressive, they lose generality and inclusive appeal, though they gain in intelligibility. Thus the word "God," when it can be used with naturalness and freedom, is vastly more expressive and evocative than a term like "Value," or "the Infinite," "Power of Being," or "Creative Event." On the other hand, when the contemporary frame of meaning offers experiences or analogies which can refresh and revive these terms of ultimate reference, thereby adding to their generality of meaning concrete reference as well, intelligibility can heighten the intensity of their meaning and wrest them from a purely formalized discourse. This is what is happening today in regard to many Christian terms such as "Spirit," "revelation," "sin," "redemption," "grace," 'forgiveness," "the Suffering Servant," and other words expressive of Christian faith.

Now one asks: why is this so? The answer is in part that the canopy that has insulated the modern Western mind from the kind of meaning conveyed by such terms has lifted. But this is only half the story. The more exciting half is that experiences expressive of these terms, comparable to events which initially brought them forth as a concrete vocabulary in history, have become characteristic of the living situation in our time.[1] That is to say, an imagery internal to experience or to the living event has resurrected these terms from their formal interment. Of this I shall have more to say later.

The imagery suitable for commonplace discourse in day-to-day conversation between people, say in the town square, at the market or shopping center, in the factory, or even at the village church, can remain fairly stable

1 The most direct evidence of this fact is to be found in the creative literature of our day, both in poetry and in fiction. Two writers in the field of theology who have been particularly helpful in conveying the theological significance of current writing are Amos Wilder (cf. his *The Spiritual Aspects of the New Poetry*, Harper, 1940, and *Modern Poetry and the Christian Tradition*, Scribners, 1952), and Nathan A. Scott, Jr. (cf. his *Rehearsals of Decomposure*, Columbia, 1952, *Modern Literature and the Religious*, Harper, 1958, and "The Bias of Comedy and the Narrow Escape Into Faith," *The Christian Scholar*, Vol. XLIV, Spring 1961). Cf. also *The Tragic Vision and the Christian Faith*, of which Scott is editor, Association Press, 1957.

from generation to generation, though some variations will occur. But in these instances the level of discourse requires no high degree of precision in the relating of terms. The terms used apply to experiences which are familiar to all—family life, children, illness, death, the price of food, or the latest headlines. If discussion should deepen to include politics, economics, or religion, stereotyped terms or phrases might suffice for the occasion.

The mortality of imagery is most acute in areas of the culture where precision of meaning is preferred or is imperative; and where the routine experience is itself experimentation, exploration, or evaluation. Here new terms are constantly being created to provide a ready discourse to designate precisely the new objects, the new process or procedure, or to note the shade of meaning intended and to point out subtle distinctions.

The gap between specialized and unspecialized groups in society has always been recognized. The age-old distinction between "town and gown" is one expression of it. Professional groups such as lawyers, doctors, clergy, and scientists within the community as contrasted with lay people who do not speak their technical language present another aspect of it. As long as these specialized groups, in their role of specialists, could remain apart from general community discussion, no one got hurt. But we have come into a period of history when all such barriers are being removed. Unspecialized minds are seeking to be informed on technical subjects, or are demanding that the specialist tell them about his subject. They are insisting upon hearing or participating in discussions of Great Books, or on being lectured to on profound subjects. "Give it to me in a layman's language" or "in a few simple sentences" have become common pleas. These outrageous requests shock the specialist or the intellectual into realizing that he is not of this world. That is, in pursuing his work, he has, of necessity, enveloped himself in a wrapping of esoteric imagery peculiar to his special mode of inquiry or research which has little or no currency beyond the laboratory, the medical center, classroom, or study. But conversely, he realizes, too, that the imagery that is current in the community, say in any representative gathering at social clubs, in churches, on radio, or on television, is hopelessly inadequate for carrying on even the simplest kind of discussion that moves toward a critical or reflective level of analysis or inquiry. When he does yield to the demand to "give it to them in a few simple sentences," and succeeds in doing so to their delight or satisfaction, he feels like a cheat or a charlatan, for he knows he has betrayed them into thinking they know something about his subject when he has done no more than to give them a shoddy caricature of it.

Usually the impasse in understanding or in negotiation between groups, or the failure to find a solution to problems that arise at this general level of discussion, stems from a clash of stereotypes. Often the experience of seeking to resolve issues on a thinking level, where only stereotyped terms and phrases are available to a discussion, results in utter disillusionment. The only way out then seems to be to reduce the negotiation to the level of sentimental, emotional, or even visceral appeals. Much of political and religious discourse is at this level. And of course the world of advertising makes capital of it.

The tragedy of the matter is that creative opportunities for fresh negotiation and for new understanding and deeper insight into the living situation await a people at the level of discourse where new imagery is at work. But the lag between the general culture and the technical or creative areas of thought where such new imagery occurs is considerable. This becomes evident when one realizes that transitions in thought which led to the revolution in scientific thinking that is now radically altering our world occurred before the end of the nineteenth century; yet not until 1945, with the falling of atomic bombs upon Hiroshima and Nagasaki, did all this revolution in scientific thought come to the notice of the community at large as a public fact; and then, not as a change in the mode of thinking, but in an event of destruction.

We may summarize these general observations on the imagery of thought, then, in saying that each period of history that is set apart by creative or disruptive events has its own distinctive imagery. The imagery of a period is at once the source of its distinctive illumination and insight, and a mode of channeling thought, by which it restricts its vision and defines the bounds within which events can take on meaning. No period is singular in its vision; for while it has its own distinctive imagery by which innovation comes into experience, it embraces strands of meaning within its structure of experience which persists from previous periods. Some of these strands exist as precedent, custom, moral sensibility, or simply style of behavior, defining the conduct of life that is acceptable or unacceptable. Each of these strands, in turn, stems from a distinctive imagery of an earlier period which initially gave it insistent meaning, and which brought it about as a rational act or judgment. The insistent meaning behind the act or custom may in time fade; but the precedent, custom, or sensibility will then acquire a new rationale, or will persist simply as an authoritative act. Imagery from the past appears also in the formalized meaning of religious rituals and in political generalizations or assumptions, many of which will have become stereotypes.

In addition to overt and widely disseminated meanings forming the discourse of a period, there are strands of meaning within the structure of experience existing as undercurrents of protest and nonconformity which often give intimations of future disruption or mutation. Thus during that period of modern Western history in which Kant and Hegel dominated European and American thought, recalcitrant currents of thought and imagery were forming within this very matrix of Idealism with

83

Marx, Kierkegaard, Nietzsche, and later William James. At the time they represented marginal protests or centers of disagreement with what was commonly held; but in persisting they became undercurrents of dissolution, ultimately breaking forth as major alternatives to the very formulated meanings out of which they initially arose.

The dominant imagery of a period which gives it drive and purpose, however, is always that which arises out of immediate cultural circumstances in response to a major event, a crisis, a decisive discovery, an innovation, or the fruition of long-range developments in which social consequences have become explicitly recognized.

When something of all or several of these strands of meaning tends to shape the mode of life of a people, the total effect of the intermingling of the diverse perspectives within a given period is one of indecision, confusion, and frustration. This all-over effect may generate a cultural mood expressive of these feelings. But within every generation there are decisive minds which adhere sharply to a single strand of meaning. They provide the assertive attitudes and drives toward objectives and, in large measure, carry the load of responsibility as far as day-to-day planning and designing of action is concerned—in government affairs, in business and industry, in education, and in the life of the churches. The indecisive minds form a large fringe of partially committed participants. Among these one finds significant critics and prophetic voices, as well as reflective minds, all of whom provide sobering restraints or even open resistance to what is clearly in ascendancy in an age; but the vast majority of this indecisive fringe simply vacillate between alternative convictions and objectives, or bask in their own reticence, awaiting the necessity to act. What this cultural confusion represents, therefore, is itself diverse and of varying degrees of significance; for it gathers in the lethargic, the indolent, the traditionally reactionary along with the seasoned, sophisticated, and judicious minds who tend to look to the bal-

84

ancing or correlating of needs and values, rather than to the single-minded pursuit of some one decisive path of meaning or action. What appears to be confusion is thus only partially so, for it harbors the critical and reflective currents of society as an incubating nucleus or as a backlog of creative resistance.

Our own age reflects all these crosscurrents of thought and opinion. We give evidence of the kind of confusion and frustration that follows from the interplay of such diversity in conviction and judgment. Running through the whole of this maze of contemporary thought and expression and seemingly redirecting our vision are recurrent and insistent reminders of newer ways of looking at old problems as well as startling suggestions warning us of new problems ahead. These are the emissaries of a new imagery of thought and the formulators of new fundamental notions underlying thought.

II

The two most decisive sources of the present change in the imagery of thought are scientific exploration and the violence and suffering of a world at war. Each has had the effect of terminating one era of thought and its imagery and of evoking fresh imagery; in some instances the result is a reconception of terms long discarded or lying dormant for generations, and in other instances an introduction of radically new terms and determinations of thought.

Current scientific exploration in its total span, extending from the microscopic exploration of atomic structure to more recent ventures into outer space, constitutes in its way a counterpart of the discovery of new continents in the fifteenth century. In that earlier period of geographical extension by sea travel, the expansion of the horizons of thought among the European communities and, as a consequence, the intrusion of alien or at least of uncalculated realities into the cultural experience, brought a vivid sense of insecurity to the established ethos of thought and faith. In a similar way nuclear science and space exploration today have awakened vague and unanalyzed fears, along with specific misgivings concerning the continuing relevance of Christian faith. These premonitions are not wholly unfounded today any more than they were in the fifteenth century. Certainly the expansion of the European community beyond its historical shores brought immeasurable change in its mode of life, and along with this change, unmanageable responsibilities as Europe sought to capitalize upon its new opportunities. The sense of dread, however, was prescient of opportunity and promise as well as of hardship and dismay. And so may be the misgivings and anxiety of the present age in the face of nuclear experimentation and automation.

The one fear that was not wholly miscalculated in the fifteenth century was concern about the possible threat to the Christian ethos, resulting from the new conception of land and sea space and the mobility of life that could be expected to follow. Within a few generations the range of observation was to extend to stellar space as well, as Galileo's telescope surveyed the heavens and Newton's newly fashioned instruments of measurement could calculate the movement of the planets. Arnold Toynbee, as we have already noted, sees in this "secularizing" development "the discrediting of the West's Christian heritage," and the elevation of a technological civilization that has only tenuous connections at best with that heritage and ethos.[2] The assessment of what followed between "the beginning of the eighteenth century and A.D. 1956," to use Toynbee's designation of time, will vary from scholar to scholar, and possibly from Christian to Christian. One thing is clear, however; the formative image of the world, and ultimately of man himself, that became a controlling factor in the thought of Western culture, followed in the

[2] Arnold Toynbee, *An Historian's Approach to Religion*. Oxford University Press, 1956, p. 184.

wake of Newtonian science. It was to alter radically the vision of human resources and the capacity of Western man to apprehend realities beyond the scope of his own formulations. In a word, under the spell of the Newtonian image, the facilities for exact thought and prediction became so perfected that it became literally impossible for nineteenth-century man to distrust his human powers and ideals. Reality for Western man thus became the human equation writ large.

One can put down as a theological premise, supported by aeons of human experience, that a recognition of the limits of man offers clues to his possibilities. Conversely, it follows that a disregard of the limits of man will invariably lead to an idealization of the human equation which must eventuate in a serious impairment of vision and capacity to recognize man's possibilities. What is this but the doctrine of the Fall seen in its cultural implications? And it is vividly exemplified in the cultural and intellectual history of Western man following the seventeenth century. I am not inferring here that liberal thought alone manifests the fall of man in Western history. The idolatries of the church in the history of the West from Nicaea to Augsburg present their own version of it. The usurpation of authority in exercising the power of grace in post-Reformation doctrine prior to the seventeenth century is eloquent in its witness to it. Wherever the literal word of man has been given the weight of an ultimate declaration, whether in philosophy or in theology, in science or in piety, the Fall has been made manifest. We are no more immune from it than were our forebears, though our own failings in this regard are not so readily detected. It is, in fact, one of the truisms of history that a people of any generation is able to see the sins of its immediate fathers most vividly, and to be oblivious of the perils and pitfalls immediately upon it. This is applicable to the imagery of thought as well.

When we look to our immediate period of history we

confront such a maze of assertive and conflicting forces, ideologies, and judgments vying for ascendancy that we are discouraged at the outset from trying to discern any pattern of events, not to speak of a formative imagery, which defines and delimits our range of meaning. The structure is there, however, though much of it is in fluid state, defying designation or definition. We who are its living participants are least of all able to form a clear picture of our world of meaning simply out of the immediacies of our vision. What can be made vivid to us are the sharp points of departure from a previous imagery. This never gives the full story of constructive events or of emerging insights. In fact it may exaggerate our tone of reaction and represent us to ourselves as people in revolt, or as an age in transition. This is due in part to the fact that, while we may consciously dissociate ourselves or our world of meaning from that of the previous age, we are as yet unready or unable to enter decisively and knowingly into the world of meaning that is forming all about us in day-to-day events, some of which are decisive in shaping our immediate mode of existence.

The sharp points of departure from the previous age thus take on the character of tiny apertures through which we can look in two directions, causing us, as it were, to peer from side to side. The one direction opens up an increasingly vivid picture of the path of culture out of which we have come. This portrayal is deceptively clear and fixed. That is because, in the portrayal of past events, the turmoil of the living situation has been stilled. Only the marks of battle and the delineation of the line of march remain to give hint of the contours of civilization as this was once known and lived. The other direction opens up, not an expanse of events, but a close-up view, disclosing the immediacies of existence which, from this view, appear precipitous and urgent, as if the turns in the road were sharp and required the most anxious negotiation. Out of this duality of vision, which each of us possesses in one form or another, come conflicting judgments and decisions which in turn tend to generate opposing movements of thought and action in any period.

Now it is not only a historical interest that turns our minds in this first direction to look at the path of culture we have just been following. For in looking in this direction we are made sensitive to the origin of much that forms our present structure of experience. In fact, looking at the immediate past is like spreading out this living structure of experience that now forms our own depth into a vivid, observable surface. Such past as we possess forms a depth of motivation and restraint in the living present; but equally significant is the fact that, in looking at this immediate past in terms of the imagery that once gave it its distinctive world of meaning, we prepare the way for sharpening our own sense of imagery, and for seeing the closures of mind which once acted as barriers to belief in the realities which now take on new meaning in our own immediate existence.

This very ability to discern the closures of mind in a period of thought preceding our own should heighten our sense of mans limits. Such sharpened awareness as we may now possess of our human limitations is, as it were, a gift out of the disillusioning debacle of recent history to which the excess in human enterprise and idealization in our previous cultural history led. We may not ascribe this sharpened Christian realism to our greater wisdom, or to our superior astuteness in analyzing man, though of course we speak from a vantage point in this instance which provides us with vision that hitherto was not available. To a remarkable degree each of us speaks out of the circumstances of our immediate history. For it is given to us to bear our witness to truth as this calls forth to us from out of the creativities and tragedies of man in any generation. We then, in turn, are the voices of history, of this history that now transpires. When we speak we echo forth both the earned and the unearned increment of truth we are able to bear, or more specifically, are able to discern, to which we are able to respond, and in which we are able to participate. Thus one may say God speaks to us out of history through the very travail of thought and experience as we wrestle with the heritage of our forebears which now appears to be in conflict with the demands and vivid perceptions of our own immediate structure of experience. Insight is born at a price. Revelation comes with the swiftness of sight, a gift of the occasion for which no antecedent is a proper measure or a surmise of what it purports.

We stand beholden to the judgments of history for whatever newness of vision has come forth in our time, but if we are realistic we will not gloat over the point of vantage to which we have come or dissociate ourselves from the folly of our forebears which made such judgment possible. In a real sense we are they, but with the years of reckoning added. We continue to think and feel with them, even as we disavow what they affirmed. For we carry the nurture of their thought in our memories and shaping and, possibly, the ethos of their faith and expectations in our persisting sensibilities.

To affirm our identity with what we now dispute, however, need not intimidate us, or cause us to recoil from speaking candidly. Our vocation as modern men and women is to speak out of the circumstances of history which now bring the consolation of judgment and vision to our age. In this sense we are no more immune from the restrictive force of immediacies that are upon us than our forebears were to the enclosure of concerns that were immediately upon them. Yet it is given to each succeeding generation to stand in judgment upon what has preceded it. This it must do, not out of egoistic reaction, but out of continuity with what is insistent in the immediacies of history. It must, in fact, do so in response to what claims them as prophetic spokesmen of its historical advance. But this means, does it not, that the protests to which we are able to give voice as a judgment out of history may be more nearly the voice of truth for our situation than the formulations we undertake as an alternative to what we reject? This follows from the fact that our perceptions of what has transpired can be more precise and complete than our perceptions of what is now taking form, or of what may yet ensue. Thus what we do within the restrictions of immediacies that are full upon us are also under the impending judgment of those through whom the realities of a subsequent history will speak.

III

But now we need to speak more explicitly of that one aspect of our cultural experience which has contributed directly to a sharpened realism in our time. I refer to those agencies of thought which have brought forth a new image of man through a dissolution of the Newtonian image which so sorely distorted the estimate of our human powers.

It is one of the remarkable though ironical facts of modern history that the processes of scientific invention and discovery which led to the horrors of Hiroshima and Nagasaki, and to the explosive possibilities of the present cold war, also initiated the new era in science, and with it, an imagery of thought which has released Western thinking from its Newtonian captivity. The year of innovation was 1895, when Roentgen discovered the X-ray. The revolution in the conception of the atom occurred toward the end of the nineteenth century, about 1896, when Becquerel and the Curies discovered radioactive elements. Just after the turn of the century Rutherford discovered the proton and came upon the surprising disclosure that the atom is planetary in character, "a merry-go-round in miniature," as one physicist described it. This was the beginning of the shift from an atomistic conception of reality to the ontological notion of the individual in community, which is the basic formula in Whitehead's metaphysics. The break in imagery, separating the Newtonian-Cartesian age from that of the new vision of science, occurred as early as 1870. Yet as late as 1920 the new imagery of thought remained relatively unknown in many circles of theology and philosophy. Gestalt psychology was launched in 1925, and emergent philosophies began to appear about the same time. Suddenly scholars, insofar as they were susceptible to scientific influence, broke out with the markings of field theory and other holistic notions. Relativity was in all this, too. The theory had been set forth by Einstein in 1905, although it was not until Heisenberg announced the principle of indeterminacy in 1931 that these new theories in physics, relativity and quantum mechanics, assumed wide currency outside scientific discussions and highly technical philosophical speculations. Not until 1945, however, with the falling of atomic bombs on Hiroshima and Nagasaki, did all this revolution in imagery become a public fact. Thus the age of atomic power did not burst upon us out of the blue. Its antecedents can be fully studied. They had been widely known throughout scientific and industrial circles before the turn of the century. But to the man in the street they came as a gale in the night, bringing death and destruction.

What is now heralded as the new age of power is publicly acknowledged and acclaimed through the periodic launching of Sputniks, Vanguards, moon rockets, and man, into outer space. Beneath this visible physical display of scientific genius, however, there is a sobering human fact. It is that a radical reorientation of scientific thinking itself has occurred, affecting the way the scientist approaches natural events and the way he assesses his means of observing them. If the imagery of Newtonian science rejects any assumption that the realities of existence might elude the forms of human thought, the imagery of present-day physical science acknowledges the mystery and indeterminacy of events in certain respects.

Unlike the Newtonian scientist of an earlier age, who could assume that his formula employing Euclidean geometry expressed a well-defined measure, the modern physicist knows he is using a tentative formulation of his own making, based on the geometrical theories of Gauss and Riemann rather than Euclid, thus explicitly acknowledging the experimental uncertainty of his effort. And he employs these geometrical equations as tentative models by which to test out certain possibilities and to verify theories or judgments to which his own reasoning from evidence has led him. What has disappeared from this mode of inquiry is the imagery of a mechanistic order in nature and the doctrinaire assumption of an absolute mathematical measure. In a word, the imagery and method of science, as these are presently understood and employed, compel recognition of some discontinuity between manageable and unmanageable aspects of events in existence. The very meaning of what in current terms has been called "the dimension of depth" is that the realities of any experience are to be accounted deeper than, or in some aspects resistant to, man's powers of observation and description. This is not to imply the rejection of reason and observation, either in science or in religious thought, but to acknowledge their limitations, and to recognize that the structures of reason which we are able to formulate and employ are but tentative ventures in apprehending the meaning of those realities. They may not be taken to be definitive and final descriptions of them in the sense of earlier mechanistic presuppositions.

Recognition of the dimension of depth has become commonplace in many of the disciplines of modern thought, including certain areas of the social sciences and psychology, as well as in modern physics, metaphysics, and theology. What is to be noted here is that depth has the connotation of complexity as well as discontinuity or indeterminacy. In this respect, field theory has as much, if not more, to do with intruding the notion as does quantum mechanics or the principle of indeterminacy. As employed in holistic thinking from James to Whitehead, such relational thinking resists the assumption that an examination of parts abstracted from its dynamic or living context can give full and adequate meaning to the reality of these parts in a relationship. Relationships thus provide a dimension of meaning and possibility of creativity which exceed the reality of parts taken as isolated data. It is this mystery of relationships, giving to events or phenomena their incalculable quality even as they yield to our apprehension of them, which contributes to a sense of depth in dealing with the living situation in any of its aspects.

Now within the ethos of thought in which these disciplines move, there is room for acknowledging or even pointing to imperceptible depths of meaning bearing upon observable events, made vivid intermittently by innovations, or by intimations of novel occurrences within the concrete events of history. In such an ethos of thought the doctrinaire dismissal of dimensions of reality which are unavailable to inquiry, or unresponsive to the logic we have been able to formulate, cannot be considered critical thought. One may choose not to concern himself with such dimensions, preferring to confine one's thought to manageable areas of experience; but the penumbra of possible meaning persists as a remainder of the unmanageable aspects of events which nevertheless attend one's thoughts, if only as a judgment upon one's formulations, and upon the clearly defined range of meaning one is able to establish within his norms of thought.

In such an ethos of thought, on the other hand, there is encouragement to be as attentive as we wish, to pursue the bearing of such dimensions of experience and their complexities upon the clearly formed judgments of thought. One is not justified by science or by critical theological opinion in simply affirming mystery and indeterminacy as controlling notions, as if critical and judicious inquiry made no claim upon the religious mind. But awareness of the dimension of depth, and a response to its judgment and to its extended range of possible meaning, appropriate to critical inquiry, is itself to be accounted the exercise of critical judgment in all inquiry.

Now it is in such an ethos of thought that the idea of "the mystery of the Kingdom" or "the New Creation" expressed by the notion of eschatology in theology and in New Testament research has again become relevant and intelligible. Intelligibility in this context is not the same as reasonableness. In the ethos of an earlier liberal thought that leaned heavily upon the imagery of the Enlightenment, reasonableness implied grasping realities "within the bounds of reason alone." Intelligibility as it may be employed in the present context implies no such domestication of the realities apprehended. Rather, it implies apprehending a margin of meaningful experience within an infinity of mystery which time and again, and for the most part, eludes our human measure. Intelligibility provides a basis for our human orientation toward what is more than human in the realities that hold us in existence.

IV

The processes by which this new climate of thought emerged in present-day disciplines, and those by which the doctrine of eschatology reappeared as a vital notion in New Testament study and theology, appear to be wholly unrelated, though one cannot be certain of this. It is tantalizing to reflect upon the fact that during the very decade in which Biblical scholars were turning attention to the Jewish eschatological writings of the *Apocrypha,* which were eventually to reawaken interest in the eschatological references in the Gospels, physicists were coming up against problems in their experiments, while exploring the nature of the atom, that were forcing them to create new models. In both instances, new discoveries of the period had propelled investigations, and in both instances a refinement of the instruments of research had facilitated new findings. Each line of inquiry was to result in challenging predilections of an earlier age of modern scholarship, and to lead to a common vision of nature and history wherein concern with understanding existence within the depth of its complexities replaced a rationalistic distillation of clear and distinct ideas.

Whether or not recovery of the notion of eschatology in recent theology is in any way related to the establishment of a dimension of depth in scientific thinking and in related disciplines, may not be easily established. Nevertheless, the relinquishment of this notion, or its transmutation, in earlier liberal theology, as it assumed a singularly ethical emphasis, appears to have been in accord with a prevailing concern of that period to establish the rationality of events in human experience as well as in nature. Basically it partook of a reconception of the nature of existence and of the meaning of history. This reconception was dictated structurally by the method and imagery of the sciences as they were then understood and and employed, and by the problems which this view of nature raised for the spiritual life of man. The controlling imagery of science by which nature was interpreted was that of mechanical regularity and orderliness as Newtonian physics had established it. Modern Idealism, which was the prevailing champion of the spiritual life of man as against the determinism of this mechanistic view of nature, was in part created out of the ethical reaction to this scientific understanding of physical things, including the physical dimension of man himself. Its valuation of personality impelled resistance to an application of the notion of determinism to personal existence, and thus the idea of freedom was given the significance of an ontological notion, identifying the condition under which personal existence could endure. But while freedom so defined was assumed to be the antithesis of determinism, its meaning in this context really took form within the imagery of a deterministic science and was thus defined in relation to the Newtonian view of nature. Accordingly, the concept of ethics took on a meaning which was expressive of the kind of relationship between persons which acknowledged and preserved the condition of freedom so understood. In this way ethics took on ontological import, conveying the sense of an ultimate sensibility at work in the immediacies of experience. Once one sees this point one comes nearer to assessing the force of the ethical dimension as the liberal theologian and philosopher understood it. In effect, ethics was the Idealist's alternative to eschatology; that is, it was a way of taking account of final ends in the shaping of the means and processes within immediate existence.

Yet all this implied a presupposition concerning personality itself, and a doctrine of man which equated the human dimension in its personal aspect with ultimacy. In this view there was no category or dimension of good beyond that of the human and moral good known in personality. Thus while modern Idealism and liberal theology provided an ethical alternative to eschatology, and thus retained something of its scope and vision in defining the religious life, insinuated into the meaning of this alternative was a doctrine of man which in effect deprived him of a source of judgment, or of holiness beyond that of human goodness. This view of existence and history, therefore, like this conception of nature, partook of an imagery of thought that rendered it manageable within established canons of interpretation. Among nineteenth-century liberals and modernists who sought to accommodate theological thought to evolutionary thinking, a closer correlation of nature and history was effected. In this way the imagery of Newtonian science, as it had been assimilated by Darwin in his theory of evolution, was more directly applied to the liberal-modernist view of history.

Now it is customary among many who are concerned to defend the procedure of historical liberalism to insist that modern man can do no other than to allow the imagery and method of the sciences to inform his conception of facts and history. What one often overlooks in such insistence, however, is that within modern history the imagery and method of the sciences have undergone radical, even revolutionary, changes. Simply to insist upon taking the imagery of the sciences seriously in religious thought, without taking account of these shifts and innovations in scientific imagery, is to incur obsolescence in religious thought of a more serious nature than that which can follow from an unexamined adherence to tradition. Tradition at least tends to be dynamic, though its susceptibility to change is subtle and slow moving. Adherence to a scientific imagery that has ceased to provide the working models for scientific experimentation and inquiry can generate a closure of mind that is defensive and rigid in its adherence to what it presumes to be established fact. All liberal thought needs to guard against such folly.

One can apply this analysis also to the problem of Christianity and history. When the theologian or historian of Christian thought presses for a return to historical method in theology, the question needs to be asked: In what sense is historical method to be understood? Historical method, as theologians a generation or more ago employed it, and as is frequently implied when this question is raised, presupposed a scientific view of history which came into prominence in the nineteenth century, but which had antecedents in eighteenth-century developments regarding nature and human existence.[3] Here again the formative imagery and, in part, the starting point were derived from Newtonian science, implying events in freedom and decision set over against the mechanistic and deterministic processes of nature. After Darwin, historical description took on a more explicit concern with environment and social adaptation, and

[3] Cf. Rudolf Bultmann, *History and Eschatology.* Edinburgh University Press, 1957.

98

changes consequent to such external adjustment. Thus the conception of history and of historical method became more openly that of a descriptive account of the mechanisms of change and development as these affected or determined the course of human decision, and their consequent action in initiating social forces or in establishing institutions. In this evolutionary view of history, the presupposition of orderly experience as a mechanistic science had formulated it entered more directly into the historian's understanding of social adaptation than it had in earlier Idealistic theories of history. It was this direct correlation of procedures that enabled historical study of that period to assume the appearance of scientific inquiry itself.

The question to be asked, then, of the scholar concerned with the historical nature of Christianity is: How is history in the present context of Biblical and theological study to be conceived? Until it is clear that, in pressing for a return to the historical method in theology, one is not simply reasserting a conception of history that cannot be defended on critical grounds, one will be doing theological interpretation a disservice, rather than restoring it to a more scholarly level.

Any recourse to historicity today, if it is to participate in the relevant imagery of the modern idiom, must take seriously the revolutionary changes in fundamental notions as these bear upon an understanding of man's existence. History, like physical processes in this context, is seen to be a matrix of partially definable events and relationships occurring in a deeper context, of which only intimations and intermittent apprehensions are afforded within human experience. The initial and superficial impression is one of absurdity, even irrationality; yet the studied view reveals a margin of correlation between structured experience in thought and action and this deeper dimension of existence. The notion of order persists, in historical and theological inquiry as in the sciences; but it is a vision toward which we move, not a visible reality which we may readily measure or describe.

V

Without meaning to defend all that is implied in their positions, for I have reservations with regard to several of them, I venture to suggest that it is precisely this kind of reconception of historical existence that underlies, and in part has motivated, the thought of our major Protestant theologians in recent years. This is especially true of Barth and Bultmann, Richard and Reinhold Niebuhr, Paul Tillich, and Henry Nelson Wieman. Each of these men, in his own distinctive way, has sought to avail himself of the new image of existence which has issued from radical innovations in modern history and thought and to take account of the dimension of depth in human relations and in history. For example, the very stance with which H. Richard Niebuhr undertakes to restate the doctrine of Revelation assumes and takes seriously the notion of relativity. And the manner in which he reformulates the meaning of Revelation as "inner history," "the story of our life," partakes of Bergson's intuitionism. Richard Niebuhr has acknowledged his indebtedness to Bergson's influence, though he points out that his use of relativity owes its stimulus, not to physics, but to studies in social science and history. Reinhold Niebuhr has made more frequent reference to his indebtedness to Existentialist writers, to depth psychology, to Marxist social criticism, not to speak of earlier Christian sources such as Augustine and Kierkegaard, in accounting for his use of a dimension of depth in his analysis of human existence. And in his discussions of history he frankly acknowledges that it is the Biblical faith, with its perspective of an ultimate meaning attending man's existence, which provides the presupposition and vision for observing historical events in their "larger frame of meaning." [4] Nevertheless, one

[4] Cf. Reinhold Niebuhr, *Faith and History*. Macmillan, 1949, pp. 102-119.

cannot read his essay, "The Truth in Myth" [5] without realizing that the depth of meaning which the Biblical faith brings to Niebuhr's observations of historical events partakes of a notion of internal meaning that is peculiarly contemporary in its character and origin. In fact the similarity in imagery and argument between Niebuhr's analysis of the truth in myth and the delineation of intuitional knowledge in Bergson's *Introduction to Metaphysics* is striking. Myth, for Niebuhr, has the value of intuiting internal meaning which cannot otherwise be known or apprehended. Thus his use of Biblical faith is made a conceptual way of envisaging the fullness of historical events as "lived experience" set in its larger frame. [6]

Paul Tillich has been particularly successful in conveying the sense of depth in history and existence; though it must be said that he has been able to do so by appealing to the pictorial imagery of myth and symbol, rather than by dealing directly with the relational and structual character of experience. By employing a measure of holistic thinking, drawn from Gestalt psychology and from certain aspects of Bergson's thought, he has been able to insinuate into his symbolism a substantial degree of process analysis, though his preference all along has been to stay within a symbolic discourse when discussing problems theologically. In this he follows in the path of Schleiermacher and Rudolf Otto, seeing the eschatological dimension as a numinous depth in existence. Amplified and structured with the help of Schelling's mythological idealism, this becomes a philosophy of "New Being." Thus, by employing both numinous and holistic notions, Tillich has been able to combine what is historically familiar within the mystical and sacramental tradition of thought with what is distinctive and current in depth psychology and Existentialism. His method of correlation, lifting up ques-

[5] *The Nature of Religious Experience.* Edited by Bewkes *et al.,* Harper, 1937.
[6] *Faith and History.* Macmillan, 1949, p. 119.

tions concerning human existence as they are being formulated in Existentialist philosophy, and bringing to them the answers of Christian faith, is consistent with his ecstatic view of nature and history. And it concurs similarly with his conception of the interrelation between Biblical religion and classical philosophy.

Although Rudolf Bultmann is intent on bringing clarity to the Biblical view of human existence through his effort to demythologize the New Testament,[7] he is equally insistent upon retaining the dimension of depth in his interpretation of history given to it by the notion of eschatology. For Bultmann belief in eschatology is simply a way of acknowledging the mystery of the end which attends every present moment of time. And this, he reminds us, is to "live from the future." For "the historicity of the human being is completely understood when the human being is understood as living in responsibility over against the future and therefore in decision." [8] I submit that this unencumbered and venturesome quality of experience which Bultmann succeeds in conveying through the act of faith is highly contemporary in feeling as well as in orientation, recalling an imagery consonant with the plight of modern man and with the role of the modern scientist in pursuit of his elusive quarry. He has sought to capture the mystery of the eschatological dimension in history through the act of faith, conceived in Existentialist terms—a "living forward" within the freedom of decision. The intermittent nature of this encounter with the mystery of depth is expressed by Bultmann in saying that "Faith is to be renewed every morning."

Of all modern theologians, Karl Barth is perhaps the most subtle and elusive mind in dealing with problems of

[7] Cf. *Kerygma and Myth,* edited by Hans Werner Bartsch. S.P.C.K., 1953; John Macquarrie, *The Scope of Demythologizing,* Harper, 1961; A new and searching critique of Bultmann's theological method has just come to hand in Schubert Ogden's *Christ Without Myth.* Harper, 1961.

[8] Rudolf Bultmann, *History and Eschatology.* Edinburgh University Press, 1957, p. 136.

faith and history, or nature and experience. His utter disregard of historical structures, either of thought or form, has earned for him the severest criticisms for his disavowal of the relevance and critical control of historical inquiry. My own experience in reading his works, however, has led me to believe that one needs to take a more judicious attitude toward this aspect of his thought. When one does, one will detect in it quite an orderly and consistent theological procedure consonant with his stress upon the freedom of God. But, of greater significance in this discussion, is his appeal to the mystery and spontaneity of each occasion in its concreteness in which decisions are made. Here there is almost a direct parallel between the way Barth uses Biblical and theological formulae and the way the modern physicist employs his mathematical formulae. In this respect Barth impresses me as being indeed a modern man, however much his concern to let the mystery of Revelation remain a mystery, uninterpreted and unaccounted for, appears to lead him into a kind of neo-orthodoxy. In fact, it is this very tenuous grasp of what is mightily upon us in the act of faith, and the very tentative stance which he ascribes to the Christian as he persists daily in the path of faith, which reminds one most forcibly of the modern scientist as he deals with the mystery of physical realities. One can blur, or even obscure, these distinctly modern qualities in Barth, calling them symptoms of a sophisticated evangelicalism, or insisting that they simply bespeak a contemporary version of the Reformers' emphasis upon the Christian's direct access to the working of the Holy Spirit. These associations can be pointed out with propriety. But the style of his effort, if not its intention, I am persuaded is more pertinent to the present situation than these characterizations would suggest. Whether or not Barth is mindful of the newer imagery and method of thought in science and metaphysics, he appears to be participating in it in his own way with relish and abandon.

I am not persuaded that we have as yet seen the full

fruition of theological thought that can issue from this reorientation in imagery. Modern Protestant theologians, who have to some degree spoken out of this reorientation, have often been more conscious of being in reaction against Idealistic solutions to the problem of faith, than of speaking knowingly and with purpose within a newer imagery forged out of a new situation in history. These Idealistic solutions presupposed the Newtonian image of nature, and thus religious faith and the theological task were defined over against this mechanistic view and against the determinism it implied. To a considerable degree, even in the way they have expressed their reaction to Idealism, or have sought to go beyond its idealizing process, contemporary theologians such as Reinhold Niebuhr and Karl Barth have imported into their constructive formulations something of the Newtonian image, if only as a lingering shadow in the way they conceive of man and of history as opposed to the realities of nature. Furthermore, through their indebtedness to Kierkegaard and to contemporary Existentialism, modern Protestant theologians tend to continue the stance and strategy of thought that was initiated by Kant, despite all that they undertake as a reconception of reason and Revelation in their reconstruction of Christian doctrine. Their participation in the new imagery of thought is unmistakable. But I think we must say also that their participation is partial, often incidental, and mostly indirect. This, in part, is what gives them power of expression in the life of the churches; but to some extent and in some instances, it is also what short-circuits their effectiveness in shaping the modern ethos.

For a number of years Henry Nelson Wieman was considered the most expressive advocate of that form of theological reconstruction that took account of the dimension of depth in experience and history as it had been formulated within the revolution in modern science. His was the first theological voice, in America at least, to speak out in behalf of this new orientation and imagery of thought. He did so, in fact, even before Whitehead's major contributions in metaphysics and religious thought had been made. In retrospect, however, one must come to the judgment that Wieman's participation in this new vision of science and metaphysics was also partial and often reluctant. Something that he retained from his earlier allegiance to Roycean Idealism, along with what he derived from the influence of Dewey's instrumentalism, kept him from going the full way in reconceiving the role of reason in religious inquiry. Thus, while he has acknowledged with considerable passion that "God is more than we can think," and that there are unmanageable depths of reality that elude our grasp and even our apprehension, his method of religious inquiry and verification adheres to a mode of empirical observation and verification that somehow disregards the caution of restraint applied to observation and reason in relativity theory. In this respect, Wieman reflects more the imagery of Newton and Locke than of Einstein and Whitehead. And while his view of history conveys the complexity of events, seen in relation to depths of creativity, his method of inquiry results in isolating a specific structure of meaning as being normatively expressive of that depth, and thereby tends to foreclose the import of what is unmanageable and hidden in the depth of historical realities.

It might be argued, on the other hand, that Wieman is doing no more in this method of responding selectively to the unmanageable and hidden depth of historical realities than any theologian does in appealing to a doctrine of Christology. It is his way of averting mysticism, yet of continuing to be responsive to the mysterious depths of historical existence which as he says, "can transform us as we cannot transform ourselves." [9] In this respect Wieman appears to be pursuing a process of demythologizing comparable to, yet more radical than, that of Bultmann,

[9] Henry Nelson Wieman, *Man's Ultimate Commitment*. Southern Illinois University Press, 1958. p. 10.

employing, instead of Existentialism, his own form of rational empiricism to attain apologetic results.

I have commented upon these theologians simply for purposes of illustration. My concern is not to assess any other theologian's theology, or to pontificate concerning his participation in the contemporary idiom of thought. Nor do I mean to argue that a theologian's effectiveness in conveying the Christian Gospel to modern culture turns fully upon the degree to which he employs this modern idiom. There are many subtle factors that enter into this problem, not the least of which is the one that has concerned Karl Barth all his life, namely, the language that is appropriate to conveying the proclamations of Scripture, even in carrying forward the theological task. My intent here has been more confessional than polemical or normative. I have meant simply to lift up the opportunity that has been offered to us out of the accidents of history and the creative developments within the sciences to convey a fuller witness of faith than the discourse of culture customarily affords, certainly than the discourse of Western culture during the past three hundred years of our history has been able to make possible. I mean by this not only that the realism with which we are made aware of our limitations of human forms and formulations can enable us to experience the stark realities of grace and judgment to which the Christian faith bears witness, but also that the very thought-forms that have been made available, the very context in which our complexity as creatures is made vivid, in which the depth and mystery of our being is impressed upon us, can enable us to grasp with more concreteness and conviction the fullness of the Christian evangel which the Biblical witness has sought to proclaim. As a result of the vision of human experience and of the natural realities of existence which the imagery of our time has opened up to us, the very notion of Christ as a New Creation can speak to us with a vividness of meaning we could hardly have imagined in an earlier Newtonian imagery. As a result of this vision of existence, the very observation that "the mystery of the Kingdom" is simultaneously a present reality in our midst and a promise of our ultimate meaning and hope, can be made insistent, can impel us to cry out with new wonder and excitement as we discern these intimations of the holy and of ultimacy in the immediacies of our existence. With this vision we are able to recover the notion of the church as a witnessing community, an ambivalent, yet forgiven community. Such a community can awaken us to the reality of ourselves and to the reality of spirit in which our lives are cast. The realization that the grace that is offered can be received in relationships with our fellow human beings, with all human beings, can stab us awake to the immediacy of the work of the spirit.[10] As a result of the vision of existence that has come to us out of the travail of history, the very depiction of Jesus Christ as the Suffering Servant becomes a compelling symbol of the gentle might that transforms and saves in the face of the most formidable threats of our existence.

In the last analysis, what has occurred in this reorientation of mind has had the effect of extricating us from the tyranny of our own human formulations, and has thus enabled us to reaffirm the freedom of God with new meaning. We still have the task of adequately assessing these formulations. They are not to be devaluated or discarded simply because they are unequal to the effort or the attainment which Rationalism and Romanticism once envisaged for them. Rather, they are to be seen for what they are: offerings of the human spirit, faithful efforts of the human mind to pursue man's problem of meaningfulness and structure, under the judgment of an ultimacy that will not be contained within any human formulation. As human beings whose very structure demands the discipline and

[10] An arresting statement of this point has recently been made by Joseph Haroutunian in "Grace and Freedom Reconsidered," *Journal of Religion,* Vol. XL, No. 2, April 1960, pp. 59-79.

integrity of honest inquiry, we may not forsake this quest for intelligibility. Something seriously debilitating seizes our humanity when we do so. Something degrading infects our religious sensibilities when we forego or forfeit the occasion to pursue this responsibility. But intelligibility and integrity demand also the humility which a clear sense of our complexity can bring to our thinking. For this is to take a proper measure of ourselves as inquiring minds, and of the mystery of the fact that our life is in God, in whom the measure of all thought is found.

In this chapter on the imagery of thought, and in the two earlier chapters, I have intended to set forth in a general way the problems as well as the opportunities that confront Christian thinking in the present period of cultural revolution and nuclear science. We need now to look more closely at the transitions in thought which led to the new vision in the sciences and to revisions in the imagery of thought as these bear upon Christian thinking.

IV Evolution and the
Imagery of Religious Thought:
from Darwin to Whitehead

In the spring of 1926 an incident occurred at the University of Chicago which may well be considered symbolic of the shift in perspective about which I am to speak in this chapter. Whitehead's book, *Religion in the Making*, had just appeared. From the title of the book and its chapter headings one had every reason to assume that it would speak directly to the concerns of any student or scholar in the field of religion for whom the evolutionary point of view had become basic. Yet, to the dismay and irritation of many who were then with the Divinity School of the University of Chicago, including such students of the history and development of religious doctrine and institutions as Shailer Mathews, Edward Scribner Ames, and Shirley Jackson Case, this book was wholly unintelligible. Shailer Mathews was heard to remark, "It is infuriating, and I must say, embarrassing as well, to read page after page of relatively familiar words without understanding a single sentence." The fact that other members of the Divinity faculty and their colleagues in other theological schools who had read the book felt likewise lessened the embarrassment, but it hardly lessened the irritation. Shirley Jackson Case was able to set the book aside as being another instance of a metaphysically burdened philosopher stumbling through unfamiliar terrain, creating problems and giving explanations where no real problems existed. Shailer Mathews, however, was less inclined to dismiss it so readily. At one moment he would bristle with indignation at being put in such a predicament; but then as the humor of the situation seized him his face would light up with a marvelous smile and he would say, "Of course, 'the fault could be in ourselves.' Whitehead may be telling us something we ought to know about."

It was this hunch that led Mathews to invite Henry Nelson Wieman to the Chicago campus to interpret Whitehead's book. Wieman had just broken into the field of philosophy of religion with an equally startling book, *Religious Experience and Scientific Method*. He had been attentive to Whitehead's writing long before the latter had addressed himself to problems of religion or metaphysics. He had read Whitehead's *Inquiry into Principles of Natural Knowledge* (1919), and *The Concept of Nature* (1920), and through these and other works [1] had become acquainted with what was occurring in the new physics. He had adopted the principles of Gestalt psychology as being especially relevant to current issues and problems in religion. He was aware also of the theories in emergent evolution that were then appearing,[2] and considered these to be of a piece with the configurative thinking which the new physics and modern metaphysics were employing. In short, Wieman was attuned to the very notions which had been shaping the imagery of Whitehead's thought, and thus words which appeared to be mere abstractions, or awkward combinations of

---

[1] Notably *Principia Mathematica* (with Bertrand Russell), 3 vols., Cambridge University Press, 1910-1913; *The Principle of Relativity*, Cambridge University Press, 1922; *Science and the Modern World*, Macmillan, 1925.

[2] S. Alexander, *Space, Time, and Deity*, Macmillan, 1920, and C. Lloyd Morgan, *Emergent Evolution*. Henry Holt, 1923. In 1926 three more significant studies in emergent evolution were to appear: C. Lloyd Morgan, *Life, Mind, and Spirit;* J. C. Smuts, *Holism and Evolution,* and Edmund Noble, *Purposive Evolution*. Behind these works and underlying their organismic philosophy were Bergson's *Creative Evolution,* which had made a deep impression on Wieman, and the radical empirical writings of William James, especially *Pluralistic Universe* and *Essays in Radical Empiricism*.

otherwise familiar words to some readers, conveyed significant new depth of meaning which Whitehead was at pains to present to his readers.

The occasion of Wieman's interpretation was a meeting of the Theology Club of the Divinity School in the Swift Common Room. Edward Scribner Ames, Shirley Jackson Case, Gerald Birney Smith, and Shailer Mathews, and their colleagues were all there, most of them in the front row, and behind them a packed audience extended to the rear of the room, all awaiting the miracle of interpreting "this book." The miracle was performed. With deftness and patience, and with occasional sallies in poetic imagination, Wieman took the key phrases and their basic concepts and translated them into the more familiar imagery of the pragmatic Chicago school. It was as if shuttered windows in one's own household had been swung open, revealing vistas of which one had hitherto been unmindful. Needless to say the act of interpretation in this context was impressive, and the response of the audience was equally so.

I

Now it is what underlies this memorable occasion that is my concern at the moment. I would venture to say that it marked the coming together of two distinct eras of imagery and their consequent perspectives. The Chicago School of Mathews, Ames, and Case was essentially shaped, both in imagery and interest, by the biological notions that had come into general usage through the stimulus of Darwin's *On the Origin of Species*. In fact, one may say that the issue between science and religion had been posed for these men within the ethos of thought which Darwinian evolution had largely created. Not that they depended in any immediate sense upon biological science for their concepts or method, or that they had any conscious concern with Darwin, but the "modernism," "environmentalism," and "functionalism" that were explicit in their methodology and emphasis had been implicitly derived from the Darwinian theory of natural selection. For while, to the popular mind, natural selection conveyed a sanctioning of competitiveness and assertiveness in the interest of survival, to the more specialized mind in psychology and sociology and in the study of religion, it revealed the decisive role of environment and the importance of functional adaptation. Modernism can be understood best, I think, as a blanket term covering the gamut of functional adaptations in response to the demands of a changing environment and the forward-moving perspective consequent to it. And I would claim that modernism, in the technical sense of that term, began with Darwin. Or perhaps one should say that Darwin's theory of evolution gave it its essential impetus precisely in the way that Rousseau sparked the Romanticist era and Descartes and Newton launched seventeenth-century Rationalism.

To be sure, it took more than a biological theory to set in motion all the cultural forces which were beginning to reshape the ethos of the West in the mid-nineteenth century. The industrial age was in the ascendancy, ready to take full advantage of technical contributions from the physical sciences then coming into their maturity. Through the creation of "invention factories," of which Thomas Edison's laboratory was the precursor, scientific invention was being consciously correlated with industrial needs. The opportunities, both for industrial and for scientific advance, were of such magnitude that nothing, not even the surviving sensibilities of an idealistic age and a mature artistic sense (in retrospect, least of all, these), could restrain the accelerating drive to bend human energy to the task of meeting the immediate demands for adaptation in the service of function, either elicited by opportunities of a changing environment or imposed by current demands. The times were ripe for precisely what did happen in Europe and America in 1859. Darwin's theory did not create the era; it provided it with the rationale that enabled it to give "full speed ahead" to the process of adaptation, accentuating the concern with practical demands and function. It brought to fruition, or at least to a period of full growth, the bent of mind which had been initiated by Francis Bacon,[3] directing inquiry as well as cultural effort to the idea of achieving mastery over the forces of nature, and turning the concern for knowledge into a zest for power. Pragmatism was to be the philosophy best suited to serve this awakening power culture, and it can be said to have been evoked by the issues which were brought to light by its problems. Similarly, functional psychology was the mode of inquiry into human behavior calculated to yield understanding of the human response to environmental demands, replacing introspective or subjective psychology whose interests were more internal and even mystical. The earlier Chicago School of Theology availed itself of both pragmatism and functional psychology and made these determining factors in its methodology.

Harry Overstreet has said that "there are two kinds of challenge that life makes to us, the challenge of needs and the challenge of the unknown." [4] The imagery of thought provided by the era of Modernism, following from the stimulus of Darwinism, clearly expressed a response to the challenge of needs. It would be misleading to say that the challenge of the unknown was wholly absent from this modernistic mode of thought. Even in the Darwinian theory of evolution something of this challenge was acknowledged. In nineteenth-century philosophies elaborating the evolutionary theory it appears as an overtone of agnosticism, as in Herbert Spencer's reference to the Unknowable.[5] Even in modernist theologies like that of Shailer Mathews's one senses this agnostic note accom-

[3] Cf. *The Advancement of Learning,* 1605.
[4] *The Enduring Quest.* Chautauqua Press, 1931, p. vii.
[5] Cf. his *First Principles.* D. Appleton Co. 1862.

panying the formulation of its practical or functional rationale, as when he wrote,

> Like a vast parabola, the personality-evolving activities of the cosmos touch our little circle of experience. We know not whence they come or whither they go; but we cannot evade them. *We set up relations with them* similar to those which we set up with persons. And thus we derive new strength and courage and moral motive for facing the tasks of life.[6]

The modernist, whether scientist, philosopher, or theologian, was content to confine observation and inquiry to the immediate data at hand and to offer judgment based upon experimentation within these limits. All concern with ultimates was to be excluded from such inquiry, for these lay outside the scope of the method.

This understanding of the limited scope of scientific method had been generally accepted since Kant's *Critique of Pure Reason* (1781); but in nineteenth-century evolutionary parlance it took on the specific meaning that "all beginnings and endings are lost in mystery," a phrase that became commonplace in the sciences and social sciences as a way of dismissing or circumventing probing questions that sought to assess the larger implications or consequences of scientific analysis. What this meant was that, as long as the sciences or any related form of inquiry attended to the immediacies of nature or experience, no ultimate question need intrude or be considered. One can see now that this was a judgment dictated by the modernistic imagery which a confirmed trust in evolution provided. Sanguine modernists could accept this dismissal of ultimate questions because their faith in the evolutionary process was such that they need have no fear of its implications. Usually in such instances there was imported into the scientific view something of the ethos or sensibilities

[6] *Growth of the Idea of God.* Macmillan, 1931, p. 230.

of modern Idealism. The mode of thought described as "theistic evolution"[7] which came into prominence in America during the late nineteenth century simultaneously with a resurgence of Hegelianism, spoke of evolution as "God's way of doing things." This was tantamount to identifying God and evolution, which had the effect of insulating the man of faith from whatever dire effects might seem to follow from the scientist's study of the process in the immediate data at hand. Certain scientists, too, were ready to adopt this assumption as an "over-belief," either as men of faith or simply as scientists at work, only too glad to subscribe to whatever might keep the issue between science and religion in a state of quiescence. For many other scientists, however, and for people of a modernistic bent of mind who saw in the sciences "a new messiah," or at least a directive of life displacing both religion and philosophy, this preoccupation with the immediacies to the exclusion of ultimates meant frankly a secularizing of life, that is, a relinquishing of all ideal or transcendent aspects which hope and wonder might evoke. Preoccupation with practical problems and present needs, as science and industry pursued them, offered a way of life that provided incentive and zest enough. This, I should say, is the true meaning of secularism—living shorn of its ultimate dimension and sensibilities. It would not be too farfetched or inaccurate to say that Darwinism in its deeper and persistent effects, as these became manifest in science and industry of the nineteenth and twentieth centuries, and, through them, in other cultural disciplines and activities, contributed to, if in fact it did not create, a new ethos in Western society,

[7] John Fiske was one of the earliest exponents of this view. His most substantial work was *Outlines of Cosmic Philosophy* (1874), though smaller works such as *The Destiny of Man* (1884), *The Idea of God* (1885), and *Through Nature to God* (1899), were more influential. Other works contributing to this view were Newman Smyth, *Old Faiths in New Light* (1879), Henry Drummond, *Natural Law in the Spiritual World* (1883), and Lyman Abbott, *The Theology of an Evolutionist,* (1897).

dedicated to the task of dealing with the immediacies of existence in their practical aspect.

II

Now the shift in mode of thought and sensibilities which has marked our recent thinking as a post-Darwinian era has to do chiefly with the reconception of this pre-occupation with immediacies. I am not concerned here with detailing corrections and modifications of the Darwinian theory of evolution. There have been many such changes,[8] so significant, in fact, that one wonders if Darwin must not be regarded, even by the biologists themselves, more as a precursor of developments leading to present-day evolutionary thinking rather than as a continuing historical source of our scientific understanding of man. But this may be putting the matter in the extreme. However that may be, it is Darwinism as the scientific sanction of the modernistic ethos with which I am now concerned. The shift in thought and sensibilities to which I refer reveals, not an abandonment of immediacies, but a reconception of them. In this reconception ultimacy and immediacy are seen to be inseparable, as inseparable as space and time. Ultimacy is seen to be in the immediacies of existence, not a remote aspect which is to be designated by the mystery of beginnings or endings. This is what is meant by the much-used phrase in our present discourse, "the dimension of depth." For many of our day, of course, this phrase has only the connotation of a mystifying irrationalism. Actually, however, it stems from serious renovations in the mode and structure of modern thinking.

It all began with modern physics, we are wont to say. In large measure this is true. That is, it is true for many of

8 These revisions of the Darwinian theory of evolution have been interestingly summarized for the general reader in George Gaylord Simpson's *The Meaning of Evolution,* Yale University Press, 1949, and in 1958 published as a Mentor Book in a paper-bound edition.

our most influential thinkers such as Einstein, Planck, Eddington, Millikan, Whitehead, and others. The discoveries and scientific creations of recent years in the field of nuclear energy, transforming our period into a new power age, are directly traceable to the discoveries of radioactive elements by Becquerel and the Curies, inaugurating the new physics.[9] A new depth of relations and energy revealed in both earlier and more recent experiments has routed the world-view of mechanism which Newton and his followers through the nineteenth century had come to take for granted. Writing in 1927, Robert A. Millikan reported,

I was present in Berlin on Christmas Eve, 1895, when Professor Roentgen presented to the German Physical Society his first X-ray photographs. Some of them were of the bones of the hand, others of coins and keys photographed through the opaque walls of a leather pocket-book, all clearly demonstrating that he had found some strange new rays which had the amazing property of penetrating as opaque an object as the human body and revealing on a photographic plate the skeleton of a living person.

Here was a completely new phenomenon—a qualitatively new discovery and one having nothing to do with the principles of exact measurement. As I listened and as the world listened, we all began to see that the nineteenth century physicists had taken themselves a little too seriously, that we had not come quite as near sounding the depths of the universe, even in the matter of fundamental physical principles, as we thought we had.[10]

[9] A full account of these developments leading to the new physics is given in Ernst Zimmer, *The Revolution in Physics,* Harcourt, Brace, 1936, and C. D. Broad, *Scientific Thought,* Routledge & Kegan Paul, 1923. See also Max Planck, *The Universe in the Light of Modern Physics,* W. W. Norton, 1931; Albert Einstein, *Essays in Science,* Philosophical Library, 1934; and Albert Einstein and Leopold Infeld, *The Evolution of Physics.* Simon & Schuster, 1938. Readable accounts of the general situation leading to these developments are given in J. E. Boodin, *Three Interpretations of the Universe,* Macmillan, 1934, pp. 144ff., and in W. C. Dampier, *A History of Science and Its Relations with Philosophy and Religion.* 3rd ed., Macmillan, 1946.
[10] *Evolution in Science and Religion.* Yale University Press, 1927, pp. 7ff.

But while physics has been the most formidable source of this sense of depth, developments in other areas of modern thought have also contributed to the new ethos. At the very time that Roentgen and Becquerel were bringing to a close the Newtonian era in science, Henri Bergson and William James were introducing, into philosophy and psychology respectively, the notion of relations as being internal and experienceable; and this was to alter radically the terms of philosophy laid down by Descartes, Kant, and Hegel.

Bergson has often been dismissed by scientists [11] and philosophers [12] alike, possibly for different reasons; but in most instances he has been criticized for his irrationalism and his vitalism. In my judgment both these criticisms have been overdone to the point of neglecting what Bergson was really about. I shall not delay the discussion here to defend Bergson against his critics, except to point out that what is frequently termed "irrationalism" in Bergson is precisely what he has in common with all modern disciplines that take the dimension of depth seriously. Concern with internal relations means, not that one disavows structured meaning to which intelligible inquiry can address itself, but that, to attend to it with any sense of reality, one must employ a mode of inquiry that is appropriate and adequate to deal with structure that is living, that is, dynamic in an organic sense. Bergson distrusted intellect as it was commonly conceived and employed in scientific and philosophical circles precisely because of its abstractive procedure in forming any cognitive judgment. What he was seeking for was a way of apprehending any fact within the living situation so as to capture what was wholly its reality in that living situation. That he chose intuition as a mode of apprehension best calculated to seize such true images of things as they are

[11] Cf. George Gaylord Simpson, op. cit., p. 131.
[12] Cf. W. T. Jones, *A History of Western Philosophy*. Harcourt, Brace, 1952.

in their living context simply meant that, of the tools available, this, in his judgment, was best suited to accomplish the intellectual task in its most realistic and vital sense. He was vulnerable at many points, as we are now able to see; for the art of thinking forward, as we live forward,[13] or of perceiving holistically, or relationally, not only was as yet undeveloped but hardly acknowledged as being legitimate in Western thought during Bergson's earlier years when he wrote *Creative Evolution* (1911). What has since become commonplace in modern psychology as field theory under the influence of the Gestalt school and subsequent modes of holistic psychology, and in the new metaphysics since Whitehead,[14] was scarcely manageable or even definable, except as one associated it with the intuitive act.

It must be said, of course, in order not to blur the fallacy in Bergson's method, that he chose intuition as being a mode of apprehension most appropriate to a concern with internal relations precisely because he failed to note or to acknowledge the structural or contextual character of such relations as an external pattern of existence as well. His insistence that that which defied abstraction was simply internal within the living experience precluded a satisfactory conception of the thought process and led him to employ what was available as the antithesis to abstractive cognition, namely, intuition, or, as it is sometimes put, imagism. William James, who sensed the importance of Bergson's effort and shared his impatience with abstract metaphysics and scientism, saw the problem

[13] This observation that we live forward but think backward was first made by Kierkegaard, and quoted by Harold Hoffding in an article in *The Journal of Philosophy, Psychology, and Scientific Methods.*, II, 1905, pp. 85-92. James took up this notion of Kierkegaard's and advanced the notion of thinking forward as we live forward in his *Essays on Radical Empiricism*, p. 238.

[14] Cf. also Dorothy Emmet, *The Nature of Metaphyscal Thinking*, Macmillan, 1945, and *Function, Purpose and Powers*, Macmillan, 1958; Susanne Langer, *Philosophy in a New Key*. Harvard University Press, 1958.

with more proportion. For him relations were experience-able in a way that could make them designative as well, as in speaking of an experience of transition, or the flux of experience.[15] A persisting positivism in his thinking, however, prevented James from doing full justice to the rich perceptions he had, in his effort to convey the "thickness of experience." What he and Bergson failed to do, Whitehead undertook to accomplish through his method of rational empiricism. However, Whitehead was brought to his metaphysics of relations through the revolution in the new physics; this fact has given to his thought, in designating the nexus of events, more externality than he really means to convey, or should imply. Nevertheless, a close study of his doctrine of prehension will reveal that he is really struggling with the same problem that challenged and excited Bergson and James in their insistence upon relations being experienceable. In Whitehead, the sense of structured meaning in the creative flow or living situation is more marked, and thus less suspect of being a detour into mysticism. One needs the corrective of Bergson and James at times in reading Whitehead, however, lest the formative notions of the new physics implicit in his imagery render one's understanding of this creative nexus more external and rationalistic than it actually can be. There is a depth in the living situation that resists formulation. It was this that Bergson knew well and meant to take with the utmost seriousness and realism. The followers of Whitehead who take his imagery literally without pondering this important insight are inclined to be more rationalistic than Whitehead intended, and than the method of rational empiricism requires.

Again, to speak of another criticism which modern biologists often make of Bergson, I think that we are not

[15] Cf. his *Psychology*, Vol. I., esp. chap. IX, and chap. VII, and *Essays in Radical Empiricism*, chap. VI.

to take his formulation of *élan vital* simply as a statement of a vital principle to explain the history of life, as George Gaylord Simpson seems to assume.[16] It is his way, not only of depicting the evolutionary character of all existence, but of accentuating the dynamic context in which all existence is cast, in contrast to the mechanical space-time imagery of pre-evolutionary science and philosophy. It is, as George Herbert Mead has said, a way of "taking time seriously" [17] to the point that no definable space in the mechanistic sense can be designated, or fixed, except as a supposition for purposes which require one to arrest the process, which is to assume that time does not matter or that it does not exist. Bergson's term "duration" is a space-time notion which implies that space can be conceived only in the context of time; and this means that every point of space is in process of passing into a subsequent point, etc. *Élan vital,* then, is no catchall phrase to explain evolution, in Simpson's sense of that term, but a notion lighting up the dynamic or process character of reality.

The notion of depth as a dimension of the living situation resisting abstract thought, or at least qualifying its relevance to every situation, which we find so dominant in Bergson and in subsequent forms of organismic thinking, is traceable also to other anti-Hegelian developments. The one that has received most attention in our time is that stemming from Soren Kierkegaard and issuing in modern Existentialism.[18] I shall not develop this point

16 Op. cit. p. 131.
17 George Herbert Mead, *Movements of Thought in the Nineteenth Century.* Ed. by Merritt H. Moore. University of Chicago Press, 1936, pp. 311ff.
18 Important as Kierkegaard is in the recent history of Western thought, especially in theological thought, it is a mistake, I think, to single him out exclusively as if he alone stemmed the tide of abstract thought and opened the way for the "Existential" stance. This is to exaggerate his role. The critics of Hegel were legion, and their contributions took a variety of directions. The scope of this variety can be indicated by the mere mention of the names of men who figured in this historical revolu-

beyond suggesting that here, too, concern with the ultimate import of the immediate situation associates ultimacy with immediacy in its concreteness. In Existentialism the living situation is no mere center of practicality, shorn of ultimate concern. It is the vivid arena of decision and act, carrying the risks and burden of their ultimate meaning. Although the mode of thinking here is radically different from that of modern metaphysics, by following the lead of the new physics, it converges toward the latter in countering the positivism and the practically oriented modernism following from Darwinian evolution, with its stress upon "environmentalism" and "functionalism" as modes of adaptation within a secularized immediacy, an immediacy shorn of depth and ultimacy.

III

There is yet a further aspect to be noted in contrasting Creative Evolution, as it has taken form within the newer ethos, with evolutionism in its Darwinian and modernistic meaning. Darwin was in every respect indentified with what is now designated *nineteenth-century science*. Now nineteenth-century science is to be understood as the summit of the scientific movement which had begun in the seventeenth century, fulfilling its vision of a mechanistic world order and its dream of the human conquest of nature through measurement and predictability. The success with which physicists particularly had been able to expand, verify, and utilize the image of a world machine provided by Newton led more and more to an assumption of a dependable mechanism underlying every natural phenomenon including man and society. The notion of orderliness in nature had become a dogma. And this at once gave assurance of a wholly rational interpretation of its

tion in fundamental notions, for example, Schelling, Herbart (a contemporary of Schelling), Schopenhauer, Feuerbach, Marx, Hartmann, Nietzsche, Freud, Bergson, and William James.

processes and the growing conviction that mechanism and materialism as a final reading of the nature of reality were indisputable. Darwin's theory certainly followed within this tradition. In fact it was said to exemplify it decisively in the human realm.

We have already noted what happened in physics late in the nineteenth century to upset this dogma of orderliness and to shatter the imagery of mechanism as a controlling notion. "The childish mechanical conceptions of the nineteenth century," declared Millikan in recalling his eyewitness account of Roentgen's report on his experiments, "are now grotesquely inadequate." [19]

The new vision of science to which modern physics was forced to come was not to be universally accepted throughout the sciences. The imagery of mechanism proved to be useful to sciences, such as biology in the late nineteenth century, which were only beginning to achieve measurability and predictability. The younger sciences, bent on attaining precision in these matters, were reluctant to give up the very facilities that assured them such results. It must be said in their defense that often the kind of problem being investigated could be well served by assuming an imagery of mechanism. Modern physics abandoned this imagery precisely because it no longer enabled this science to explore the kind of problem that presented itself, once radioactivity was envisaged. Nevertheless, the lag between other sciences and physics in these matters and the persistence of (the) mechanistic imagery in psychology and the social sciences have been real obstacles to taking this revolution in fundamental notions seriously throughout the various disciplines.

Such a notion as emergence, for example, which is closely allied with the principle of indeterminacy and uncertainty and which was later to develop in physics, actually assumed more credence in physics before it took

[19] *Evolution in Science and Religion.* Yale University Press, 1927.

root in biology and psychology; yet it has more significant implications for the data of the organic and social sciences than for physics. But here again measurement and prediction were at issue. When biologists could see that emergence and structure go together, that the one is present wherever the other appears, there were grounds for seeing that emergence did not preclude measurability, though predictability was to a degree radically lessened. Yet the notion of emergence opened the way for biology really to take the living character of its data seriously.

Harry Overstreet wrote in *The Enduring Quest:* "Professor Jennings has hailed the doctrine of emergent evolution as 'the declaration of independence of biology.' It is not difficult to understand why. As long as biology was headed for a complete predictability, it was necessary to believe that 'the only method of learning about the organic is to study the inorganic.' In short, biology was forced to become physics. Every living creature had to be studied, not in terms of its own unique configuration, but in terms of its constituent physicochemical parts." [20]

The contrast between Darwinian evolution and the creative or emergent evolution of recent years may be sharpened if we look more closely at the decisive notions which are seen to be formative in each case. It was common in the nineteenth century and even later to set Darwin over against Lamarck or vice versa, and by this means to point up the contrast between the inner and the outer orientation of evolutionary thinking. Lamarck was supposed to have ascribed to the internal condition of the organism itself, its inheritable side, a good deal of the initiative in the variations observed. Thus evolution could be said to be inherent in the organisms of life themselves. Environmental conditions could be said to be the occasions of change in the activities of the organism; but the decisive thrust of evolutionary change was internal process of

[20] Op. cit. pp. 61-62.

a sort. One can see how Vitalism could draw upon such an orientation and why Bergson preferred Lamarck to Darwin. Lamarck believed in a single life process which expressed itself in many forms. Organisms behaved in certain ways under the pressure of circumstances in the environment. Every activity of the organism, as Mead has observed, "altered the form of itself, and the form then handed on the change to the next generation." [21] The effort of the organism to adapt itself to these circumstances may, as Bergson has said, be simply mechanical and external; but it may also involve consciousness and will. Thus Bergson was moved to say that "Neo-Lamarckism is therefore, of all later forms of evolutionism, the only one capable of admitting an internal and psychological principle of development, although it is not bound to do so." [22]

Darwin, on the other hand, tended to look solely at the external phenomenon of the organism's response to conditions in the environment and to ascribe to such response the initiation of change or variation in the species. All internal factors were set aside, for these presumably, according to Darwin, played no significant role in the evolutionary process.

The issue between these two orientations was not so much discussed as acted upon. The scientist assumed one or the other stance, and, accordingly, moved in the direction of a mechanistic naturalism or in the direction of a more organic view of evolution, often veering toward mysticism or vitalism.

The orientation which best describes the stance of emergent evolution is neither internal nor external but a subtle interplay of both aspects; but this can make sense only if one takes into account the whole discussion of form and structure which has dominated the holistic

---

[21] *Movements of Thought in the Nineteenth Century.* University of Chicago Press, 1936, p. 159.
[22] Henri Bergson, *Creative Evolution.* Henry Holt & Co., 1911, p. 77.

thinking of those who speak of emergence and field theory. The imagery of organism in relation to environment seems altogether too simple and external to express what is envisaged in these various formulations of a dimension of depth. As Boodin has said, the new intellectual renaissance into which physics has led us in the twentieth century is marked, not only by the emancipation from mechanism, but "the discovery of form or structure as fundamental in reality." [23] In this context, variation, or let us say emergence, is no mere chance response to a condition in environment, as if miscellaneous parts were going their own way, conditioned only by incidental or accidental factors in environment. To quote Boodin again, "Nature is not a mere random collection of parts, but a whole-making activity is manifest in nature." [24] Thus it is emergence with structure.

Now this, I should say, points up the basic difference between the way evolution was conceived in Darwinism and the way in which it is understood by the emergent evolutionist. In Alexander's words, it is nature as a whole that manifests the "nisus toward deity," [25] deity here being simply the level beyond any presently established structure, and thus the lure toward which the evolutionary thrust is directed. In less metaphysically motivated disciplines the nisus, or the movement toward novelty, is simply expressive of the Gestalt itself. This is a way of saying that relationships carry within themselves a potency that is creative of new situations. They yield a "More," in William James's words, that is not the sum of the parts but a new creation, an emergent quality or character.

Here one will see that the external and the internal have merged, as it were. Or one may say that mechanism has yielded to organism, to the creativity of relationships

[23] Op. cit. p. 178.
[24] Ibid.
[25] Op. cit. Vol. II, Book IV.

which are at once internal and external, yet neither one nor the other at any one given moment of time.

V

The implications of this shift in perspective for theology are quite marked. Darwinian evolution, we noted earlier, created a serious problem for all religious inquiry in the nineteenth century, and, to some extent, continued to do so beyond the turn of the century. A perusal of the literature in religious and theological journals following 1859 throughout the 'sixties will reveal a resounding sense of despair and denunciation. The linkage of man with an animal heritage on grounds of variation dictated simply by his response to environmental changes introduced a dominance of physical influences which could in no way be squared with the Christian doctrine of man. What ultimately turned the tide in a direction which could accommodate theological thinking to the evolutionary view was a resurgence of Personal Idealism which purported to see the entire process of evolution, animal as well as human, in the context of a cosmic drama presupposing a Creator God. Hermann Lotze's philosophy in *Microcosm*,[26] provided many a theologian and churchman of this period with the key to resolve the issue between religion and evolution. For while he took mechanism seriously as a physical base for all phenomena, including man and society, he was able to show that even the formation of this physical base in each instance took place within the cosmic ground of a higher purpose. Thus the material was a function of the spiritual and, to a degree, a manifestation of it, not its ultimate ground or directive.

It would be difficult to find any one individual of the

---

[26] Rudolf Hermann Lotze, *Microcosm,* 3 vols., Leipzig, Verlag von G. Hirzel, 1872. (This work was actually written between the years 1856-64.) Eng. trans. 1884. Lotze's work was in medicine before he turned to philosophy, and in these writings as well as in the early volumes of *Microcosm* he actually anticipated Darwin's theory.

nineteenth century whose thought proved more basic in resolving the issue between evolutionism and religion than Hermann Lotze. In philosophical circles, especially in nineteenth-century America, the resurgence of Hegelian Idealism was to have wider influence in dealing with this problem. Among theologians, however, Lotze's thought, either directly or as mediated through the Ritschlians and the Personalists, had the greater impact. Lotze, in placing emphasis upon the disclosure of the spiritual reality in its effects, cut a path between a mechanistic science and an abstract metaphysics and thus was more immediately available to the religiously motivated mind of the period, say from 1880 to the early nineteen twenties. He was the basic source for the American Personalist movement founded by Borden P. Bowne; and the frequency with which he was quoted in the writings of other liberal theologians would indicate that his influence was pervasive. I would even claim that the procedure by which Shailer Mathews resolved the issue between evolution and religion, in which he conceived evolution to be a personality-producing activity in the universe continually making the world more personal, partakes of this personal idealistic vein. Mathews's "Noble Lectures," published under the title *The Spiritual Interpretation of History*, were an eloquent account of the march of human history toward this personal end. And in his "Ingersoll Lectures," *Immortality and the Cosmic Process*, he saw this movement of life toward the personal continuing beyond death. Immortality was itself another stage in the fulfillment of personality.

Edward Scribner Ames was more cautious than Mathews about injecting even so tenuous a metaphysical notion as "personality-producing activities" into the empirical discussion of religion. He was willing to settle for what he called "practical absolutes," [27] that is, visions of

[27] Cf. his "Religious Values and the Practical Absolute," *International Journal of Ethics*, Vol. XXX, 1922, 347-65.

the mind or idealizations which, at any given time, had the value of an ultimate directive in decision or action, but which were clearly to be understood as being apiece with man's own nature and experience. It was man acting with full commitment to idealized dimensions of his experience. One will see, even here, the shadow of Idealism. And this was generally true of the Pragmatist when he expressed himself even tentatively in the ontological vein. For it must be said that, while the Pragmatist considered himself to be departing from Hegel and from any explicit ontology, it was generally the abstract, universal notions from which he was departing. The process of idealization remained intact at the empirical level. Thus Pragmatism must be seen as a truncated Idealism. The superstructure of the Absolute or of a Personal God may have been relinquished, but the idealization of the human equation, consonant with such a superstructure, was as decisive as ever. This was as evident in Dewey as it was in Ames and Mathews.

The Chicago School of Theology made much of its opposition to philosophical Idealism; but its strategy of thought in transmuting evolution into something other than mechanistic naturalism was actually dictated and directed by the vestigial remains of its own personal Idealism. It could hardly be otherwise, with "environmentalism" and "functionalism" playing so large a role in the formulation of its critical method. There was nothing in the method itself to justify a religious or a Christian resolution of problems that emerged. Some recourse to Idealism, as a counterpart or corrective of the mechanism implied in its environmental and functional method, was demanded, whether implicitly or explicitly employed.

The change that has come about in theologies that partake of creative and emergent evolution can be described in this way: since mechanism is no longer the base of their evolutionary thinking, Idealism is no longer essential as a strategy of thought in resolving the tension between science and faith. The relinquishment of the dichotomy implied in the issue between mechanism and Idealism has been followed by a reformulation of the meaning of man and nature. Whether one speaks of this as a new naturalism or a religious naturalism, or abandons these terms altogether, choosing to see the world of reality in its dynamic and creative character as being "dimensional," and expressive of many stages of creative emergence, the correlation of man and nature, in contrast to their antithesis in earlier evolutionary and idealistic thinking, seems evident.

The notion of dimensions or levels of reality within nature has introduced into this later mode of evolutionary thinking qualitative distinctions which alter one's understanding of the conditions under which evolution occurs; such a concept also alters the implications of the notion itself. To put it sharply, discontinuities appear between levels or structures by reason of the something new that has occurred to create the one level which transcends the other. "Emergence with structure" thus implies structural change and qualitative innovations which, as it were, set the one apart from the other, even as their continuity in nature is acknowledged. The novel event is never reducible to its antecedents, once emergence has occurred; it is not simply the sum of its parts, but real innovation. Spirit, personality, community, individuality, psychical qualities, organic processes, each in its own way manifests a *More,* a novelty in quality and in structure by which it transcends its antecedents. Yet transcendence is never separation or alienation, for the higher subsumes the lower. Thus dimensional thinking provides a context of continuity within which discontinuities are constantly occurring.

This more complex evolutionary picture reduces mechanism and fixity to the minimum, yet retains them in forms appropriate to the level or dimension of emergence. It accentuates the role of freedom, thus extending the

130

range of flexibility; yet it sees all freedom and flexibility as being within a field or structure of relationships.

Such a complexity at once alters the fundamental imagery from which implications or consequent meanings are formed. For example, the notion of automatic progress, which seemed to follow rather naturally from nineteenth-century Evolutionism, cannot be deduced so readily from this context. The simultaneity of continuity and discontinuity within any dimension or level, of mechanism and freedom, of moral and rational qualities of personality and the grace and forgiveness of spirit, of individuality and community, bring to each event or existing situation the tension and contradiction inherent in the complexity of each structure. What Kant perceived as "radical evil," rendering the freedom of man subservient to the mechanisms of nature that persisted in him, takes on an even darker and more subtle turn in this emergent situation. For the issue is not simply between freedom and mechanism, as in the Kantian view, or between the personal and man's vestigial animal heritage, as nineteenth-century Personal Idealists viewed it. Rather, it is a variation of these along with the demonry of personality itself, of man's moral and rational capacities in tension with the sensitivities of spirit as a higher dimension of freedom and goodness which grasp him as a novelty of grace within his human structure, judging him, yet summoning him to that which is beyond his own human order of good.

This sense of tension and contradiction is not of necessity a movement onward and upward. It is fraught more with frustration, dissipation, pride, and pretension, and the anxiety which must inevitably ensue from these human failings demanding resolution in a doctrine of Redemption.

Or again, it does not follow from this emergent reading of the human situation that the structure of man, that is, "personality," is dominant and sovereign in value.

Moral and rational good, expressive of man's ideal aspects and thus characteristic of this human dimension, stands under the judgment of a sensitivity more consonant with the freedom of spirit, a structure of sensitivity and grace transcending man's level. The grace of the spirit evident in acts of love and forgiveness, though present in the human structure, is not to be subsumed under its category. Thus any idealization of the human equation or projection of it as an absolute or ultimate good becomes a voluntary act of illusion, making absolute a level of reality which is patently relative and thus insulating the characteristically human structure of personality from its sensitive frontier where it might otherwise encounter the dimension of spirit, expressive within its own structure, yet not of it.

The Darwinian theory of evolution took form in a period of history when individuality was itself at a premium. It was often expressed as the "primacy of the person," a dictum which had been affirmed since the time of Descartes. Obviously, some of the qualitative overtones of this liberal dictum were seriously threatened by the evolutionary theory, principally because its ideal aspects appeared to be dissipated under the disclosure of man's animal antecedents. Furthermore, in its concern with the species, the priority of the individual person tended inevitably to be obscured. Nevertheless, the virtues of individuality as such were enhanced. Individualism, in fact, gained a new status, encouraging aggressiveness, if not ruthlessness, in the pursuit of individual enterprise as adaptability and the competitiveness it entailed. What natural science stimulated, industry furthered in the very mode of activity it promoted and the ethos it tended to generate within communities and within culture as a whole.

What has followed from the creative evolution of emergence and the accompanying notion of field theory, on the other hand, is a radically different view of individuality and of human fulfillment. It would be a mistake to say that it reverses matters, setting up community in opposition to individuality. To some extent this has followed; though when it occurs, it represents an exaggeration or even a perversion of what is implied in this newer image of man. For while relations are real and can be experienced, forming the context of man's being and providing resources of energy and power which are greater and other than he, himself, can effect, they are also expressive of what he, in himself, represents. The truer imagery is the one formulated by Whitehead, in saying that the topic of religion is "individual in community," [28] which is to see individual values empowered through relationships, and the community expressive of freedom and qualitative differences. In this context the meaning of men enlarges because selfhood itself widens and deepens its bounds. Freedom also changes in meaning. In addition to connoting a measure of independent judgment or decision as well as flexibility, it means, in this context, freedom to have relations, freedom to avail one's self of the grace and power which relationships can bestow. The atomism of the autonomous self thus gives way to a sound sense of the community of being and the responsibility, as well as the opportunity, of being fulfilled within such a creative nexus.

One can see, then, that the theological significance of this reorientation of evolutionary thinking could be considerable. However, the relevance of the imagery provided by such notions as emergence and field theory to the theological task will be judged variously. Those theologians are who persuaded by present discussions in analytical philosophy will insist that even a consideration of the

[28] *Religion in the Making.* Macmillan, 1926. Whitehead, in using this phrase, was reaffirming a notion well known in classical Christian thinking, as expressed in the Covenant and in the *Imago Dei*. But his metaphysics sets forth a new rationale for it, giving it added contemporary force.

problem of their relevance to theology is misguided; for this is to confuse two different areas of discourse, the scientific and the religious. Others, open to the suggestion that some interrelation between discourses is permissible, will object to intruding these particular notions into current theological thinking on the grounds that they are not significant or even legitimate notions in the biological sciences themselves. Again, theologians who are persuaded of their usefulness in conveying theological meaning to the contemporary mind may have gone so far as to claim emergent evolution to be a theological symbol by which Biblical events of history as well as subsequent doctrinal formulations may be explicated. This view was implicit in the theological writings of the late Archbishop William Temple, particularly in his volume on *Nature, Man, and God*. It has been explicitly set forth by another British theologian, L. S. Thornton, in his trilogy on *The Form of the Servant*,[29] in which he virtually equates the terms "emergence" and "revelation." A more recent exposition of this position appears in a paper by John Hayward entitled "Evolution as a Theological Symbol."

The problem of how scientific, philosophical, or even common-sense notions are to be employed in bringing intelligibility to the Christian faith intrudes here. I would venture to suggest that to apply them so directly and completely as to subsume all theological meaning under these notions is to make too much of them. They are at best analogies that can help the modern mind to take such Christian concepts as "revelation," "grace," and "spirit" more seriously than is possible within the monolithic discourse which our contemporary disciplines provide. This applies particularly to many of our time who have been schooled in the thought of Western culture, say from the period of the Enlightenment through nineteenth-century

[29] This trilogy includes Vol. I, *Revelation and the Modern World*, 1950; Vol. II, *The Dominion of Christ*, 1952; and Vol. III, *Christ and the Church*. Dacre Press, 1956.

philosophy and science. The imagery of thought provided by this period literally closed the modern mind to dimensions of meaning which such terms as "revelation," "spirit," and "grace" convey. The aversion to supernaturalism or to any appearance of dualism that seemed to threaten or to undo the assumption of "one-world order of meaning" has rendered the modern consciousness peculiarly insensitive to the great themes of Christian faith that have meant to point beyond man's own human powers and resources. And with no imagery available, other than that of supernaturalism, to suggest such nuances or sensitive ground for pointing toward dimensions of grace or spirit, Christian faith could mean for the modern consciousness only confidence in the resources of man's moral Idealism. The radical turn of Protestant thought in recent years, motivated largely by a rediscovery of Kierkegaard's critique of modern Idealism, represents one serious reaction within Western culture against this impasse and self-enclosure. But the protest extends beyond specifically theological literature. For example, what has come about in the shift of imagery exemplified in the new physics and in emergent thinking generally represents not so much a reaction as a radical reconception of fundamental notions, altering the modern consciousness itself. In so far as one partakes of this deepened mode of modern consciousness, one is made aware of depths and nuances in the complexities of man's existence which at once sober one with the limits of man's reason and perceptive powers, and awaken one to the very dimensions of experience to which the themes of the Christian faith bear witness.

It is quite possible that, when one has been awakened to the import of the Christian witness through a distinctive imagery, partaking of specific philosophical or scientific notions, these notions will affect one's speech and even condition one's understanding of the witness to faith. It was so with Augustine, for whom Neo-Platonism served such a role, enabling him to take the Gospels seriously, whereas previously they had offended his disciplined taste. But it does not follow that one is necessarily subjected to these thought-forms in his effort to understand the witness to faith. Insofar as they are assumed to be "instruments of vision," lighting up realities of the spirit which would otherwise remain obscure, or even nonexistent, they will be understood to be subservient to the realities disclosed. What is thus seen and heard within this more sensitive stance will bring its own occasion of judgment and understanding.

To speak specifically on this point, the fact that form and relationship have been restored to the current image of man, both in the new metaphysics and in the sciences of man, enables us to be more understanding in our anthropology of what is being conveyed in such historically Biblical notions as the Covenant and the *Imago Dei*. Care needs to be exercised, lest we make the correlation between these Biblical notions and contemporary ideas too complete and simple. There are differences to be noted, respected, and seriously pondered. Nevertheless, the recovery of these valued notions in the current discourse is a decided gain. Where the dialogue between this newer modern consciousness and the Biblical witness is sensitively pursued, it can yield the kind of critical insight into our understanding of man which we desperately need in this age of yearning and conflict.

V   Relativity and Ultimate Faith

Basic as the formative imagery of modern thought is to a repossession of what is insistent in the Christian ethos, we must acknowledge that apprehending the realities of faith is not simply a matter of imagery. It involves the intricate depths of the human psyche as man relates to his fellow human beings; it involves his own self-understanding, his sense of need and dependence as well as his freedom, and his capacity to correlate these aspects of his existence. These all contribute in subtle ways to influence man's capacity to receive the grace that is given. Ultimately this capacity may not be man's to determine or to shape in decisive ways; but insofar as he is his own obstacle to the ministries of a good not his own, he has something to do with removing that obstacle. To these matters we shall be turning our attention presently.

But there is yet another problem that plagues the modern man as he concerns himself with the Christian ethos, and then looks to disturbing events about him. It is a gnawing uncertainty about what could be implied in these day-to-day events which lead us further and further into the perplexities and anxieties of this nuclear age. We have no perspective with which to view this aspect of world revolution. We are still victims of our own wide-eyed wonder, listening to reports of one scientific miracle after another as rockets and satellites are being shot into orbit. It is quite likely that millions of this generation will go down into the dust of the years stunned into insensibility by the magnitude and threat of its meaning. Our technicians and clearheaded scientists, for whom much of this nuclear display is routine, will continue in stride, laying the groundwork for the age of power that is emerging; but the peoples of the earth, for whom there are neither tools of thought nor tools in hand with which to grasp the simplest reality to which this nuclear and space talk refers, will continue in their role as the stunned generation.

The uncertainty which such ventures into space precipitate is of a different nature than the disorientation attending industrialization and secularization, where cultural moorings are being dissipated; although space exploration, too, involves the kind of peril to which we referred earlier. For in our decision as nations to project the exploration of this frontier of outer space we are catapulted to a staggering new level of mechanization. Yet the uncertainty we feel here goes beyond this. It is the feeling of leaving a firm base of familiar ground and of being propelled irresistibly into uncharted areas. What is often unexpressed, though vaguely felt, is the suspicion that the relinquishment of familiar ground, the sense of this one earth to stand upon, implies much more than a transitional mood of psychical dislocation. It suggests radical philosophical implications. And, these strike at theological assumptions, or in some way undermine the foundations of faith.

Now one assumption that underlies these misgivings is that our planetary history defines the bounds of our heritage of faith. In most instances the range is defined more closely than that. At times it is spoken of as a *"heilsgeschichte"* occurring within a particular sequence of cultural history within the Tigris-Euphrates Valley, and subsequently within the Mediterranean world and the Atlantic community. It is what relates to this nucleus of space-time that constitutes the faith. Furthermore, this *heilsgeschichte* is made universal in application. Thus while it speaks for God's people, it speaks forth to the world. The juxtaposition of so circumscribed an image of the heritage of faith and the expanding universe prompts many to feel the ground of this faith slipping from under them.

This is not the first time in Western history that such an experience has come to Christian people. Every expansion of visible horizons has evoked such misgivings. Striking instances were: the launching of the Crusades in the eleventh century, breaking down protective barriers which, for some at least, had enclosed the familiar world of Christendom; geographical expansion beyond European shores as ocean travel developed in the fifteenth century; discoveries in astronomy in the seventeenth century, opening up the study of planetary movements; and the widening of the historical consciousness in the eighteenth and nineteenth centuries, when new facilities for reckoning time and development impelled revisions in man's understanding of the natural world as well as his own history. The present experience of the nuclear age, however, has dimensions of dismay and possible destructiveness which none of these earlier periods of expansion presented. Somehow the very notion of its vastness, and of the degree of innovation we may yet encounter in exploring these unknown regions in space, fills us with misgivings as to how anything so fixed within historical experience as the Christian witness can continue to have relevance to this baffling new world now opening up before our eyes. Whether we use the word or not, we sense the relativity of every situation that it presents, and this has the effect of loosening the moorings by which clear and dependable judgments of value and meaning in existence have been made. Plainly, what we are worried about is the dissolution of a sense of order and of orderliness in the processes of life upon which we depend. Christian faith means, for many of our contemporaries, faith in the orderliness of existence governed by an unfailing Providence. The suspicion that this sense of order is being threatened, or taken from us by the innovations that begin to crowd in upon us, evokes the haunting question: is such a faith any longer tenable or relevant? The problem here is basically relativity itself—whether this stance of multi-relationships to which the most recent scientific inquiries have brought us, offering a variety of perspectives upon these scenes of facts, can sustain as well an ultimate faith. To this problem we must now turn.

I

It is odd that uncertainty concerning the orderliness of nature should be the issue evoking the question of the relevance of Christian faith. For it was precisely the scientific confidence in this notion that created the problem of faith in earlier periods of our history. As critical thinkers in the eighteenth century became persuaded that Newtonian physics could describe the processes of nature with utmost accuracy and faithfulness, many of them came to the conclusion that science itself offered the only reliable and satisfactory basis for philosophy and religion. Thus they were ready to dispense with all other forms of philosophical or religious thinking, including that of Christianity, and simply attend to the sum of the sciences.[1] On the other hand, theologians of this period and after, recognizing that Newtonian physics presented a mechanistic image of nature implying an inescapable determinism, sought to extricate the life of faith from the realm of science, even defining religion as being the conquest of the human spirit over nature. Gerald Birney Smith, after

[1] Positivism was the name given to this turn of thought in the nineteenth century with which the names of Auguste Comte, John Stuart Mill, and Herbert Spencer were most often associated. As evolutionary thought became more pervasive following 1900, this turn of mind, subscribing to the priority of the sciences in matters of knowledge and belief, became increasingly influential among educated people. It continues to be formidable as a mode of thought, though among discriminating minds today a distinction is made between taking the sciences seriously and making them autonomous in matters of faith and knowledge.

describing the way Ritschlian theologians in the nine-teenth century managed this problem, wrote:

> It was with a sense of relief, therefore, that many perplexed thinkers turned to the way of escape held out by the Ritschlian theologians. Here was a proposal to do away entirely with the embarrassing entanglement between theology and science. Each could now go on its own way with entire freedom.[2]

As theologians sought to come to terms with evolution in the latter decades of the nineteenth century, however, they defined theistic evolution in such a way as to correlate orderliness in nature with God's providence. They were aided in this effort by the work of the German scientist-philosopher Herman Lotze, who had undertaken to show the interrelation between the mechanisms of nature and personality, and to ascribe both levels of reality to the creative work of God in nature and history.[3]

It will pay us to recall some of the history of this no-tion of order as it has developed in Western thought so as to see its relation to the problem of faith in this pres-ent period of relativity and quantum theory.

George Herbert Mead has said that "the premise that nature is uniform" is a postulate taken over by science from Christian theology.[4] Obviously he meant Scholastic theology. This would carry its initial formulation, as we have known it in the West at least, as far back as Aris-totle. In its present form, however, the presupposition goes back to Newton and Spinoza, each of whom in his own way sought to trace the universal, rational structure in the world and in the life of man. Enlightenment philos-ophers, no less than Renaissance thinkers, treated this postulate of order as if it were dogma. Mead writes that

[2] *Current Christian Thinking.* University of Chicago Press, 1928, p. 104.
[3] *Microcosm.* 3 vols., 1856-64; Eng. trans., 1884.
[4] *Movements of Thought in the Nineteenth Century.* Posthumous publica-tion edited by Merritt H. Moore. University of Chicago Press, 1936, p. 7.

"Descartes, Spinoza, and Leibniz . . . gave to the mathematical interpretation of nature an almost religious value." [5] He might have added Newton as well. Voltaire was Newton's principal popularizer. It was he, in fact, who gave wide credence to this theme, equating the measure of universal order with ultimate truth. The thesis which issued from this presupposition was that nothing is defensible as an ultimate truth or value unless it can be shown to have universal application. On this basis Voltaire was able to prove to his own satisfaction that no one of the historical religions, nor all together, could be said to have any truth in them. In the face of this universal test of truth, the force of concrete demands, "truth for me" in particular situations, as well as specific cultural traditions and heritages, lost much appeal.

With the development of the science of mechanics, as physics was then known, order in nature became increasingly mechanistic in implication. Under Newton there developed the well-known image of nature as a world machine. The perfection of calculus provided for precise measurements of the movement of objects in space. So long as one was dealing with the manageable phenomena of nature, there was little point in speaking of the orderliness of nature as a postulate. It was a fact which was being demonstrated again and again. This assumption, even when interpreted as fact, could do little harm so long as it applied to physical mechanisms. Even Newton, who was inclined toward the Cambridge Platonists in his philosophy, remained open to intimations of Revelation beyond this ordered world. But as the notion assumed popular currency, discriminations disappeared. With the help of popular thinkers like Voltaire, the notion of order was elevated to the status of a basic category. To be sure, there were rationalists among philosophers and theo-

[5] Ibid. p. 8. Cf. also E. A. Burtt, *The Metaphysical Foundations of Modern Science,* Doubleday Anchor Books, 1954 (originally published 1924), pp. 237ff.

logians of the period who gave full support to this procedure.[6] Hence reason, itself, became an infallible mechanism, perfectly attuned to the reading and measuring of
every aspect of knowable reality.

The interim of Kantian Idealism and the theology consonant with it can be looked upon as an insistent effort to
wrest the human spirit, and the moral will in particular,
from the machinations of reason within this ordered and
determined realm of nature. Kantianism, however, did
not alter the concept of nature as a vast mechanism in
which man, to his chagrin and peril, was involved. And
for every theologian since Kant who has adhered to the
Kantian strategy of thought, nature has continued to assume the impersonality of the machine.

Hegel, to be sure, found it possible to go beyond Kant,
not only in elaborating a structure of thought expressive
of the human spirit, but in expanding the teleological principle of nature to the point of approximating an organic
view of nature. It is sometimes claimed that Hegel anticipated evolution in his dynamic view of history. One can
speak this way as long as one keeps in mind the point that
sharply distinguishes Hegel's organicism from that stated
in modern cosmologies. R. G. Collingwood has expressed
this point clearly in saying that the difference between
Hegel's cosmology and most of those current today "concerns the significance of time."

Modern cosmologies are in general based on the idea of evolution, and represent the development not only of one natural species
or order as a development in time, but also the development of
mind from nature as a development in time. Views of this kind
were already being canvassed in Hegel's days, and he considered
them, only to reject them with emphasis. All reality, he says, is a
system of strata or grades, higher and lower; this is true both of

---

[6] *The Deists*—Arthur Bury, *The Naked Gospel,* 1690; John Toland, *Christianity not Mysterious,* 1696; and Matthew Tindal, *Christianity as Old
as the Creation,* 1730—were the extremists.

mind, where there is a lower stratum of sense and a higher one of intellect, with subdivisions, and also of nature, where the inorganic or lifeless and the organic or living are the two main divisions; and in nature, which is the realm of externality, the living and the lifeless instead of interpenetrating must exist outside one another as separate classes of things. But he insists that there cannot be a temporal transition, but only a logical transition, from the lower forms in nature to the higher.[7]

The reason given for this decision on the part of Hegel, Collingwood explains, is

that a purely dead and mechanical world of matter, as conceived by the physics of his day (which he accepted as his starting point) cannot conceivably produce life by doing the only thing which it has the power to do, namely, redistributing itself in space. There is a new principle of organization at work in living things, which differs qualitatively from that of dead matter.[8]

So long as the science of mechanics remained the dominant form of scientific inquiry, it was understandable that a mechanistic conception of the order of nature should prevail. What is surprising is that the advent of biology [9] and other organic sciences did not break through this mechanistic image and demand a model more expressive of the data with which the organic sciences had to deal. But the method of scientific inquiry prevented this. One might even say the vanity of the organic sciences precluded it. In any case, the compulsion to attain controlled conditions conducive to precise measurement and prediction, carried the day, and thereby kept biology within the

[7] R. G. Collingwood, *The Idea of Nature*. Oxford, The Clarendon Press, 1945, p. 131.
[8] Ibid.
[9] The invention of the achromatic microscope in 1825 made biological research as we now know it possible. The cell theory of animals, which is "the fundamental notion of biology" was formulated in 1838. (Cf. F. Sherwood Taylor, "Scientific Developments of the Nineteenth Century," in *A Short History of Science, A Symposium*. Doubleday, 1959, p. 82.

traditional scientific imagery of seventeenth- and eighteenth-century physics. Thus the evolutionary theory formulated by Darwin presupposed the mechanical orderliness of nature, and adhered to a reading of the organism's external behavior of functional adaptation to environment. In this respect, Darwin's evolutionary theory was a summary exemplification of the science of mechanics and marked the summit of scientific inquiry as it had developed through the seventeenth and eighteenth centuries into the nineteenth.

II

It remained for physics to break this mechanistic model and to initiate a mode of inquiry clearly more suitable to the dynamics of living things. Yet what it formulated was for the purpose of dealing more precisely and adequately with dynamic relations within the structure of the atom.

The magnitude of the change involved in shifting from nineteenth-century physics to the new physics of radioactivity, relativity and quantum theory can be gauged by the late Alfred North Whitehead's striking comment as recorded in one of his communications.

When I went up to Cambridge early in the 1880's my mathematical training was continued under good teachers. Now nearly everything was supposed to be known about physics that could be known—except a few spots, such as electromagnetic phenomena, which remained (or so it was thought) to be co-ordinated with the Newtonian principles. But, for the rest, physics was supposed to be nearly a closed subject. Those investigations to co-ordinate went on through the next dozen years. By the middle of the 1890's there were a few tremors, a slight shiver as of all not being quite secure, but no one sensed what was coming. By 1900 Newtonian physics were demolished, done for! Speaking personally, it had a profound effect on me; I have been fooled once, and I'll be damned if I'll be fooled again! Einstein is supposed to have made an epochal discovery. I am respectful and interested, but also sceptical. There is no more reason to suppose that Einstein's relativity is anything final, than Newton's *Principia*. The danger is dogmatic thought; it plays the devil with religion, and science is not immune from it.[10]

Nevertheless, Whitehead was to take the theory of relativity seriously. As a mathematical physicist he had no choice. Years later, writing his magnum opus, *Process and Reality,* relativity was to provide the perspective from which he developed his metaphysics of the event.[11]

Perhaps at this point we should try to acquire some understanding of just what happened in the revolution in physics at the close of the nineteenth century and during the early years of the present century. This is no easy matter. For a precise statement of changes would entail a description of experiments and an elaboration of their consequences, both for physics and for metaphysics. And while a general acceptance of the major ideas and theories expressing these changes can be assumed, the differences in judgment among physicists, and more particularly between physicists and metaphysicians, or even among metaphysicians themselves, on important points having to do with the bearing of these changes on human thought are far-reaching.[12] The first thing to note is the change that occurred in the scientific understanding of what previously had been called matter. The familiar assumption prior to

---

[10] *Dialogues of Alfred North Whitehead.* As Recorded by Lucien Price. Mentor Books, 1956, p. 277.

[11] It should be noted, however, that Whitehead differs radically in certain respects from Einstein regarding the theory of relativity and its implications. Cf. his article 'Einstein's Theory; An Alternative Suggestion,' *The London Times Supplement,* Feb. 12, 1920; also his work, *The Principle of Relativity.* Cambridge University Press, 1922. A full discussion of these differences appears in *The Philosophy of Alfred North Whitehead,* edited by Paul Schilpp, Tudor, 1951, pp. 170-207.

[12] See F. S. C. Northrop's discussion of Whitehead's Philosophy of Science, *The Philosophy of Alfred North Whitehead,* edited by Paul Schilpp; also J. E. Boodin's discussion of Bertrand Russell's metaphysics as it relates to the theory of relativity in *The Philosophy of Bertrand Russell,* edited by Paul Schilpp, along with Einstein's 'Remarks on Bertrand Russell's Theory of Knowledge' and Russell's reply, ibid.

the discovery of radioactivity was that physical reality, when traced to its most minute entity, would turn out to be multiple, tiny, autonomous pellets. Indivisible bits of matter could thus be said to form the physical substance of every entity. Materialism was an easy deduction from this path of analysis; but even more seriously, the notion of interrelatedness appeared wholly fictitious. The fact that things held together was acknowledged to be a mystery, though it was assumed that something invisibly cohesive would be found to account for it. The disclosure that came through radioactivity was indeed something cohesive, though not of the sort that was initially imagined. The model that seemed best to account for what was there apprehended seemed to describe reality, not as a mass of indivisible pellets, but as *fields of force,* suggesting a van Gogh landscape. Relationships loomed as dynamic, experienceable realities. This was the first advance beyond the earlier Newtonian imagery.

The second advance came in the formulation of the theory of relativity, which Einstein first announced in 1905. The meaning of relativity may perhaps be more readily grasped if it is thought of as countering the common mode of thinking of things as being either at rest or in motion. This is a habit of thought that goes far back in our history, but in its present form it partakes of a rationale which was established by Newton at the end of the seventeenth century. Newton presupposed the existence of absolute space, which provided an absolute base from which measurement and description of natural forces could proceed. The prevalent belief during Newton's time that Euclidean geometery defined the structure underlying the universe, and that mathematical laws directly and precisely described the laws of motion within this absolute sphere of reality, led to a correlation of human rationality and the orderly processes of the universe. Man's formulations could thus be taken to be a precise expression of the rationality inherent in reality, that is, in the vast cosmic machine whose parts, it was supposed, moved unerringly on a surface of absolute space. Accordingly, scientists could speak of scientific laws as universal laws of the universe.

The theory of relativity has found Newton's conception of space implying absolute rest to be false. In its place it envisages a vast space-time continuum comprising fields of energy, within which motion is measurable only in relation to other moving centers of force. This loss of a fixed base of reference, and the recognition that there are many frames of reference from which phenomena or movements are observable, is what has contributed to a sense of disorder, if not chaos, in one's thinking as one contemplates this change. For our habits of thought and perception incline us toward thinking in terms of contrast between rest and motion. To shift to a way of thinking which involves no such contrast, at best implying relative rest and motion, and which compels one to relate one mobile situation to another, presents a complexity which appears unstable. And in fact it is.

But an aspect of modern physics which tends to be even more disturbing to the modern mind committed to the notion of orderliness in nature as Newtonian science envisaged it is the apparent prevalence of chance, and the use of it in the normal course of scientific investigation. This feature of scientific inquiry relates to the theory of quantum and to the later principle of indeterminacy. The discovery by Max Planck and others at the turn of the century that radiation and absorption of light take place discontinuously, that is, in separate, minute quantities called "quanta," dispelled the notion, held since Leibniz and Newton had established differential calculus, that physical thought was based on the continuity of causal connections in the natural world.[13] In the nineteen twenties quantum

[13] A full description of Planck's experiment is given by Ernest Zimmer in *The Revolution in Physics*, H. Stafford Hatfield trans., Harcourt, Brace, 1936, pp. 54-55. See also Albert Einstein and Leopold Infeld,

physics was to advance to another degree of uncertainty with regard to the description of physical processes when it was found that velocity and position could not be measured simultaneously. This introduced the element of indeterminacy in measurement in a way that struck the final blow at the mechanistic imagery of classical physics and its mode of measurement and description. The significance here lay in the effect of this principle upon the classical view of causality. In effect it means that the specific grounds upon which determinism rested in the earlier view of Newtonian physics have disappeared; hence determinism is no longer tenable in modern physics.

As a consequence the whole scene in the scientific portrayal of natural events changes. Instead of a procedure based upon the investigation of observable objects which could yield direct description of natural phenomena, modern quantum physics has become a science of statistical measure as applied to large masses, not to individual phenomena or events. As Karl Heim has observed, necessity in natural law has given way to probabilities, and this alters the nature of the measurement and the kind of precision it can provide. For example,

The manager of an insurance company . . . can calculate statistically the number of road accidents to be expected annually. . . . Yet it remains true that no insurance company can tell a single one of its clients the probable date of his death.[14]

Nevertheless, Heim goes on to say,

The company is able to apply a rule for the average number of deaths among its large clientele, and to do it with such accuracy

The Evolution of Physics, Part IV, Simon and Schuster, 1938 (paper, 1961) ; Karl Heim, *The Transformation of the Scientific World View.* S.C.M. Press, 1953, Chap. IV.
[14] Karl Heim, *The Transformation of the Scientific World View.* S.C.M. Press, 1953, p. 138.

that the business of insurance can be firmly founded thereon. The law of large numbers which is so familiar in the field of vital statistics has its application also in the field of natural science.[15]

In this mode of scientific thought and calculation, probability replaces precise description. Human supposition in the form of statistical law replaces the formulation of natural law based on direct observation of physical objects. This serves well enough for exploring most scientific problems; for the law so formulated is "exact enough in practice in virtue of the law of large numbers" [16] which implies that at that mass level the probability of deviation is practically nil. Yet the deeper, metaphysical question of ultimate orderliness is not settled by that kind of resolution. For the question as to whether statistical laws point to and in some sense approximate ultimate law in nature, or rest more on the rule of chance, still remains unanswered. This question is vigorously debated among scientists themselves insofar as they concern themselves with the metaphysical problem. The role of chance is emphasized more by scientists who tend to draw radical implications from the quantum theory and the principle of indeterminacy, as did Jeans and Eddington, and Max Born. Einstein, on the other hand, held out for the vision of ultimate law. Thus in 1944 he was moved to write to Max Born, saying,

In our scientific expectations we have grown as far apart as the poles. You believe in God playing dice and I in perfect laws in the world of things existing as real objects which I try to grasp.[17]

This statement is perhaps suggestive of the variations in judgment one finds in scientific literature regarding the scene and nature of its inquiry.

The issue as to whether a vision of orderliness is to pre-

15 Ibid.
16 Ibid. p. 140.
17 Quoted by Levi from *Albert Einstein: Philosopher-Scientist,* edited by Paul Schilpp, Tudor, 1941, p. 176.

vail in this maze of scientific conception appears to turn, as Albert Levi has observed, on whether a model of continuity or discontinuity shall ultimately be used in giving representation of physical reality in space-time.[18] And on the resolution of this issue turns also the epistemological question as to whether the sciences, particularly physics, can grasp realities as they really transpire unobserved, or "are confined to making statistical predictions." Scientists appear to stand strongly on one or the other side of these issues. On the one hand, physicists such as Max Born, Eddington, and others, for whom glimpses of discontinuity in nature as disclosed in quantum theory and resistance to accuracy in measurement as indicated in the principle of indeterminacy, appear to be decisive, are led to emphasize a theory of probability. This resolution of the matter appears to leave room only for a kind of tentative mystical Idealism as in Eddington's thought or for a philosophy of chance which some would interpret as encouraging the mood of meaninglessness that pervades much of contemporary thinking. On the other hand there persists a substantial realism as sustained by Einstein and exemplified by the writings of Whitehead. It may be possible to include Bertrand Russell's neutral monism as well. While these men are not able to affirm an order of nature as Newton and the nineteenth-century mechanists envisaged it, they see a rationality at work in its processes; or more precisely, they find the formulation of thought a useful instrument in apprehending and exploring instances of orderly events and the projection of experimental inquiry effective in verifying some of their expectations. To this extent orderly occurrences are experienced and known. Some physicists who have become adjusted to the subleties of relativity theory are inclined to argue that the notion of the space-time continuum offers possibilities of a higher form of orderliness than was en-

[18] Albert William Levi, *Philosophy and the Modern World*. Indiana University Press, 1959, p. 265.

visaged under Newton. Nevertheless, it would be a misreading of their views to assume from these remarks that they rest easy about the discrepancies that continually intrude, or the inaccuracies which appear unavoidable. The immediacies of scientific inquiry give ample grounds for pause. Yet, as Einstein has said in speaking of the question of an ultimate order of nature and reality, it is his faith that such an order of laws exists. It is a faith that the experimental scientist must assume, he would argue. And it is a faith that is periodically rewarded.

A fresh statement of this thesis, correlating commitment to a universal vision with the partial endeavors of scientific research, has recently appeared in a book by Professor Michael Polanyi entitled *Personal Knowledge.* Polanyi is concerned to establish the role that the personal framework of commitment of the scientist plays in his research and his so-called objective inquiry. He is persuaded that no amount of objectivity rids the scientist of this "fiduciary framework"; that, in fact, the framework enters vitally into inquiry itself, giving to inquiry an attendant dimension of motive and intent ("universal intent" he calls it) which reaches beyond the prosaic effort at hand, though at the moment this intent may not be directly in focus. (Is this not reminiscent of Einstein's admission of "faith" in an ultimate order of reality?) Polanyi writes strikingly:

An empirical statement is true to the extent to which it reveals an aspect of reality, a reality largely hidden to us, and *existing therefore independently of our knowing it.* By trying to say something that is true about a reality believed to be existing independently of our knowing it, all assertions of fact necessarily carry *universal intent. Our claim to speak of reality serves thus as the external anchoring of our commitment in making a factual statement.*

The framework of commitment is now established in outline for this particular case. The enquiring scientist's intimations of a hidden reality are personal. They are his own beliefs, which—owing to his originality—as yet he alone holds. Yet they are not a subjective state of mind, but convictions held with universal intent, and heavy with arduous projects. It was he who decided what to believe, yet there is no arbitrariness in his decision. For he arrived at his conclusions by the utmost exercise of responsibility. He has reached responsible beliefs, born of necessity, and not changeable at will. In a heuristic commitment, affirmation, surrender and legislation are fused into a single thought, bearing on a hidden reality.[19]

This passage from Polanyi leads us to a final comment on the revolution in modern physics, affecting our mode of thinking and our understanding of how scientific inquiry proceeds. A consequence of singular significance, one which Weizsacher speaks of as "the central point of quantum mechanics," [20] is the realization that in any scientific inquiry or observation, observer and object are simultaneously involved. Polanyi's remarks were not directed specifically to this point, but they speak eloquently regarding it. This is a point that must follow from relativity and quantum theory alike. Thus "objectivity" as we have come to associate it with scientific inquiry is, in effect, denied to nuclear science. The common image of the scientist impartially observing or studying his object becomes an illusion. To be sure, he is more disciplined in attaining such detachment than most of us, but this, too, is relative. For the very nature of his inquiry, as both Polanyi and Weizsacher have made evident, draws the scientist as subject into what motivates and qualifies his effort.

For many scientists and scientific workers, however, these questions of personal involvement, and what they

---

[19] Michael Polanyi, *Personal Knowledge*. University of Chicago Press, 1960, p. 311.
[20] Quoted by Heim, op. cit. p. 133. See Weizsacher, *The World View of Physics*. University of Chicago Press, 1952.

portend of a faith in an ultimate orderliness, are of no avail in the work they pursue; and they rarely if ever intrude to complicate their research. The orderliness they acknowledge is the day-to-day regularity of mechanisms as these yield up their counters and pointers. Margins of error and miscalculations are taken in stride as they go through their paces. The high dependability of intricately fashioned instruments and machines heightens their sense of being part of a highly orderly enterprise which moves within a sphere of physical realities that are remarkably responsive to their technical inquiries. All this generates an atmosphere of technical precision and dependability strikingly reminiscent of the earlier mechanistic science. Thus in the midst of the indeterminacies and discontinuities which attend rarified regions of pure research, a firm and uninterrupted confidence in the orderly processes of scientific experimentation can persist. But clearly this is confidence in the orderliness of the mechanisms of research and of scientific thought formulated within a circumscribed sphere of activity. Except for the fact that these orderly processes of inquiry and research yield occasional breakthroughs of surprising significance and consequences, one can hardly say that they address themselves to the ultimate question of orderliness in nature. Success in scientific effort gives assurance that human formulations and efforts have experienced a correlation of the orderliness of human thought and its assisting mechanisms with the orderliness in realities beyond man's conceptual world. This is always a time of rejoicing, and, interestingly enough, a time marked by surprise and elation. If one examines this mood a moment, I think one will detect in it some acknowledgment of the distance that exists between these orderly mechanisms of scientific research and the vaster order, the order toward which Einstein and Planck looked with faith, but which in daily encounter but marginally apprehended.

Order in this ultimate sense can be said to be a structure

of meaning toward which inquiry and thought continually strive. It is not immediately given as orderly processes to be measured and described. The scientist, in marginally apprehending such orderliness, and intermittently in decisive ways, has a sense of participating in depths of meaning which are more ultimate than the immediate tasks at hand. To this extent, vision and faith are dramatically verified, and confidence in the ends one seeks, reassured.

III

What is of concern to us is the very real change in climate of thought resulting from these innovations as the basic assumptions of science. We may put it this way: Newtonian physics literally established a climate of thought from the seventeenth century onward which created barriers to belief in anything outside the monolithic order of meaning provided by our own human mentalism. The security of rational inquiry and description was such that no exception could be taken to the definitive conclusions of observation and reason. The interim of Kantian Idealism can be viewed as a marginal respite from this rigid enclosure. It countered mechanism and determinism by establishing a realm of freedom through the practical reason. It did not, however, counter the enclosure of mentalism. On the contrary, it accentuated this very habit of mind. One of the casualties of the modern revolution in physics appears to be this very strategy of thought which Kant devised.

"Modern philosophers are by no means completely agreed upon the matter," writes Albert Levi.

Reichenbach believes that with Einstein and Planck the *synthetic apriori* is forever banished. Cassirer holds that Kant can be adapted to modern scientific requirements. The consensus, however, supports Reichenbach. It is generally assumed that modern physics is the refutation of Kant; that the redefinition of space, time, causality, and matter has made imperative reassessment of the categories which Kant derived from his predecessors. For the great physical revolution of the seventeenth century was Newtonian, and Kant's ideas are saturated with presuppositions of Newtonian dynamics.[21]

The return to an all-enveloping naturalism in the nineteenth century, based upon a conception of orderliness in nature which simply transferred the basic notions and methods of Newtonian physics to biology and the social sciences, consolidated these Newtonian barriers to belief. With the advent of industrialization and the intimate correlation between science and industry, the impact of the Newtonian image of thought upon all areas of culture was complete.

The revolution in physics can be said to have demolished these barriers of mentalism and mechanization. In effect, it as if a new critique of reason had been written, not by one man, but through the collaboration of many men working individually, and co-operatively, to determine the status and possibilities of human inquiry. The consequence seems to be, not the abolishing of reason from these most profound areas of concern, nor the abandoning of such inquiry, but a wholly new estimate of our human powers and facilities and of the results we are able to achieve.

The judgment as to the status of our human powers of reason is decisive enough. However, our contemporaries, who take this revolution seriously, differ in what they conclude as to their possibilities for interpreting the life of man and the realities beyond his vision and grasp. The judgment of modern science concerning our human powers of reason is clearly that they are limited in what they can apprehend of ultimate reality, and that their formulated structures of meaning are expressive of a realm of experience which answers to the report of our senses. Yet the modern physicist points up a radical discrepancy between what this world of sense can report, or that human reason

[21] Albert Levi, op. cit. pp. 267-68.

can describe, and the reality which underlies yet persistently evades observation. An intermittent grasping of these evasive realities through chance formulae has enabled science to perform miracles in the harnessing of energy and in the use of it to conquer space. Yet all of this achievement, and it is overwhelming indeed, does not justify the conclusion that we know about this reality. So conclude some of the major voices of this scientific revolution. The discourse we have and are able to understand, they assert, is the language that speaks of this relatively superficial sphere of experience and formulation—a language largely of mathematical symbols and statistics.

What then remains as to the possibilities of language and response to what meets us in this ambiguous arena of intermittent apprehension and mystery? Here the paths of disciplined inquiry diverge sharply. On the one hand, the modern positivists, commonly designated logical positivists, decisively rejected metaphysics as a venture of mind going beyond the realm of experience. We have only the world of experience to which we can appeal, they asserted. Whatever we claim to have as intelligible meaning must be able to prove itself so by the tests which scientific verification provides.

In the context of Newtonian science, this position could still retain a concern with ultimate meaning or value, for the report of experience was presumably a faithful account of what was observed. In present-day physics, modified by relativity, quantum mechanics, and indeterminacy, the situation becomes a voluntary abdication of any such concern. For by definition in the newer physics, experience, as this comes through the senses, cannot be assumed to be a direct and faithful account of what is thus apprehended.

Under pressure from logical positivism, modern philosophy has tended to become identified with the discourse and work of the sciences at the utility level, within the scope of a human language which willingly settles for the restrictions in meaning and impact which this orientation of thought imposed. Logical positivism was a determined stand to remain, at all cost, within the sphere of discourse where clarity of meaning could be assured. Whether or not significance and ultimate implications attended these meanings could not be determined.

Meanwhile the successors to the logical positivists in language analysis have come forth with heartening revisions that would seem to argue that all such rational venturing beyond the specifically technical realm of verifiable experience need not be rejected per se, though they are equally adamant in holding to a course of precise inquiry in philosophy at whatever cost this role may imply in defining human problems.

Over against this firm repudiation of metaphysics and of a concern with problems of ultimate faith are modern philosophers such as Whitehead and Hartshorne who, on the basis of the new physics, along with other formative influences, have reared an impressive structure of thought under the title of a rational empiricism. The intent here is to take the relativity of the event with utmost seriousness, yet to see that there is a generality of meaning issuing from each concrete occurrence that can be formulated as a true vision of experience. Such a vision is a venture in imagining first principles which will adequately express the world in its essence. But the Rational Empiricist, mindful of the warning of modern physics, recognizes that

Philosophers can never hope finally to formulate these metaphysical first principles. Weakness of insight and deficiencies of language stand in the way inexorably. Words and phrases must be stretched towards a generality foreign to their ordinary usage; and however such elements of language be stabilized as technicalities, they remain metaphors mutely appealing for an imaginative leap.[22]

[22] Alfred North Whitehead, *Process and Reality*. Macmillan, 1929, p. 6.

There is neither the enclosure of the concrete event within pre-established universal categories, nor enslavement to a "rigid empiricism" which presumes to gather adequate description from the direct observation of immediate experience. Whitehead writes:

The true method of discovery is like the flight of an aeroplane. It starts from the ground of particular observation; it makes a flight in the thin air of imaginative generalization; and it again lands for renewed observation rendered acute by rational interpretation.[23]

There is both tentativeness and bold, imaginative exploration in this mode of generalization, accepting the elusiveness and complexity of the data of immediate experience, yet venturing a formulation within the scope of adequacy that seems available and presently justifiable. "The danger," as Whitehead himself has said, "is dogmatic thought." Even so tentative and explorative a venture in generalization, in the hands of less imaginative and sensitive philosophers, can assume a finality and rigidity which belies both the philosophical method which initiated it and the physical theory upon which its bold imagery rests.

It should be seen, then, that the disparity between the concepts and language in our minds or on our lips, and the reality which intermittently reaches, but mostly eludes us, is not to be taken as a justification for irrationalism. In a way we have said that ultimate truth escapes our grasp. And this is what we must say if we speak within the imagery of the new vision of science.

We have our choice, then. We may say, as some of our contemporaries have said, that we shall ignore all discourse, save as it moves within the logic and syntax of recognizable and meaningful speech. This is to dismiss the complexity of existence as if it were nonexistent, and to

[23] Ibid. p. 7.

remain, at all cost, within the prim world of intelligible discourse. Or we may choose to live on the boundary of meaningful discourse, and the depth of reality which is ever present, yet resistant to our constantly seeing eye, except as our formulae or formulations of meaning accomplish the unexpected and thus receive in structured form what is otherwise denied to formulation. The scientist will speak of a chance equation that momentarily, and in a once and for all fashion, fits a fleeting occasion; and from this there issues a chain of insight, or possibly accumulative energy that can be transmuted into power. The philosopher will say, "However far our gaze penetrates, there are always heights beyond which block our vision." [24] And the theologian will speak of being "grasped," of having the reasoning thoughts of his mind arrested or overwhelmed by reality aggressively declaring itself as a "Word" beyond reason. Are these the same, or in any way related? It is difficult to say. They represent different forms of speech; yet they seem to convey one kind of borderline situation in which reality that will not be aggressively seized comes into the human situation as a gift of the moment, or as an unexpected working of grace.

But now a further point can be made. Reason directed toward reality, as a scientist projects his chance equation, can be a persistent and highly costly way of entreating the realities beyond mind to yield to its demands. The modern scientist, offering up his mathematical equation before the Silent Process of outer space, recalls to one's mind the wonder-worker or magician giving his full measure of devotion before the inscrutable mystery. But there is a third way that is neither indifference toward this ultimate faith, nor a direct attack upon its resources. It is the conscious use of reason in a way that renders it indirectly a vehicle of this ultimate faith. What does this

[24] Whitehead, Ibid. p. 519.

mean? It means accepting human reason for what it is, employing it within the limits of our human experience, and directing it to ends that serve to discipline thought and to clarify immediate ends; employing it, that is, as Whitehead has said, to create and to promote the art of life.

The art of life, whether simple in its demands, or highly subtle and complex, becomes a way of fulfilling the human structure within the dimension of its manageable realities. This, to be sure, can be made to degenerate into a trivial concern with well-being, or, as we mentioned before, into allowing conscious interest to shrink to the dimensions of our prim world of intelligible discourse. It may, on the other hand, be the stimulus which gives zest to imagination, and impelling it to large generalities by which both thought and sensibilities are fashioned to extend their range and reach. It is not simply that man's inquiry impels him to search the heavens, but that the sensitivities of his nature open with a wide awareness to receive what can be given to him out of the fullness of events that may reach him when he has lived faithfully and wholeheartedly as an adequate human being.

Being a reasonable creature can mean living heartily and responsively within the human structure of sensitivity and vision, thus employing reason to the end of being a *good* human being—an adequate human being. But in doing this, one does more. One fulfills one's creaturehood in such a way that the act of being human becomes an offering of intelligibility before whatever is more than human. This is to allow the reality of what is more than ourselves to exercise judgment and rewards of grace upon our human reason and upon the reasonable life.

The change in stance which this way of thinking implies does not warrant the abandonment of reasoned and orderly inquiry. It does, however, uproot the ingrown fixation that has set the presupposition of "order" against every intimation of spontaneity, vitality, and mystery that might challenge the structures of reason or the mechanisms of scientific research. The imagery of the sciences in their mature expression takes account of both reason and unreason, both ordered relations and indeterminate dimensions of experience. In the language of the day, depth and nuance have once again entered the discourse of disciplined inquiry.

The fear that this could create a break in the dam of ordered discourse and flood us with irrationalism is an understandable one. The pressures of phantasy and hope, frenzy and violence, are all too real to ignore. Yet the force of reality is equally assertive and compelling; and once it has broken free to lure men's minds, the appeal to what are merely protective measures loses force. Reality once free will not be downed. Restraint is a proper caution—but not disavowal of what is real.

Thus it has come about that in every major discipline relevant to the sciences of man and to the life of the spirit, this imagery of depth and of internal relations has awakened the modern mind to new dimensions of mystery in its existence. The fact that, to some degree, they are unmanageable is not the disturbing discovery that one might suppose. Wherever the dogma of order persists and where there is tolerance only for "clear and distinct ideas," even as ultimate truths, this unmanageable aspect of our existence can be a plaguing thorn. But the maturing of the modern consciousness in relation to its complexities and to its indeterminacies is bringing about greater poise, proportion, and power in dealing with what can be approached only indirectly and with a measure of faith mingled with doubt.

Order has not vanished, nor has reason; but each has assumed an importance proportionate to the function it can serve, and to the capacities in man to employ it. What has vanished is the easy access to a measurable stance, on the basis which judgments of ultimate value can readily be declared. Reason is deprived of this power precisely because reason has access only to a limited sphere of orderly process. It can make judgments appropriate to this manageable sphere. Beyond this structure of meaning available to human inquiry reason itself is under judgment.

What is thus beyond the judgment of reason, however, insofar as it is made expressive through human acts, must be recognized for what it is—an ambiguous bodying forth of reality within the living situation, bearing simultaneously the truth of faith as actuality and the dubious, even idolatrous claims of the finite persons bearing the witness.

There is no faith that may claim ultimacy in the sense of possessing or conveying absolute truth. Yet there is no faith devoid of ultimate reality in what it bodies forth. This is to say that all faiths are relative in what they are able to embody and express of ultimate reality. The point that we need to grasp if we are to assume a constructive stance in this new imagery of thought is that relativity is itself a witness to ultimacy.

Relativity, however, is a humble stance to which the modern mind has been brought through man's realization of the depth and complexity of reality, of man's existence, and the partial, even fragmentary character of each man's perspective or vision. But relativity does not necessarily mean the loss of all decisive norms or of decision in the judgment of meaning or value. Neither does it mean indifference to these concerns. It does not imply that one thing is as good as another, one faith as good as another faith. On the contrary, it denies simply the reality of arbitrary absolutes and invests absoluteness in reality itself, wherever it occurs, under whatever guise it appears.

Relativity does not mean the disruption of all ultimate truth. This is a negative deduction based upon the assumption that only a fixed order of things, either on the Aristotelian model, or in the manner of the Newtonian world machine, can give assurance of ultimacy. Relativity as a constructive doctrine means that every concrete situation bears witness to an ultimacy peculiar to the interplay of circumstances and the limitations or resources that attend its witness. The infinite variety of good has its own claim upon us; and each situation can best be judged by a measure capable of dealing sensitively and genuinely with these concrete circumstances.

But the universal measure is by no means inapplicable, or nonexistent. For relativity implies interrelatedness. And within this purview, relations are real and experienceable, not simply superimposed by universal categories of meaning. The connections are concrete, not abstract idealizations. Their truth or untruth may be known through the encounter with differences.

This universal measure may best be conceived as the relational dimension which summons all concrete situations to see their own values in the context of other values. This can mean both the lessening and the heightening of concrete goods, revealing both their limitations and the judgment of the communal ground upon them. And at the same time it can point to the degree of correlation that is achievable beyond the differences that must be accepted and lived with.

IV

H. Richard Niebuhr has written,

No other influence has affected twentieth century thought more deeply than the discovery of spatial and temporal relativity. The understanding that the spatio-temporal point of view of an observer enters into the knowledge of reality, so that no universal knowledge of things as they are in themselves is possible, so that all knowledge is conditioned by the standpoint of the knower, plays the same role in our thinking that the idealistic discoveries of the seventeenth and eighteenth centuries and the evolutionary discoveries of the nineteenth played in the thought of earlier generations.[25]

25 H. Richard Niebuhr, *The Meaning of Revelation*. Macmillan, 1952, p. 7.

Niebuhr then adds:

Theology ... is concerned with the principle of relativity as this has been demonstrated by history and sociology rather than by physics, and if it is developing into a relativistic theology this is the result not of an effort on its part to keep up with natural science or with the popular linguistic fashions of the day but rather of an attempt to adjust itself to a new self-knowledge.[26]

But do these two expressions of relativity necessarily come to the same thing? Insight into the cultural relativity of religious institutions, values, and beliefs has been invaluable in providing a critical grasp of the processes at work in religious history, and in understanding the phenomena of religious faith. The zeal with which cultural anthropologists, sociologists, and historians of religious thought set to work early in this century to uncover these facts is what gave zest and enterprise to the modernist era of religious liberalism. In retrospect one must acknowledge that much of this study served to dispel the ultimate appeal of religious movements and to assimilate them into the stream of social institutional history as humanly conditioned culture groups. To be sure, this is what they were in large measure. This reading of them, however, had the effect either of nullifying their claims to an encounter with an ultimate dimension of reality, or of dissociating them from such claims. Conventional sociological analyses and the history of social thought accomplished the first; theology, in so far as it took their judgments at face value, accomplished the second. Concern with ultimate value in theology was thus taken to be a matter that must transcend ordinary historical religious groups, just as absolute value itself was assumed to be a

[26] Ibid. p. 8. Professor Niebuhr's own work, *The Social Sources of Denominationalism,* is a significant application of this sociological view of relativity to the history of Christian churches in America.

reality transcending history. The turn which current "relativistic theologies" has taken in modern Protestantism, for example, in stressing "religionless" Christianity becomes a way of seeking to evade cultural relativism by discounting the religion of the churches and elevating the abstraction of pure Christian faith, devoid of cultural involvement. The illusion here is that Christians, when they are apprised of the folly of cultural accommodation, can escape the taint of cultural relativism. But this illusion stems from an inadequate grasp of the implications of relativity itself, and from a persistence of Absolutism that has not really come to terms with the current judgment of relativity theory upon the Kantian apriori and the mathematical assumption underlying it.

The truth of the matter is that cultural relativism was never a thoroughgoing relativism. That is, it employed relativity as an instrument of social and theological criticism, as applied to cultural institutions and practices; but it did not give serious attention to its meaning as a radical revision in stance for reassessing the basic notions underlying all thought about these institutions and practices. In a word, cultural relativists were not themselves self-critical in applying their criticisms. Attention to the relativity of physics would have alerted theologians to the fact that there is no hiding place within spatial-temporal existence from the truth of relativity. The theologian, in acquiring the critical understanding which insight into cultural relativism afforded him, often assumed that he was thereby enabled to think and live beyond these relativities. He was helped toward this assumption by the very strategy of thought which Kant had devised for propelling man beyond the contingencies of determinism. What seems to have been at work here is a deep-seated dissociation of man from nature, or of thought from its physical involvements, which contributed to an estrangement of man in his freedom from the contingent relationships with his physical existence. If it turns out to be true that Kant's assumption of the transcendental apriori, upon which this strategy of thought rests, presupposed the ultimacy and absoluteness of the forms of Euclidean geometry, the present recognition that alternative geometries and perspectives are possible and in fact underlie relativity theory will have struck a serious, if not fatal, blow at the strategy of thought being employed to attain a transcendental and ultimate reference. An impressive body of judgment among scientists and philosophers has been forthcoming to the effect that the Kantian apriori does stand or fall with the assumption of the absolute character of Euclidean geometry. And on this basis, the apriori is rejected. In any event, the space-time perspective which is now proving fruitful, and which made possible Einstein's general theory of relativity, is informed by a non-Euclidean geometry. More and more one is made aware within this perspective that the transcendental escape into an ideal moral subjectivity, immune from involvement in cultural relativity, is not an available option to the relativist who clearly understands its implications. For one can sustain this option only as one insists upon making absolute the geometrical perspective in the way that the Kantian apriori does. Any effort to insulate theological or moral thinking from the ambiguities of its own involvement in culture and in the physical universe must be doomed to failure. And any purist effort toward this end must be seen to be illusory.

Left without such an entry into the sphere of Absolute rationality, or to an absolute value, one is compelled to make peace with one's involvement in concrete history, and with the contingencies attending such concrete experience.

But to accept one's involvement in these contingencies is not to forego all sense of ultimacy. For while the minds and consciences of men are not up to apprehending this holy of holies, ultimate reality comes to them in the very commonplaces of their own ambiguous experience. That is to say, there is no immediacy in history or experience that is without its ultimate depth, its ultimate reference. The appeal from any religious witness, while it exudes the conditioning of its cultural environment, speaks also out of the depths of its own encounter with what sustains and judges its witness. Ambiguity implies an intermingling of our immediacies with ultimacy, not insulation from it. The fact that our human formulations in thought and effort are not to be taken as direct accounts or descriptions of what is ultimate and real in experience is not to be understood to mean that we stand dissociated from these depths of reality in experience. This is a point which the theory of relativity in physics makes clear, whereas cultural relativism does not.

It is to the credit of Richard Niebuhr that he has discerned this truth, even while insisting that relativity in theology was acquired from history and sociology rather than from science. His distinction between "history lived" and "history observed" opens up for him a depth of understanding which speaks through "the story of our life" as a confessional witness having revelatory meaning. But he would be the first to acknowledge that this important insight draws, not upon the analysis of cultural relativity in sociology and history, but upon the Bergsonian distinction between "time lived" and "time observed." That he has seen fit to follow Bergson also in speaking of this as "internal history," as distinct from "external history," seems to me to cause him to forego insight which process thinking and relativity science since Bergson's time has made available to our thought, interrelating internal and external meaning in a structure of experience rather than dissociating them, or of separating out the internal strand of history as if it stood dissociated, transcendent, like a concrete apriori to speak independently of its revelatory word.

Nevertheless, the recognition that in history, and out of the concrete structures of experience, an ultimate word speaks forth amidst the ambiguities of culture and of physical involvements is of signal importance, and must not be lost from sight. This is the present-day reply to all despairing with relativity doctrine, and to the concern lest relativity deprive us of an ultimate faith.

VI Revelation as Depth and Judgment

The realization that ultimacy reaches us through the immediacies of experience has once again brought the notion of revelation to the fore as an insistent word for the man of faith. Nevertheless revelation is a hard word to assimilate into the vocabulary of modern men and women for whom the notion of order has been formative in their habit of thought. Orderliness and Revelatory acts seem mutually exclusive terms. It is a fascinating experience to work through the literature of seventeenth- and eighteenth-century writers who had become enamored of the philosophical and scientific works of Descartes and Newton, yet who felt compelled to hold to a doctrine of Revelation. Almost without exception they were able to sustain some connection with this term, however tenuous or guarded its relation to reason might become. Both Descartes and Newton were able to justify a place for it in their systems. Even Locke, who is generally known for insisting upon subjecting every claim to knowledge to the test of sense data, found it necessary to retain the concept in *The Reasonableness of Christianity*.

By the end of the eighteenth century Revelation had either been abandoned altogether as being irrelevant to theological discourse, or had been assimilated to the notion of religious experience. What made the notion of Revelation particularly difficult to incorporate within the discourse of earlier liberal theologies was the conception of it as propositional knowledge which was thought to

170

have been delivered through Scripture, and which thus either confirmed or stood in defiance of man's reasoned word. The transitions of thought leading to present-day reforms in Protestant theology have brought about a reconception of the term Revelation. It still conveys the thrust of a dimension of meaning beyond man's own reason and effort. Yet it is not propositional knowledge comparable to, yet defying man's reason. Rather, it is an event which transforms or re-creates man's sense of knowing and brings to judgment what man's own reason has wrought. In this context Revelation is the encounter with the depth of God's reality in history, an event which man's reason or experience did not, or even could not, apprehend on its own initiative.

The appeal to the revelatory in our time is of a piece with the dynamism of events as over against all formalism; only it repudiates as well, or at least seeks to get beyond mysticism and religious experience on the grounds that these, too, tend to restrict reality to our human measure. The sense of the *otherness* of God's reality, or reality over reason, or reality seizing us with the sense of shock, of innovation, with judgment and redirection, gives to the word revelatory or revelation its distinctive, contemporary meaning.

The word Revelation is important not only to our theological vocabulary but to our modern vocabulary. We would be able to speak more profoundly of so many things if we could employ it with a full sense of its meaning in any field of discourse, but this is quite impossible as yet.

I am impressed by the fact that a modern psychologist like Rollo May chooses to speak of ontology and psychoanalysis, by which he means to point, as far as field theory will permit, to a complex or depth of the human reality which quite obviously extends the meaning of man's existence beyond the psychologist's observable data. Yet the awareness of this depth, Rollo May tells us, can in no way affect the method he must employ in dealing with his people as a psychoanalyst. In his words, he must deal with them in terms of their "centered existence," which is to confront them as individuated persons. If any ontological term such as "Being" is to intrude at all, it must do so only minimally, as an inchoate backdrop against which each "centered existence" is interpreted.

Now the term "Revelation," like the term "Being," requires an image of the human situation that is not available within our general discourse. The moment we intrude it into such discourse, we shift the imagery or we draw upon one alien to the conversation at hand; and this is to confound matters utterly. It is my concern in this chapter to try to indicate how this notion of Revelation may become intelligible within our modern discourse; and why it seems important, not for theological purposes alone, but for the purpose of getting at the truth of the reality that meets us in experience, and that holds us in existence as living beings.

When experience is taken to mean "the living situation," and the report of experience is understood to be a witness to what is apprehended in that context of events, it is difficult to see how the term "Revelation" can be viewed in any other way than as an empirical notion. That is to say, it is the encounter in experience with a depth of reality simultaneously as a judgment and as a new resource which sharply qualifies and, at times, puts to rout the formulated meanings which men have come to accept as being descriptive of the world as presently understood and thus normative for ordinary communication. The event of Revelation, then is always one in which the shock of reality impresses itself upon a people. Revelation is always noted as an experience of shock precisely because it has the effect of breaking through the existing framework of meaning, both to shatter its pretensions and to deepen or to enlarge its apprehensions. Revelation breaks upon the human situation as an experience of shock, further, because it is always climactic as well as innovating. It is the final thrust of accumulative occurrences which, in a way, had been noted, but were not recognized or acknowledged for what they were.

Why were they noted, but not recognized for what they were? This question calls attention to our habits of perception and apprehension. And this, I think, is what Kant rightly saw in speaking of the forms of sensibility and the categories of the mind, though, in my judgment, he made too much of their subjective character and thus drew the wrong conclusions. Perception is simultaneously a bodily event in which the data of reality are freshly encountered through participation, and a valuating event coterminous with the act of individuation by which what is encountered is felt, grasped, apprehended, valued, and finally interpreted within a frame of meaning that is organic to the conscious life of the person. These frames of meaning which each one possesses as a conscious person are both illumining and limiting in their effect upon the perceptual vision. They bring to bear the full effect of one's accumulative history. They set bits of experience in a context and thus expand and enlarge their implications of meaning. When an object is encountered that has not received conceptual characterization within the tradition of a people, it will be labeled with meaning that best accords with what has been visually perceived and interpreted. Thus the American Indians of the West in frontier days, on first encountering the steaming, puffing locomotive of a train going west, fled from it as from a monstrous beast, and later tried to attack it. This has happened more recently among other primitive peoples on first sighting an airplane. Conversely, young anthropologists, who had become skilled in the technical apparatus of their own science, but who had never lived on an Indian reservation long enough to acquire rapport with its mode of life, or some internal identity with its symbol-making, have been known to go wide of the mark in interpreting what they saw.[1] They were victims of an interchange between two frames of meaning which were in no sense congruent with one another. What stands in the way of apprehending realities for what they are is often the very cognitive forms which are employed, at times quite unwittingly, in apprehending what is occurring at any given moment.

Societies, communities, or regions within any culture, and within any given generation, tend to depend upon certain fundamental notions for their basic forms of apprehension. These have generally been provided by a few seminal or assertive minds. Thus Plato, Aristotle, Descartes, Newton, Kant, Hegel, Peirce (or James), Bergson, Dewey, Husserl, and now Kierkegaard and Whitehead may be said to have provided the fundamental notions which have fashioned the frames of meaning most commonly employed through which perceptual experience in the West has been apprehended and interpreted. Now frameworks of meaning are, at best, tentative ways of attaining a synoptic view of experience, and of gathering fragments of experience into an ordered and disciplined discourse of explication. At its worst, a new frame of meaning, or a new vocabulary expressive of such a frame of meaning, is an imposition of current sensibilities, or a current vision of the mind, made possible by a fresh orientation of thought and experience and by a new imagery that now suddenly lights up the landscape. The discovery of gravity in the seventeenth century, with its consequent formulation of a solar system moving within regular orbits, laid the ground for conceiving of the order of nature in a peculiarly mechanical way. The very word order, so understood, became a basic notion, defining as well the nature of ultimacy and establishing an ultimate ground for rationality and the appeal to reasonableness. Newton was to give more precision and decisiveness to

[1] Hartley Burr Alexander, "The American Indian" in *Mythology of All Races*, edited by Louis H. Gray. Vol. X. Marshall Jones Co., 1916.

this mode of thinking with his image of a world machine, working with mechanical accuracy and regularity. The discovery of relativity and the quantum theory in the present century, as we have said, has radically altered the imagery of disciplined thinking and promises to become formative of our thinking in more radical ways at all levels of discourse.

At their worst, then, we may say, new frames of meaning exert a highly contemporary influence in that they impose what is presently novel and exciting as a new vision of experience. At their best, however, they exercise a critical judgment upon all previous frames of meaning by disclosing what has been left uncalculated in their surveys of experience. And this critical judgment is always very much to the fore in any new frame of meaning. For while a seminal philosophy in any period generally arises under the stimulus of new insight and new conceptual resources, which together provide a more adequate explication of experience, it invariably reflects reaction against previous formulations, or at least defines the new stance over against them. Thus Aristotelianism is a revision of Platonism. Cartesianism, Kantianism, and Hegelianism are critically refined restatements of Platonism, implying rejections of Aristotle's revisions. Peirce, James, and Bergson are self-conscious reactions against Descartes, Kant, and Hegel, being in turn radically revised expositions of Aristotle. It is difficult to decide whether Whitehead's genius was that of a seminal or a synoptic mind. Doubtless something of each was present in his reformulations, though he, himself, conceived of his work as that of completing and fulfilling the innovations of James and Bergson and Dewey. Kierkegaard's contribution was largely critical in nature, but the way in which he posed these critical issues radically altered the philosophical stance itself, and reoriented both philosophy and theology. Both modern Existentialism and Process philosophy represent a rejection of the Cartesian-Kantian preoccupation with consciousness and a return to the notion of Being-in-the-world. The one stresses subjectivity or authentic selfhood; the other, the nexus of internal relations as the communal ground of selfhood.

Now all this is by way of saying that the frameworks of meaning which people live with and work within through any period of time, or possibly through a generation or more, are modes of illumination providing them with a degree of intelligibility and understanding. They are more or less tentative, drawing as they do upon immediate insights and discoveries; but at the time of their usefulness, they provide the best possible illumination available to the mind at a given time and place. And each of them probably yields more durable truth than is generally recognized. The immediate moment of reaction discounts their durability; but they continue to come back in a different guise.

I come now to some deductions from this analysis; these can be discussed under the following ten points:

1. Every framework of meaning is sensible up to a point of what has been left uncalculated by some previous conceptual framework. To that extent it opens up new dimensions of meaning, or sets experience in a new light so that meanings previously unavailable become known and encountered. The intensity of reaction against previous frames of meaning, however, tends to exaggerate the relevance of the new perspective and to neglect what may be durable in older visions. Thus the new dimension of meaning suffers from loss of proportion and criticism.

2. While each framework of meaning is sensible of something which has been left uncalculated by previous conceptual frameworks, no one of them, nor all together, can take adequate account of what is left uncalculated in perception or cognition. Reality in some respects evades apprehension, or is misapprehended to some degree in every system.

James and Bergson did their best to provide an adequate mode of apprehending the living experience, and Whitehead has tried to benefit by their cautions and constructive efforts; but, in my judgment, no one of us, however faithful one may be to the realities of experience as they come into the orbit of our "centered existence," to use one of Rollo May's concepts, can escape the predicament of our limited structure of experience as a particular emergence. Nor can we transcend altogether the failings attendant upon the act of individuation, which is one indispensable mode of our being.

In saying this I mean at one and the same time to qualify Bergson's critique of intellect and to go beyond what he implied by his criticism. In speaking of the inadequacy of mind to capture the realities of the living situation, Bergson likened the intellect to a camera which seized any given moment of experience by fixing it within a particular focus. As a result, he said, intellect knows experience in retrospect through a static image. Intellect is a mechanism. As such it is unable to apprehend or grasp the subtle, mobile, or dynamic relations that form the living situation. Intuition, as an internal mode of knowing, he argued, enables us to come nearer to the realities of experience.

Now I would say that Bergson was feeling after what all organismic thinkers since him have been trying to express—namely that conceptualization, especially when it tries to be precise and critical, tends to arrest and formalize what in the nature of the case is much too fluid and subtly interrelated to be grasped in so decisive a way. For purposes of technical discussion in which clarified and manageable meanings are sought, a specification of terms and categories is made. A classification of terms follows, and the analysis proceeds in orderly fashion upon the basis of this agreement of terms. The messy flux of experience is thus brought into neat orderly blocks of subject matter, so one can know one's way around in talking about this or that. Order is the fetish of the disciplined mind. But who is "kidding" whom the radical empiricist asks.

Precise knowledge thus has its own aspect of illusion. And to this point, Bergson and James were constantly referring. Rather than ascribing its failing to intellect as such, as Bergson has done, I see it as applying to habits of thought where the "thickness" of the living situation, its complexity and depth, are not taken seriously. It must be said that the Kantian conception of the role of mind contributed enormously to the habit of thought which readily formalized the data of experience.

But I would go beyond Bergson in saying that our inability to grasp the full import of the living situation arises from a limitation in man more basic than either the mechanistic character of the intellect, or the arbitrary and formalistic character of disciplined thought. Basically, it stems from limitations inherent in the human structure itself, given its level of emergence. We do reach the point of our extremities, the edge of our being, as it were, where the mystery of being even as it meets us in experience confounds us.

3. This means, then, that at any given moment of time, and within a certain period of time, intimations of meaning are left unnoted, uncalculated, though the events and their shaping of the structure of experience will persist whether heeded or not. These events, to be sure, do not go altogether unheeded, but such acknowledgment as is given is intermittent, partial, probably not seriously regarded, for they do not come readily within the frame of meaning that is accepted as intelligible discourse.

Thus the very notion of the "law" can be a barrier to belief in what transcends law or in what implies a more sensitive order of relations. Likewise the notion of order, or of rationalities as implying one world of meaning, can stand as a blockage to a more sensitive grasp of what is perceived in experience. But I am ahead of my story.

4. The uncalculated occurrences which persist in effects

without adequate apprehension build up as a structure of reality in the historical stream of events within a given culture or people and precipitate, as it were, a decisive experience of man's extremity. Man becomes vividly aware of his own conscious failings; his frame of meaning will not encompass the events of experience. He is brought up sharp with a realization of reality overriding reason. In his distraught mood of reaction, he will speak of it as something breaking into history. In point of fact it is doing just that—that is, uncalculated events are breaking into man's conscious experience of history, though in fact they have been actual occurrences in the stream of history for years upon years of time.

It is this sharp awakening to the fact of reality over reason that gives to one's experience of the Revelatory occurrence the sense of shock—the shock of reality breaking in upon one with fresh import. Reality then speaks to the living situation out of its situation of brokenness. This is a peculiar way of speaking. Most speaking occurs within an ordered frame of meaning. Where reality overrides reason in a given historical situation, the framework of meaning is itself momentarily shattered. This has the effect simultaneously of casting the human mind into despair (it is helpless to grasp the *Kairos* of events that have come upon it) and of releasing the mind from the imprisonment of meaning in which its ordered, conscious experience has held it.

5. In such historical instances, the innovation that occurs is really more than an innovation of meaning. To be sure, it is that too, but it is more. It is an innovation of reality itself, a new depth of reality which now can reach the perceptions of men, where hitherto it could not, or at least had not done so. It is able to reach them now because now the barriers to innovation have been momentarily lifted. But even more significantly, the accumulative power of intimation and pointing is such that it assumes structured form as a full-bodied event in history, present-

ing its own nexus of historical occurrences as the Revelatory event. The Revelatory event thus enters into conscious history simultaneously as a judgment upon all formulated meaning, and as a depth of new meaning, a new reality within experience opening up new possibilities and offering new resources to human living.

6. Now speaking of the Revelation of God in Jesus Christ within this context, the notion of "New Being," or the New Testament words "New Creation," seems to me to take on force as empirical realities. In this occurrence, we are not dealing with a simple variation in the meaning of law, or a different ethic, a more permissive set of morals, or a more winsome idealism. Rather, we are dealing with a radical innovation of reality within the structured experience of this period of history, an innovation within Middle Eastern and Western history which has summoned the moral and rational consciousness to a new level of sensitivity and dedication.

7. Immediately there are many questions that burst upon us. One that is before us is the question as to whether the Revelatory event we call Jesus Christ was something wholly novel, or the fruition, the fulfillment of previous occurrences? This question, I would say, can be answered both "yes" and "no." There was something wholly novel in the sense that a new creation occurred in the form of a new level or dimension of sensitivity in relationship and meaning. This, I am persuaded, was an actual innovation in the structure of experience in Middle Eastern history and had radical consequences for all subsequent existence in this area and in the historical formation of Western life. Yet this New Creation followed upon a sequence of happenings within Hebraic and Judaic history in its encounter with a succession of world powers, the last of which was the Roman Empire. What Tillich calls the "preparatory revelation," and what Bernard Loomer refers to as "structures of particularity," was at work, generating an accumulative probability of response,

a potential or incipient matrix of sensitivity consonant with the dimension of sensitive relations inherent and explicit in the New Creation.

8. I am unable to speak of the New Creation itself as an emergence in quite the same way that L. S. Thornton tends to describe it.[2] To be sure, I see this occurrence within the imagery of emergence. But I should be inclined to speak of the human response to Revelation as being the new emergence. That is, the emergence occurred in the developing human structures of history. The energies of grace broke into history through the historical person of Jesus and in what he evoked as a community of faith in a specific time and place, because this emergence in human structures occurred. But the question I find necessary to answer is, Can one properly speak of this New Creation as an emergence out of this stream of history or a novel event that happened to this stream of history by reason of its emerging structures?

The energies of grace, I am saying, antedate all Hebraic and Judaic structures. God was not rendered more sensitive as saving love or as Suffering Servant by Jesus Christ; he was disclosed as such. This means to me that what became actual and historical through Jesus Christ and the communal witness had ontological reality prior to the emergence of structures adequate for its disclosure within history.

On the basis of a strictly empirical theology, one could not assert this; though I would assume that one could point to it as a possibility simply on the basis of generalizing the implications of one's understanding of the nature of the relation between Jesus Christ and God. If, as a means of deepening the empirical method, one avails oneself of the philosophy of experience and of events expounded in the philosophy of organism, one will be impelled to see that what appears to be a possibility in read-

[2] Cf. *Revelation and the Modern World*. A. and C. Black, 1950.

ing the pointers of this historical event is of a piece with what is given as an ontological description of God as the primordial ground of existence. That is to say, the sensitivity of relations expressed as the energy of grace and of saving love in Jesus Christ as Suffering Servant is a dimension of being, spirit, freedom, or creativity supervening or undergirding existence itself. Created beings like ourselves exist by reason of this matrix of sensitivity. We are, in fact, cradled and nurtured by it as living creatures. Apart from it we could not exist.

9. Thus Jesus Christ, in disclosing God as Suffering Love, revealed something about our creation and nurture as well as about our Redemption. In fact the Redemptive act in Christ reasserts and reaffirms the character and intent of God implicit in His creative act.

Now I mention all this with just one point in mind: to straighten out the imagery with which we seek to grasp the import of the Revelatory event. If this ontological assertion is justified, if the philosophy of organism is justified in speaking of a nexus of internal relations as a communal ground of all existence, and if this illumines what Christian thought has historically affirmed in the *Imago Dei* and in the Biblical imagery of the Covenant relationship, then we cannot speak of the Revelatory event of Jesus Christ simply as an emergence in the stream of a particular history. The structures bearing this disclosure were new emergences; but the Revelatory event, made possible at a given time and place by these emergences, was an opening into history of a depth in the ground of existence which heretofore had been put partially apprehended. It is here that one may see that this cultural innovation had decisiveness in more than a cultural sense.

10. There is some meaning given then to the notion of transcendence other than being a function of Immanence. The limits of the human structure are envisaged along with a dimension of sensitivity in relations which may be said to supervene our structured existence in the way that

a father's matured and concerned structure of mind supervenes the restive, groping, assertive, yet insecure mind of his child. James used the figure of the dog lying at the feet of his master as the man talked with his friends. The dog heard the conversation, that is, the sound and the rhythm of the voice, felt the warmth of the fire and the conviviality of the occasion; but of the structure of meaning conveyed in the conversation itself, the dog knew nothing. It was a level of relationship that transcended his canine structure of consciousness, though he participated in it in ways consonant with his kind.

I have literally blown hot and cold in regard to this analogy; for it is suggestive beyond my powers to resist. Yet it also seems too easy, too pat. My own revisions of this imagery have followed along the lines of Whitehead's doctrine of prehension, seeing this doctrine as implying a nexus of internal relations, not along Hegelian lines, which would provide a wholly immanental view of spirit, but along emergent lines which acknowledge discontinuity within the continuities of experience.

The actualization of events along with the individualizing of persons accents the limits of the human being more particularly as a structure of conscious experience. Yet that limited structure is in concourse with a creative passage that conveys to his being, as a living person, the depth and sensitivity of internal relations which hold him in existence. Each person is constantly bodying forth in his structured experience a burden of actualized meaning which he will never wholly apprehend; certainly he will not comprehend it. The complexity and mystery of living is beyond our comprehension, though we may grasp intimations of its import for us.

When we take the limits of man's structure seriously, along with the discontinuity it encounters within the continuities through internal relations, I think we must speak of the order of sensitive relations inhering in God as Suffering Servant, or as Suffering Love, or even in the more abstract notion of a matrix of sensitivity in which all life is cast, as a dimension of goodness transcending our limited structures. And the incursions of this reality of grace and judgment in our day-to-day experiences bring us moments of heightening and a new sense of freedom even as they lay bare our situation of crisis, our alienation, our sin, our inescapable need of a good not our own.

Revelation becomes intelligible to one through these very day-to-day experiences in which such need and alienation are made vivid and menacing, and in which the grace of forgiveness as a new level of freedom becomes redemptive and revelatory. This I have seen to be no incidental religious experience, but, in Bonhoeffer's terms, it is the reality of Jesus Christ as the living event—the New Creation as a dimension of our own existence.

Part Two

APPREHENDING THE REALITIES OF FAITH

VII   The New Image of Man

The developments which have been occurring in the sciences since the turn of the century, altering the imagery of thought in the West, have had repercussions in our thinking about the nature of man. What is distinctive here is the relational aspect of man's existence and the depth of meaning which arises from this holistic view of the human situation.

Evolutionary thinking, following from that of Darwin in the nineteenth century, focused principally upon individual behavior of the organism in its adaptation to environmental conditions. Through its theory of natural selection, it envisaged the social consequences of such adaptations among the physically fit insofar as it interpreted natural selection to be the mechanism by which alteration of the species occurred. This concern with the behavior of man as a clue to his nature and future possibilities has occupied the attention of geneticists and behavioral scientists for more than a generation. It continues to gather momentum as a serious mode of inquiry into the nature of man.[1] The decisiveness of their findings and the precision with which they are able to perform their research give these behavioral sciences a distinct advantage over every other form of inquiry into the human problem, enabling them to speak with a certainty about their findings which more complex forms of inquiry cannot emulate.

[1] Cf. *Evolution After Darwin*, Vol. II, *The Evolution of Man*, and Vol. III, *Issues in Evolution*, edited by Sol Tax, University of Chicago Press, 1960.

Yet it becomes increasingly clear that the study of functional adaptations, however revealing, can tell only a partial story about man. On principle, if he is true to his method and vocation, the behavioral scientist must ignore everything else about man and his situation except this one area of external and observable data. The probing of more subtle and complex aspects of man's responses as human being must appear extraneous to his inquiry. Yet a moment's reflection will suggest that, unless one can justify gathering the whole of man's meaning into this one area of functional adaptation, significant dimensions of our human existence go uncalculated in this behavioral approach to an understanding of man.

While the behavioral scientists have steadily modified and enlarged upon their methodology since the time of Darwin,[2] it must be acknowledged that the image of man that guides their research is essentially consistent with that of nineteenth-century evolutionism. That is to say, they have been reluctant to appropriate or to be caught up in the holistic vision of man, which owes its stimulus, in part, to modern physics and the development of field theory and to revisions in biological theory following from this imagery.[3] This difference is understandable when it is realized that what is chiefly the concern of holistic thinking is the phenomenon of internal relations and the *telos* that such relations convey, hinting of an internal structuring of man's existence.[4]

[2] See George Gaylord Simpson, *The Meaning of Evolution,* Yale University Press. Mentor Book edition, 1958, pp. 127-28.
[3] The ground for modern theories of field physics was laid by Michael Faraday and Clark Maxwell. Cf. Sir William Cecil Dampier, *A History of Science and Its Relations with Philosophy and Religion.* 3rd ed., Macmillan, 1946, pp. 242ff. Einstein has called the field theory "the most important invention since Newton's time." Cf. A. W. Levi, *Philosophy and the Modern World.* Indiana University Press, 1959, p. 250. Cf. also A. Einstein, *Essays in Science.* Philosophical Library, 1934; and Max Planck, *The Universe in the Light of Modern Physics.* W. W. Norton, 1931, pp. 72ff.
[4] This point of view stems initially from William James's effort to establish the proposition that *relations are experienceable* in contradistinction

We have to do, then, with two different approaches to the meaning of man: the one focusing with utmost precision upon a restricted area of functional activity with the expectation of yielding decisive information about man through such behavioral study; the other purposely standing back from these immediacies, as it were, thus widening the focus of vision. What are sought in this latter view are glimpses of broad patterns or relationships that might give hint of the large context in which specific behaviors occur. There is even the hope, if not the assumption, that something like a vision of man's ultimate meaning might thus be disclosed.

Now in the nature of the case, this holistic approach to an understanding of man appears abstract. All thinking about man that presumes to venture beyond his observable behavior will involve one in a distant view in which recognizable details recede. The venture becomes doubly abstract when, after a generation of such study, one undertakes to gather into a summary view the generalizations setting forth its image of man. The reach toward the ultimate image must always involve an obscuring of concrete distinctions, however faithful one might wish to be to its qualitative richness.

---

to Hume and Kant. Cf. his discussion of "the stream of consciousness" in his *Principles of Psychology,* Vol. I., Holt, 1890; and "The Continuity of Experience" in *Pluralistic Universe.* New York, Longmans, Green, 1909. See also *Essays in Radical Empiricism,* 1912. S. Alexander, in *Space, Time, and Deity,* Macmillan, 1920 (Humanity Press 1950), made the first comprehensive attempt to restate this teleology in modern terms. In the same year, 1920, A. N. Whitehead published his *Concept of Nature,* Cambridge University Press, 1920; and in 1929, *Process and Reality,* Macmillan, 1929, which Alexander viewed so much to be the fulfillment of his own effort that he decided to forego a third volume to his own work. See also Charles Hartshorne, *Man's Vision of God,* Harper, 1941, and *The Divine Relativity,* Yale University Press, 1948; Paul Weiss, *Reality,* Yale University Press, 1938, and *Nature and Man,* Yale University Press, 1947. In my *Faith and Culture,* Oxford University Press, 1953 (Allen and Unwin, 1955), Part III, I undertake to give a theological interpretation of man from within this perspective.

Many years ago I lived with my family in constant sight of the mountains in a charming village in southern California. Soft rolling foothills snuggled against the austere façade of rock that rose to a snow-capped peak. In the foreground, stretching for miles in either direction, we could see sunlit orange and lemon groves. Even at that distance they displayed a lush blend of color.

What we saw of the mountain at that distance, however, beautiful as it was, did not begin to portray the mountainside as it was experienced close at hand. From a distance the surfaces seemed smooth, as if on a single plane, like the hard surface of a rock. And the coloring was of one tone. You might even say it looked barren. But when we drove up into the mountain, it appeared quite different. Close up there were no smooth surfaces in sight, not even much rock. Instead, we would come upon trails leading through thick growths of trees and sparkling streams rushing over colored cliffs, disappearing into ravines, or leveling out into shaded brooks. We would see huts and cabins and people living in them. In the remote areas uninhabited by human life, we would see deer grazing or bounding quickly out of sight. The richness and depth of these concrete experiences, so abundant near at hand, were not available to us at a distance.

All distant views have this failing. You then may well ask: Why must we concern ourselves with an undertaking admittedly so bereft of vividness and interest? I must answer because we have no alternative in this matter, for to deal with these developments in thought at closer range, we would have to live through them; and this would take a lifetime, as it has with some of the men whose thought we shall discuss. So the mode of our speaking must be abstract.

Futhermore, the task to which we have set ourselves demands it. I am concerned to bring forth, in a single glimpse, if possible, the enlarging image of man which recent Western minds of a prophetic spirit and of profound sensibilities have provided our generation. The mere detailing of developments leading to this image would require many hours. And the many experiences, of despair and otherwise, which have entered into the forming of judgments and brought new insight concerning the human situation, would take us far afield. The best we can accomplish in so brief a space is to obtain a summit view of some representative features, pointing out from the vast variety of reflection significant strands of interpretation which will give some inkling of the pattern of meaning of such an image.

But in moving toward the more distant view of man we need to be aware of the kind of corrective it can bring to these more vivid, close-up experiences and observations. It is not simply an enlargement of focus as we recede, causing the concrete detail to fade, or the creation of illusory lines and patterns as the larger contours come into view. Something happens in assuming the distant view which evokes realism of a relational sort. Realities of relationship so easily obscured by the immediacies of sight and sound now press for recognition as these concrete sights and sounds subside. This, too, was our experience on the mountainside. The immediate surroundings of the summit, with their sharpened detail, form, and color full upon us, wove a spell over us once we were in this world apart. This caused us to lose all sense of its being part of a larger countryside. Even the roadways and mountain paths, connecting us with what lay below, somehow faded from view until we were ready to use them on our return to the world below. What was hidden from our view in that farther look toward the mountainside, the rich fullness of detail, color, and sound, now served to obscure the larger contours of the terrain that marked its integration with a whole region combining mountain, desert, and the thickly inhabited villages surrounding them.

Assuming this distant view of current happenings that have been changing our image of man, we may say that what separates the present generation of thought in the West from that of previous periods of the modern era is the realism with which it views the nature of man. Now realism in this case does not imply any necessary depreciation of the possibilities of man, or a negation of expectations. In fact, one might say that the new image of man which has begun to inform decision and action encompasses dimensions of human existence which far exceed the range of thinking made possible by earlier conceptions of the modern period. Present-day thought upon the nature of man partakes of a depth of being which is comparable in its range to that of the imagery of classical Christianity, say in medieval realism. I do not mean to say that it partakes of that imagery, or that it simply reclaims or repossesses dimensions of man's meaning which were lost to it following the Enlightenment. I mean, rather, that the modern mind, having been shaped by developments of thought and formulations, beginning with the era of Rationalism and culminating in modern Idealism, has broken free of the circumscribing effect of these formulations and has thus moved into a new stage of the modern consciousness.

This new stage of the modern consciousness has continuities with the modern period extending from Descartes and Newton through the nineteenth century; but it departs from it more radically than did Romanticism from the Rationalist era, or than nineteenth-century evolutionism departed from either Romanticism or Rationalism. The reason for this is that a break in fundamental notions has occurred, altering basic imagery, and bringing into play resources and perspectives bearing upon the human situation which were not even contemplated within the orderly existence of the earlier modern period.

I will not argue the question here whether or not this new stage of the modern consciousness can properly be spoken of as being of a piece with the earlier modern period which we have commonly called liberal. In my judgment one cannot make sense of it, or adequately grasp its implications and directives, except as one does consider it so.

That it is a new frontier of realism means simply that it has become alerted to realities outside of and other than self-experience, existing independently of it, though engaging it both continuously and in intermittent encounters. One insistent theme of our present way of thinking about man is that the breadth and depth of our ultimate meaning are immediately apprehended in the momentary events of day-to-day experience.

I do not say that man consciously knows this in the detached way that we are accustomed to speak of the mind attending the object; but he knows it as an act of living. He knows he is aware of himself existing in, participating in, and belonging to a cluster of interrelated events which makes up his life and the lives about him, and which, at the level of creation itself, gathers in all lives that have ever existed. Here we begin to get a glimpse of the complexity of man's existence at its ultimate ground.

In its most immediate aspect, that with which we seem to be most directly engaged, this complexity that contains and gives rise to our existence is seen to be a structure of experience. One can try to delineate this structured existence at various recognizable levels. For example, the living cluster of relations may be apprehended in the recital of certain intimate facts about the personal history of a people. It will be useful here to restate what I developed in *Faith and Culture* in speaking on the structure of experience: every family group discloses two levels of history—the one they talk about and the one they possess more hiddenly. Letters, family albums, journals, and the like provide the tangible record of events now held in memory. Except for these mementos which fix a few fragments of the past, the personal history of individuals would, indeed, seem but a perpetual perishing. Yet this is never altogether true, and this points to the second level of history; for events live on in part as bodily feelings in the sufferings and joys of those who, in ways remote or immediate, have been shaped by them. But more vividly still, these past events of the family experience, those consciously cherished as well as those but dimly perceived or possibly forgotten, live on in the character and disposition in children, and in the anguish or rising hopes of parents, for whom the past is now a living burden, or a foretaste of joy.

The family history is one thing. This may be recaptured again and again in festive moods which celebrate the passing of the years. The family character—this may be something more. For it preserves with utter fidelity as a present structure the remembered as well as the uncommon workings of destiny which no celebration or historical review can convey or apprehend. Occasionally it may be made subtly manifest in a look of anguish, or in a momentary mood of expectancy. Character speaks forth out of the spontaneous responses of the person, as well as out of the more durable traits and habits of life. Thus actuality, in any given moment of a person's life, presents history in its stark, creative residue. It is here with the blessings and benedictions of God and with his wrath as well.

In a similar way, every community and every culture carries the living burden or opportunity of this survival character as a structure of experience, which can never be readily explicated or described.

The structure of experience gives durable form to our repeated valuations. It is impossible to get at the details of this accumulative valuation which expresses itself through the sensibilities in response and action; though, of course, certain memorable events or observations, conveying such response or action, stand out in any period. The history of events presumes to tell the story of this growth of the psychical structure. But as compared with the actual, evolving structure of experience, which is the living nexus of relations in any given moment of time, recorded history is a relatively superficial and impressionistic account.

Somehow all events enter into this emerging structure of experience, but something of each event partakes of a perpetual perishing which inevitably accompanies emergence. Hence what persists as an organism of events is a selective distillation of what has occurred. The structure of experience is not a blind accumulation of inherited values. Rather, it simulates an organic unity at every stage of history. Thus the struggles and crises as they occur vividly in history, the dedications and betrayals, along with the discoveries, creations, and intellectual triumphs, become the formative stuff out of which rises the persisting structure of experience within any community or culture. Great insight at any one point becomes creative in its influence beyond calculation. Stretches of insensitivity, with their consequent impersonality, brutality, or evil, likewise affect the accumulative valuation, not just in an additive sense, but in a transformative one.

Within any nation's or community's history, then, the present moment of time is laden with qualitative meaning so complex in character, being the living distillation of decisions and resolutions of ages, so profound in implication for all existence and for all present events, that no single center of consciousness is equal to discerning its burden and its opportunity. Each new generation comes into an organic inheritance greater in depth and range than the perceptions of any living person who is a member of it. Thus people live in a context of feeling and awareness that is always beyond their grasp emotionally or cognitively. They are not automatically bound by this heritage or by these relationships; for they, too, are creative of its yet emerging structure in the way that all concrete events have influenced it. Nevertheless, all living persons carry within their conscious existence and in their perceptual nature something of the hidden drives and aspirations that rise from this accumulative structure of experience.

Thus any analysis of man's existence at any given time conveys but a portion of man's real meaning; for it presents only the strands of relationship that can meet us at a common level of human response, in perception, and in reflection and memory. But our deeper judgment, that which critically takes account of the fullness of events under all circumstances and in all moments of time, leads one to see that this cluster of relationships which we apprehend in perception, reflection, and memory, is of a piece with the creative passage that carries forward all events as a burden and promise of actuality.

The realism of the new image of man applies to the clearheaded judgment with which one is led to contemplate the limits of man as a clue to his possibilities. In this new image the setting of man's existence has assumed vaster scope, but the meaning of man, himself, has become more precise. One can say that it has become proportionate to the actualities which define his human structure. This sharpening up of the contours of human existence within the larger matrix has opened up a clearer picture of what might be called the otherness of reality, as distinct from the human equation itself. Man is viewed in a context. Man is not the whole of reality. He participates in its depth of meaning. To be sure, man is a formidable figure in the drama of events that make up this cosmic history; but he is not its creator, its arbiter, or its determiner of destiny. He is responsive to a good not his own, in which his life is cast, through which his life finds nurture, resource, and grace, and by which his life is judged.

The decisive factor in modern thinking, altering the image of man from that of an idealized portrait to one discerning of man's limits, can be said to be this sense of otherness as a real, defining, even assertive dimension of man's existence—an "out there" which may not be altered simply by wishful thinking, or evaded by circumventions of human imagination. The fact of another in concourse with the self has become the formidable factor lending depth to self-experience.

It can be said with considerable justification that for the liberal philosophies and theologies of the earlier modern period, the imagery of self-experience dominated the strategies of thought.[5] It was this as much as anything that opened the way for the mental enclosure of reality in modern Idealism. For self-experience in the philosophies of the liberal era offered no occasion of real encounter with realities other than self. Such response as might indicate contact even with objects in experience could be but the "beginning of knowledge," as Immanuel Kant put it, a stimulus to the cognitive process, the content and character of which was shaped by the forms and sensibilities of the self. Whatever the philosophical orientation, whether Empiricism, Personalism, or Absolute Idealism, the imagery informing the nature of objects, and giving content to the world of events, was that of self-experience. It was as if the climate of self was made to envelop the whole of the experienceable world.

This was more than solipsism, for the modern liberal had no sense of being imprisoned within himself. On the contrary, the self was a center (of being) from which one ventured abroad imaginatively, impressing upon all that came within the purview of experience such form and

[5] Leibniz's philosophy of monads was an early interpretation of this view. What saved his conception of the self from becoming a complete solipsism was an accompanying notion of pre-established harmony which provided a basis for assuming that experience beyond the self, say in that of another person, is akin to if not comparable to that of one's self. This view was more fully developed by the nineteenth-century philosopher Herman Lotze in his *Microcosm.* Lotze's philosophy was a major source of the thought of Borden P. Bowne who established the American movement of Personalism. In his philosophy the projection of self-experience became the method of establishing, not only the nature of realities beyond the self, but a basis as well for justifying the ultimate significance of human values and ideals, and for positing belief in God for safeguarding and fulfilling those values.

meaning as was consonant with this center of being. In this way the world took on the shape and coloring of the individual ego, or such shape and coloring as the individual mind could allow.

The shock of a reality other than this self-experience is what makes the difference in the new image of man. This may seem to be a strange and overstrenuous way of coming to an obvious point. Yet the transitions by which this kind of clear and decisive apprehension of otherness in reality has come about in the more recent period are subtle indeed. What is given to us as a climate of thought in the present period of Western history has been attained at great effort among metaphysicians and theologians alike,[6] though it must be said that, apart from creative discoveries in the world of the sciences, it is doubtful whether any progress in this direction could have been achieved except as an arbitrary act of revolt against the subjective or solitary ego. The new image of man which has arisen in modern metaphysics in the West, for example, partook first of the organic sciences, especially biology, and then of the new physics with its basic notion of a patterned reality. In both areas of research, the fact of relations as something experienceable has played a decisive role in reshaping the conception of existence. The singularity of objects, even the singularity of individual persons, ceased to be an intelligible fact in this newer way

[6] I refer here to the movement of radical empiricism beginning with Bergson and William James and continuing through Whitehead in which the Kantian-Hegelian view of the transcendental ego was critically appraised and finally rejected in favor of a revised concept of selfhood based on the view that relations are experienceable. Since James' own thinking had an Existential quality, focusing upon the concrete decisions in experience in contrast to abstract conceptualism, it conveyed a critique of Hegelian idealism reminiscent of that of Kierkegaard's. The fact, however, that James viewed relations as being experienceable, whereas Kierkegaard assumed a theory of knowledge continuing that of Hume and Kant, make for some decisive differences in their orientation and imagery of thought. These differences are what set modern organismic thinking and modern Existentialism apart, despite their common focus upon the concrete realities of existence.

198

of thinking; for things and persons are known to exist in relationship with one another. They become known, or they assume self-understanding, insofar as they take account of these relationships. Perceiving the thing in context thus becomes a newer and deeper mode of apprehending meaning. William James, and later Whitehead, gave impetus to this way of thinking when they observed that perception provides a deeper event of knowledge than analysis; for here, the complexity of man's meaning as man is apprehended. Here the richer, thicker form of experience is conveyed. The formula with which modern metaphysics expresses this truth about man is "individual-in-community." This, Whitehead has said, is the topic of religion, because this is man understood in his ultimate dimension of meaning and responsibility. By this one means understanding man in his full nature and reality. Man, stripped away from the connections which form his complex heritage of meaning, is a strange abnormality. In every instance of human existence there is a structure of experience that forms out of a sequence of occasions defining each life. Man embraces as well as reflects the social inheritance; but in each instance, it is the social heritage as it is peculiarly assimilated within an individual span of life.

The tendency of a former generation, at the turn of the century, to elevate the individual and to glory in the dream of universal man, seems, in retrospect, to suggest how oblivious that generation was of the factors which motivate our present estimate of the human situation. For both individualism and universalism abstracted man from his actual living connections.[7] And because man was con-

---

[7] Nowhere is this mode of thinking more in evidence than in the utopian prophecies of a world religion following the World Parliament of Religions held in Chicago in 1894. It continues to form the basis of much that is projected today as an argument for a world order and a world faith in so far as these concrete aspects of man's structured experience are ignored or allowed to go uncalculated. What alters matters somewhat today, however, is the degree to which science and industry

ceived to be so readily isolated from these connections that formed his heritage, it was possible to envisage him, along with other human beings, in an ideal setting, divested of inherited biases or bent of mind.

The ardent age of nationalism which we have lived to see rising in our time bespeaks a reaction against this ideal man. The disregard of concrete connections has had the disastrous effect of releasing violent, partisan forces in one national community after another until we have become confronted with aggressive national egos, highly self-conscious, fearsome, and combative, distrustful and arrogant toward other national communities, and intolerant of every internal sign of deviation from the national consensus. Partisan loyalties and chauvinistic patriotism have once again come to plague us in our national experience. An era of individualism, and its international corollary universalism, has thus precipitated a public state of mind the world over which stands ready to crush both individuality and community of universal proportions as threats to the national ego.

Now it must be obvious that a national egoism, which is the inversion of individualism and universalism, presents an equally distorted and illusory conception of man and the human situation. For however much one may concur with the sound instinct which motivates its reaction, one cannot accept the restricted and restrictive view of man which its reaction implies. For the measure implied by the phrase "individual-in-community" looks to the values of both individuation and relatedness. Each is a distinct source of meaning in itself; but, their correlation and even their tension and occasional conflict offer opportunities of creative meaning for man which are of inestimable worth

are modifying these concrete realities, establishing within the structured experience of the various cultures a strand of common meaning and experience which is beginning to form a basis within the actualities of existence, itself, for envisaging world order, and possibly for some dimension of a world perspective qualifying the individual cultural expressions of faith.

to individual man and to the human situation. The integrity and authenticity of the person present one aspect; the claims of our communal ground present another. These are not antithetical aspects merely, for their occurrence simultaneously in any society and their interaction upon one another assures a depth of freedom and solidarity which is spiritually greater in sensitivity and creative power than either individualism or communalism taken singly.

In this vision of man, metaphysically grounded in a doctrine of relations that takes structural meaning seriously, the individual, the national community, and the world community each stand for dimensions of our human meaning. One can hardly take each one singly or separately as an entity to be analyzed or described. For in each case, the one presupposes the other. There are no individuals who live in isolation from a structure of relations and these relations in some respects take on national characteristics, while in other respects they assume international connections to gather in the structural ground of every created event. Here one will see that man is microcosmic as surely as he is individualistic. The sea water flows in his veins. The chemicals and ores embedded in the earth combine to give form and frame to his visible, bodily structure. But in each instance, man is at once and simultaneously individual man, national citizen, participant in the world's community of men, and creature of creative processes that fashion the whole of existence. And this is his complexity. He lives in a depth of relations which compels acknowledgment. The demands which they impose create the tensions of his being which in some degree must be resolved, but in other respects will never be resolved. To some degree, the tension must be sustained. I call attention to this point because I believe it is one of the distinctive features of the present view of man. Tensions are real, important, and actually creative of value in existence. A life in which all tensions are resolved must mean that some relationships have been dissolved, ignored, denied, or even betrayed. Individualism, universalism, nationalism are total resolutions, each in its own way, of the tensions that form the complexity of human existence. The individual in community is the holistic, the organic, and the emergent way of affirming the demands of relationships which create, nurture, and hold each individual life in existence while, at the same time, acknowledging the needs and merits of individuation. The one points to the social ground of all existence; the other lifts up the unique value along with the limits of every concrete occurrence, including that of individual man.

If these remarks appear abstract and airy, it is because I am oversimplifying a vast amount of metaphysical talk having to do with the new understanding of the human situation, in order to light up the full background of this innovating vision with which we are concerned. Comparable changes in Western thinking about man have been coming from another source and from another combination of concerns. I refer here to the series of developments in European thought which have culminated in Existentialism. There are those among contemporary Western thinkers who regard Existentialism as the most significant turn of thought informing the human situation in the modern era.[8] This judgment would be particularly persuasive to theologians who continue in the Kantian tradition and who stand apart from developments in the organic sciences and the new metaphysics. For the Existentialist offers an analysis of the human situation to which Protestant theologians, reared in a neo-Kantian understanding of the self, find they can speak.[9] Their own

---

[8] Cf. Carl Michalson, Ed., *Christianity and the Existentialists*. Scribners, 1956.

[9] Existentialism in some form has played an important role in shaping the thought of most of the major Protestant theologians of today, notably that of Karl Barth, Emil Brunner, Rudolf Bultmann, Paul Tillich, Reinhold Niebuhr, and H. Richard Niebuhr.

affinity with transcendental thinking enables them to feel the cogency of the Existentialist description of the self. And their Protestant preoccupation with the problem of human despair and anxiety as a dimension of faith gives them confidence to point to the resources of the Christian revelation as an answer to the modern situation of despair.

Existentialism is truly a phenomenon of the present age. More particularly it is a phenomenon of Western culture, expressive of a psychical dislocation that runs deep in the modern ethos of the West. It is more than an aftermath of war and social disillusionment. It partakes of a deeper despair. Whether or not one traces its thought directly to Spengler's devastating cultural analysis, *The Decline of the West,* it echoes a similar skepticism concerning all cultural values and the heritage of insight which tradition itself bequeathes. For this reason it puts no weight whatsoever upon cultural securities or upon the guarantees of any inherited social consensus. The collapse of these guarantees is a presupposition of its thought. Man stands stripped of every vestige of support, save the capacity to affirm and to assert his own humanness in an act of decision, looking toward possible salvation in being open to the freedom of the future. There are many versions of this theme. Typical expressions are: Jaspers's "remaining free for all possibilities" and Heidegger's "possibility of being oneself."

Now what is basic in the Existentialist analysis of the human situation is not its despair with actual man, but its drive toward "authentic existence." Its positive theme is to be found in its zeal to transcend the phenomenal world of events and the concrete ego which this cultural melee invariably produces in cultural man. The dramatic motif of this mode of thought may perhaps be more readily grasped in the method of the philosopher Husserl, whose thought is considered to be indispensable for an understanding of the German and the French school of modern Existentialists.[10]

Husserl sought to establish a sense of authentic existence in what he termed the lonely transcendental self. Such a selfhood, above and beyond the natural self who partakes of the pain and folly of finite existence, opens into "consciousness in general" in a way similar to Kant's *Bewusstsein überhaupt*. It is this anonymous selfhood which, in Husserl's view, overarches all finite existence as an infinite sphere of being. Each finite existence, by reason of being in this world, is responsive to its concerns and demands, and thus becomes involved in its complexity of events. This is to live at the level of natural or common-sense existence. On this level, "one believes in the reality of the world and in one's being in the world." [11] Husserl's method of pursuing authentic existence follows in two steps: The first is what he terms the phenomenological reduction, which is to "bracket this whole world and the sciences referring to it." [12] In so doing, Husserl meant to separate out of existence the events and interests which are to be characterized simply as phenomena or of passing concern. In Husserl's analysis, this left the concrete ego, as it did for Descartes and Kant before him. But Husserl meant to go a step beyond this stage, and this his second step, is his transcendental reduction. True selfhood, he argued, requires that one undergo, not only alienation from this complex of world affairs, and the trivia of experience, but self-alienation as well.

Husserl's method was in the nature of a return to essential being through the route of transcendental loneliness. In one way or another, modern Existentialists have

10 H. Heinemann, *Existentialism and the Modern Predicament.* Harper, 1953, p. 47.

11 Ibid. p. 53.

12 Cf. Edmund Husserl, *Ideas: General Introduction to Pure Phenomenology.* Trans. by W. R. Boyce Gibson, Macmillan, 1952.

accepted the starting point of Husserl's, yet they have sought authenticity in an opposite direction: not by a return to an essential being, but by a forward thrust toward a new creation of authentic being. The transcendent is a beyond of creativity in which the self participates through decisions, acts, and the venture of faith toward the future which fears no risks.

The drive toward authentic existence in Existentialism assumes a characteristically contemporary turn in the thought of the Jewish philosopher, Martin Buber, whose work, *I-Thou*, has become a modern classic. I speak of it as a characteristically contemporary turn because in Buber's *I-Thou* the note of relationship appears to express the ultimate dimension of selfhood. Buber has, himself, moved through various stages of modern Existentialism, as he relates in his autobiographical essay in the volume, *Between Man and Man*. He began, as do all Existentialists, with affirming Kant's transcendental ego. In asserting the I-Thou relationship as the summit of his Existentialist climb, a narrow ridge spanning the two peaks of subjectivity, Buber identifies the infinite ground of spirit as social encounter. It is, in my judgment, a work of genius to have found the way to an ultimate sociality of spirit by way of the loneliness of the transcendental ego. One could say that this long arduous pilgrimage of the Existentialist has served to provide empirical grounds for a fact of existence which might otherwise have had only theoretical justification in the new metaphysic. This is a rash claim. Many who feel the force of the Existentialist's analysis may resent my making it. Yet I would insist that the metaphysics of internal relations, which takes its rise from the organic sciences, is a direct path of reaction against the abstract theory of spirit which was fashioned by Hegel out of Kant's notion of the transcendental ego. It becomes a search for the unifying bond of life in a reality deeper than consciousness, a reality in which consciousness itself participates, from which it draws its sustenance, nurture, and creative life. Step by step, the consciousness of man, and the ego of self-experience, which formed in response to acts and decisions, assumed its proportionate scope, as this deeper matrix of conscious existence loomed in the guise of a recognized other. Upon this social ground in which each individual life is cast, each developing mind was seen to assert its selfhood simultaneously as part and participant. The reality of otherness, though constituting a real alternative to every individuated experience, and thus providing a threat of alienation or estrangement to every emerging selfhood, nevertheless opens before each person a career of ultimate selfhood through its communal encounter. Man wins his larger selfhood, his larger freedom, in being responsible to the selfhood of another; for then the two together participate in a goodness of spirit which neither of them by themselves could know or experience. In the I-Thou encounter we awaken one another, as it were, to a reality of spirit that transcends our separate existence. You will see how close this comes to affirming the social character of ultimate reality, or to saying that ultimacy in spirit waits upon this social encounter.

Relationship is of the essence. It is not just a connecting link forming the parts into a mechanism; it is a live and serious confrontation of created centers of dignity pursuing the intentions and ends of self in and through the drama of communal existence.

The new metaphysics, I say, is the direct route of reaction against an era of individualized mentalism which obscured and even obstructed this deeper social sense of selfhood. Modern Existentialism, as it has come to fruition in the concept of the narrow ridge of an I-Thou relationship, is the long-suffering path of reaction within Idealism, which found it necessary to go the full way of loneliness as a transcendental ego before the limits of selfhood as a subjective experience could grasp one in the social encounter of self with self.[13] There is a bursting of the individuating forms of self-experience in this I-Thou encounter, not through any conscious assertion of self, but through a listening and looking toward another creative center which is to wrest the I from its contained and conditioned existence to a creative level of freedom where the novelty of relationship can occur. In this encounter, relationship is spontaneous, tenuous, intermittent; yet it is an unmistakable entrance of the self into its communal ground. In the empirical sense, at least, it is an entrance of the concrete self as person into the reality of spirit.

This image of man as an individual self in an ultimate ground of communal existence has become formative in the new Protestant theology of the West. Protestant theologians particularly have taken their cue from one or the other of these routes of reconceptions. The result has been a reformulation of the doctrine of the *Imago Dei* as a basis for interpreting the Christian estimate of man.

The *Imago Dei* is thus seen to be a kind of formula in Christian doctrine, conveying the fact that every man stands related to his Creator, and through this bond with every other man, as creature. Creation thus lays upon each individual man a threefold demand, which is what gives complexity to his existence. He is made for God, he is made for other people, he is made for himself. The living out of these relationships becomes man's daily burden as well as his opportunity. And it is his ultimate hope.

[13] Paul E. Pfuetze in *The Social Self,* Bookman Associates, 1954, has made a detailed study of similarities and contrasts between these two paths of thought as they bear upon the nature of the self, comparing the works of George Herbert Mead and Martin Buber.

VIII Experience, Culture, and Faith

Our understanding of the nature of man as being simultaneously an individuated self and a participant in relationships may be helped somewhat if we pause to consider the meaning of three terms which express various degrees and aspects of man's involvement in a social nexus. These terms are experience, culture, and faith.

I

Experience is the primal source of all awareness. It is not so much an interplay of explicit sensory responses as a bodily event which conveys to the living organism, in a holistic way, its rapport and participation in the nexus of relationships which constitutes its existence. Experience in this holistic sense is not immediately conscious, and much of it never becomes so; for it remains below the level of consciousness as bodily feeling or simply as duration, providing a substratum of intimate organic acquaintance from which moments of conscious experience intermittently arise. The occasion of conscious experience is always precipitated by some demand for attention. The character of the attentive stimulus will vary from the faintest intimation, alerting one to some hint or symptom, to a decisive occurrence of critical proportions in which the full powers of one's sensory facilities are brought into play.

In such moments of attention, there is always a two-way occurrence, giving definition to meanings which arise. The more obvious occurrence is the actual focusing of consciousness upon the stimulus which has alerted or awakened the sensory organism. The less articulate occurrence, but one equally significant for the creation of meaning in any situation, is the conveyance of this bodily acquaintance from the level of duration to that of conscious experience. In attentive moments, bodily acquaintance acts both as a resource of accumulative experience contributing form and character to the immediate event, and as a barrier to meaning. The problem of every attentive moment is to give due and proportionate value to each of these occurrences. The lack of critical intelligence will tend to give full sway to bodily acquaintance, causing every novel event to be absorbed into the context of accumulative meaning. In this kind of response there can be little or no emergence of new insight or meaning, for attentive moments, alerting and focusing the sensory powers, merely release the floodgates of memory or of judgments held in store through the act of duration, giving to every immediate event the value and character of meanings that have already accrued. An excess of critical intelligence, on the other hand, for example, intelligence dissociated from its bodily feelings, or possibly conditioned to distrust their accumulative report, will give full weight to each attentive occurrence. Even here, observation is not apt to be a bare event. Something of the substratum of duration persists or intrudes, even if only as a habit of thought or a limitation of sense, to qualify attention and its implications of meaning.

The interplay of duration and critical intelligence is what lifts experience to a creative level, wherein novelty and accumulative meaning become mutually qualifying. For the most part, however, one must confess that creative experience is a rarity, rather than a rule, in individual lives as well as in cultures. The more common form in which experience asserts itself is either a lethargic dependence upon the habitual routine judgments and valuations persisting as duration, or a ready response to thinly acquired data to which the creative intelligence can respond. Individuals as well as cultures thus tend either to be tradition-bound or at least tradition-bent, on the one hand, or to be caught up in an almost irresponsible gregariousness toward the frontier, toward the novel interest, or toward the latest model in ideas, theories, or practices.

Experience is always an internal ordering of responses within individual lives, but it assumes a corporate character. This is so because individuals exist in relationship with one another within certain defined geographical bounds, and partake of common occurrences which in turn give rise to specific instances of conscious experience. The inner channeling of these events in individual memories, sensibilities, and bodily characteristics which make up any individual psyche is one course which such participation takes. But this is accompanied by an outer channeling in the form of social custom, precedent, legislation, moral and religious taboo and sanction, all of which express themselves through institutions, ceremonies, and public practices. These inner and outer dimensions of accumulated valuations and meanings, together with the physical qualities that give them actuality and limited form, comprise the structure of experience that is operative in any period of time or generation within a given society.

Experience is thus never a simple sensory act or response; it is always a structured occurrence. It is never simply a subjective event, but a happening within relationships that takes on public character with social consequences. It is at once something internalized as individual meaning and a social nexus of accumulative occurrences which live on in individual lives and in the relationships between them in communities, to qualify each instance of feeling, attention, judgment, decision, or act. It is necessary, therefore, to speak of experience as the individual response to events, together with an accumulation of effects in duration within a structure of experience.

The structure of experience forms the living nexus in which all individual experiences participate, or from which they derive their public conditioning or character.

In speaking of various kinds of experience, Kroner has suggested that the sciences have introduced a special mode of experience in that scientific experience is controlled by especially designed conditions and procedures.[1] Not only that, but the person engaged in experimentation or inquiry is disciplined to be acutely responsive in certain ways and scrupulously insensitive in others. This is the meaning of the objective attitude in science which seeks to rout or to multiply subjective factors. I would suggest that the sciences are not alone in providing a special mode of experience. Mystical, religious, and aesthetic experiences have been known to develop special disciplines and procedures by which distinctive modes of apprehension and response have been made possible. And cultures, as well as periods of history, have varied in the degree to which they have given status or attention to these several modes of experience. Here lies a basis for understanding the differences between peoples and between periods of civilization.[2]

Experience under these specialized circumstances takes on a highly concentrated and exclusive character. As such, it can lead to startling and often significant results, eventuating in discoveries and in new levels of knowledge. Such experience, by the very nature of its discipline, its exclusiveness, and its dissociation or extrication from the nexus of common relationships and events, tends to deal irresponsibly with this nexus of accumulative meaning, which inheres in what has been called duration in any structure of experience.

[1] *Culture and Faith.* University of Chicago Press, 1951.
[2] The contrasts between Judaic and Greek culture, Greek and Roman, Indian and Chinese, or Japanese, as well as the marked contrast between Eastern and Western cultures are to be accounted for to some extent in this way.

211

The saint and mystic, as well as the creative artist, have always been enigmas to the common life and have generally been considered as people apart from the accepted mores and customs of society, sometimes persecuted, but usually tolerated until circumstances favored their being revered. Then the special mode of experience which had been exclusively and narrowly cherished became the source of a new communal experience at a level at which it could be assimilated into the common experience. The sciences have a similar history in their effect upon the common nexus of experience within any society. In Western history the scientist remained a wizard to be feared and opposed until he was finally revered and trusted. Once this trust in his special mode of experience was assured, both the benefit and the peril of his procedures pyramided in Western society.

II

When experience is defined in such a comprehensive and relational manner, the term culture may seem indistinguishable from it. But it can be distinguished. It is the human flowering of existing structures and facilities, becoming manifest as an ordered way of life in the imaginative activities and creations of a people, their arts and crafts, their architecture, their furniture and furnishings, their costumes and designs, their literature, their public and private ceremonies, both religious and political. It is in their formative ideas, giving direction to their educational efforts and customs, as well as to their religious notions and practices, their social graces and manners; in their habits of eating and body care; in their modes of livelihood and the social organization that follows from them.

Civilization is often used interchangeably with culture. But a moment's reflection will reveal, I think, that civilization is a particular stage of any culture, and that culture exists even though the stage of history designated as "civilization" may not have been reached. "Civilized beings," Whitehead has said in *Modes of Thought,* "are those who survey the world with some large generality of understanding, since civilization involves the understanding of the given world in respect to its qualifications."

On this basis civilization is a rarity and exists as a high degree of maturity among certain minorities in any society. Quite clearly one can say that the term "civilization" connotes a particular stage of culture in any society which partakes of something like a large generality of understanding, to use Whitehead's words. This is true primarily in the sense of providing access to individual and independent reflection upon social processes, and thus a critical sense in matters of social responsibility, social manners and practice, appreciation and judgment, such that taste or discrimination along with possibilities of differences in judgments can emerge. Here the function of a critical tradition, in contrast to a binding or moribund one which rests solely upon precedent, releases human effort for a variety of ventures, inquiry, invention, and experimentation in all areas of human endeavor.

This very freedom to explore, invent, and produce, in turn, gives rise to an expanding social horizon and to a zest for progress in the making of tools and machines as well as in science, art, and statecraft. The term civilization thus tends to be associated with societies which have actively pursued a course of freedom in human relations and the exercise of individual judgment and interests with a corresponding zest or concern for human well-being. In this way civilization has readily been associated with material progress and with conditions suitable for enjoying the abundance it can provide. The agencies principally active in providing the conditions essential to this form of livelihood have been science and industry. Hence industrialization and scientific-mindedness have been assumed to be indispensable to the civilized life. One will see that in these transitions something of vital significance to the human spirit has dropped out. Civilization has taken on the meaning of technical adequacy in the processes of society, enabling a people to live well in terms of economic abundance. This is to lose sight of the real meaning of the liberation or freedom of spirit implicit in such terms as "large generality of understanding," the force of which is to accentuate the dimension of spirit.

As a result of this change in the meaning of "civilization," the term in common usage in industrialized societies for pointing up the civilizing or spiritualizing aspect of man's life is that of "culture." "Cultural interests are in jeopardy in Chicago," headlines the newspaper, "now that the Civic Opera House has been leased to the nickelodeon company." This is at best a restricted use of the term culture. In our usage, in speaking of religion and culture, we need to be aware of the full range of human flowering that is expressive at all levels of society.

Culture will then be seen to be a more inclusive term than civilization. And both of them represent particularized fruitions within the realm of experience.

III

Faith can be defined in a way that relates it intimately and deeply with the whole evolving structure of experience and its cultural expressions; or it can be set forth as a thing apart, a magnetic pull from a transcendent source, altering the course of individual lives and directing them toward a higher order of fulfillment than experience or culture can in themselves provide, even setting them over against the fulfillments of culture; or it can be seen both in its immanent and in its transcendent aspects. One's metaphysical predilections intrude here to affect one's understanding of faith in relation to experience. My own predilections, together with my understanding of the doctrine of creation, lead me to speak of faith both in its immanent and in its transcendent dimensions.

Faith in its immanent aspect is the condition of trust which comes to dominate the psychical experiences of a people or a person, preparing them to confront the ultimate mystery of existence; or simply to find innumerable instances which awaken man to his limits, his creaturehood, and his dependence.

Faith in this primordial sense is given as a component of creation. That is, the creative act of God, in bringing life into existence, imparts to every creature the subliminal condition of being a life that is in God. In its minimum and most innocent form at this level, faith is simply a will to live, or perhaps a capacity to live, expressing simultaneously a joy in living and an organic purposiveness which impels one to seek out conditions essential to the survival of life.

Neither the joy in living nor the zest for continuing life can be considered, in and of itself, an explicit acknowledgment of faith. These simply convey, in an elemental sense, the vital intent of the creature to actualize the relationship with God in an individual life span. This is not even a conscious intent. It is deeply organic, pervading the whole of the living organism.

No life is possible without this elemental condition of faith. The dissipation of it through ennui, or the dispelling of it through psychic failure, despair, defeat, or frustration, disrupts the internal functioning and leaves the organism or personality subject to, or even at the mercy of, external forces and pressures. It also impairs, and may even destroy the person's capacity to participate in relationships. Students of the personality sciences who put a primary emphasis upon socialization of personality tend to speak of this kind of impairment of personality as a reversion to selfcenteredness, as if only the capacity to receive and to participate in relationships has been dissipated. The invalidism or failing is more pervasive than this suggests. It implies loss of concern and capacity for decision and for initiative within the personal center of existence itself, and thus loss of personality structure as well. There is no ego here to break through or to dispel relationships, as we often think; but a shattered or dissipated selfhood which needs to be restored to a holistic existence where it can be reactivated within its own centered existence, both for purposes that are integral to self-interest, and for ends that are socially shared.

The threat to this primordial condition of faith is constant in the life of every individual. Conceivably, however, where individualization is at a minimum or even nonexistent, this "vital joy," as Marett the anthropologist calls it,[3] can persist relatively uninterrupted, as in the innocence of childhood.

Apart from the disturbance of self-consciousness, of individual desires, demands, choices, acts, decisions, etc., faith, as this elemental condition of trust, might persist in the sheer act of existing without conscious appreciation or understanding of its implications.

Individuation carries with it the act of falling away from this elemental condition of trust. More specifically it implies heeding the demands of individual senses, appetites, and concerns; in short, particularized interests which may assume varying degrees of assertiveness and egocentricity. Self-awareness is in itself innocent enough. It is in fact an essential phase of selfhood. The pursuit of individual freedom given to each creature is indispensable to his realization as a self. But the fact that all selves exist in a nexus of relationships, relationships with other men and creatures, and in relationship with the creative ground of being which is in God, gives to self-awareness the hazard of becoming oblivious to this communal ground, or even alienated from it. The freedom of self-experience makes this possible and in every instance probable.

It is here that the transcendent aspect of faith as a gift

[3] R. R. Marett, *Faith, Hope, and Charity*. Macmillan, 1932.

of grace is acknowledged. That which reclaims man from the alienations of self-experience is a movement of grace out of the relationships of this creative ground which is in God. This is the New Creation of which Christianity speaks, through whom awareness of our life in God is restored, not simply as a primordial condition of trust, though this depth of our creaturehood too is reclaimed, but as a conscious commitment to the creative ground which claims us. Faith in its mature state, then, must be defined as the gift of grace reclaiming us as being related in God.

These two dimensions of faith, primordial trust (which is immanent and subject to dissolution through the individuation of experience) and the ultimate assurance that comes into the human psyche as a movement of grace (which is transcendent), are continuous in that they can be considered to have one source—namely, our life in God. The one follows upon the creative act, the other from the redemptive act. In between the two, and precipitating the split in the dimensions of faith, is the individuation of experience, intensifying the demands of self-experience, and thus dissipating the self's capacity to participate in the relationships that form its communal ground.

Faith as primordial trust, given in creation, is ultimately involved in experience; it is, in fact, its precondition. Similarly it is involved in culture inasmuch as the most meager assertion of creative and moral experience, out of which culture emerges, depends upon this elemental condition of trust in the human psyche. In all life religions,[4] therefore, one must say that experience, culture, and faith are intimately interrelated and interdependent.

Faith as the gift of grace, given in the redemptive act or in the New Creation, is a dimension of spirit which

---

[4] The term "life religions" is generally applied to religions that celebrate the vital processes of existence.

transcends both experience and culture. That is to say, it is literally a goodness other than one's own and is consciously acknowledged to be so. It does not arise out of the creativities of experience, out of a culture, or simultaneously with their emergence. Rather faith, as this transcendent condition of trust reclaiming us, issues forth out of the matrix of sensitivity that is in the life of God expressing itself through the communal ground, evoking a reconception of experience and culture and of the primordial condition of trust as well.

We should recognize, however, that the threat of self-experience centering about the vitalities of nature and man has evoked another kind of faith besides that given as a gift of grace. This is the moral faith of human idealization. The idealisms of India, of Greece, and of modern Europe and America have found in the ambiguities of human nature the basis for seeing man involved in a tension between his physical existence and his ideal self, or between his passional nature and his spiritual self. Faith in man in this ideal or spiritualized sense has never been simply a faith in the human dimension. It has been a faith in man's ideal aspect as being an element or increment of divinity in man. The assertion of this higher self through the discipline of reason and the moral will, it is believed, will deliver man from the threat of his vitalities and from the contingencies in nature which enslave his physical being. "Once a man comes to know that his life is divine," said a Hindu priest in a Ramakrishnan Mission in Calcutta, "he will live up to that conception of himself." "This knowledge of the self as being at one with the divine life," he claimed, "is itself a transforming and creative faith."

This idealization of man has been a barrier to belief in the dimension of spirit through which transcendent faith comes. In its place it has set moral faith and its ethical disciplines. Thus, historically, while the idealism of moral faith has been affirmed in lieu of a transcendent faith, it has also served to seal off the realities from experience by which such transcendent faith might be recovered. Recognition of this fact is what has prompted the reaction today in theology against Idealism. In the sense in which Christian theology has most consistently used the term, faith is to be understood as a condition of the human psyche that is bequeathed to it in primordial form in creation; and in maturity, following individuation, it is offered as a gift of grace.

But we use the term quite differently in some instances; and since these too enter into discussions of faith and culture, we need to consider them also. One speaks of faith as an attitude, or faith as act, or faith as a complex of beliefs, rules, and practices defining a cult or a religious body. Obviously the latter, faith as cult, can include all of the others; though it may not presuppose the precise theological characterization which we give as a condition of trust. When the term "faith" is employed as attitude or act, it may not imply the same meaning given to the term in its more commonplace usage. Faith as attitude can mean simply an expression of confidence, an absence of doubt. One has faith in one's spouse or friend; one has faith in some enterprise. This kind of an attitude may partake of the primordial condition of trust to which we referred earlier, or it may be more empirically based; that is, it may be a definite and spontaneous response to an accumulative experience with this person and enterprise which leaves one no basis for doubt. Even so, we may not be able to dissociate it altogether from faith in the theological sense.

Faith as attitude, however, is often used to suggest a venture of trust in the absence of evidence or of accumulative experience. It is said to be a gamble. It implies something more than risk, however. It may imply a choice of some acknowledged good in the face of its denial. Living by faith in this sense is thus more a venture of hope than trust, though one acts as if one trusts what one affirms. This too may have particular psychological aspects peculiar to the circumstances in which it arises, and constitutes something of an act of will, though again, we cannot dissociate it either from the condition of primordial trust or from the movement of grace.

Now what determines whether the response of faith assumes the form of a singular act or decision, implying a decision of trust against doubt and skepticism, or an affirmation of beliefs in a corporate sense, "the faith," as in the cultus, is the degree of solidarity that may exist with reference to any communal witness. I am speaking now chiefly of circumstances which have attended Christian faith.

The earliest records of the witnessing community express not so much a venture of trust against possible odds as an assurance of grace given in the act of Revelation to which the witness is borne. In the tradition of classical Christianity, that is of the organized church, faith loses the freshness of a response to a historical act of revelation, and becomes instead acceptance of church authority and whatever it declares of the historical Revelation. Faith here is acceptance of what is authoritatively declared to be true. Both the early Christian community and the medieval church, however, affirmed a communal trust in something given, the content of which could be stated either as a kerygma or as a body of doctrine.

In the Reformation use of the word faith, we come upon a breakdown of the communal trust and begin to see the intrusion of the individual act and attitude as a venture of trust following upon a radical experience of despair and from an individual vision or experience of God's grace. The contrast here should not be emphasized too strongly, however, else the continuity of meaning in Christian faith will be missed. The contrast in meaning here turns upon the loss of solidarity in belief among the Reformers and a fierce dependence upon "the individual's access to the Holy Spirit," as Calvin put it. Once such solidarity was recovered in a community of believers, faith took on the meaning of a communal witness to the goodness and judgment of a forgiving God and the freedom of the forgiven man.

It is possible that faith in its most critical sense never loses this tenuous character of being, in the last analysis, a venture of trust bordering upon despair—that is, a necessary laying hold of a gift of grace, a goodness not our own, against the insecurities that follow from any naked self-sufficiency. But when this is romanticized simply as a gamble, "a betting of our life that there is a God," something of the stature of faith is forfeited. It amounts to psychologizing what is in fact a more objective reality. There is a gift of assurance conveyed through this term as the Christian witness implies it. And this means, in effect, a content of meaning in which the condition of trust is restored, because awareness of the ultimate condition of our existence is recovered, namely that our life is in God.

IX   The Encounter with Spirit

In the developments which we have thus far described, altering the scientific understanding of nature and of human thought, one detects changes so radical and far-reaching as to suggest that we may have entered upon a new stage of the modern consciousness. What this may mean we as yet do not really know, for the innovations in scientific exploration continue to come with ever more overwhelming impact and effect. What is full upon us at the present moment is the realization that frames of meaning which hitherto held us to a monolithic order of meaning to which the sciences subscribed have given way to unsettled inquiry before the complexity which the new vision and the new estimate of our human perceptions and observations present to us. An impatient orthodoxy is content to say that supernaturalism has been returned to us; hence the claims of a historical faith against which the modern consciousness rebelled can now be reaffirmed. On the other hand, an unrepentant liberalism tends to assume that, with all this talk of depth and complexity, reason appears to have fled the earth, leaving us helpless before a flood tide of irrationalism, except where the liberal has stubbornly reasserted the claims of an orderly universe. Neither of these summary observations seems to me to assess our situation soundly.

What has been restored to us is a vivid sense of creaturehood which alerts us to distinctions between our thoughts and reality, and thus confronts us with dichotomies or discontinuities which may or may not imply ultimate dualities, but which certainly accentuate our human limits of vision and comprehension and thus impose upon us simultaneously that which we understand, or which is available to understanding, and that which is beyond our comprehension. But even as we acknowledge depths of realities that are beyond our comprehension, we are made aware of the fact that we participate in them at the level and mode of experience which we call duration. To this extent we know by acquaintance through bodily feeling, or through the sheer act of existing, much that we shall never know in any explicit, cognitive way. The ultimate range of meaning is not a penumbra of mystery that simply supervenes experience; it is a mystery and depth of the immediacies themselves.

My purpose in defining experience, culture, and faith as I have done was to cut through the conventional cleavage between immediate and ultimate concerns, and to suggest that what are ordinarily presented under the title, antinomies, are actually interrelated in a way that makes all living ambivalent, and all existence cast in a situation of ambiguity. This situation compels us to confront a creative tension in dealing with the problems of faith and culture. Such creative tension is the essence of a life in relationship.

Tension is never the end result. It is the condition which holds in focus competing qualitative interests and demands. In less adequate form all related life existing in tension results in unrelenting strain. In its more adequate form it results in negotiation, a pondering of significant differences with, of course, expected intervals of distress and satisfaction, of sorrow and joy, suffering and significance, tragedy and the conquest of spirit.

The chaotic expression of existence under tension is unrelenting dissonance, the unceasing encounter of opposites or differences, offering no relief through rapport, appreciative awareness, negotiation, or agreement. This is a dominant characteristic of modern existence both within nations and between world cultures. The creative or negotiable expression of existence under tension is symphonic. This, to be sure, is more ideal than actual, but in instances where a real grasp of the relational situation is achieved actual interrelational existence occurs. This occurs more frequently between individuals in an I-Thou encounter between sensitive persons, or in experiences of forgiveness or in the sharing of a common vision of life's meaning, or in the sheer act of being in community as an experienced good. There are group experiences also in which such solidarity and communion are known. All these instances release into the human situation a flood of sentiment and genuine fellow feeling which, in its more objective nature, would best be described as a working of grace in the human situation, heightening the level of existence. From within the perspective out of which I attempt to speak, these become instances of participating in a structure of sensitivity transcending our commonplace experiences, a participation, that is, in the life of spirit. I hope to be able to clarify why this heightening or deepening of experience in such sensitive encounters partakes of a transcendent level or dimension of existence.

These instances of interrelational living in which grace is experienced are intermittent. That is, they cannot be sustained, given our ambivalence and ambiguity. Thus, at best, existence is symphonic; that is, given to an alternation between conflict and resolution, evidencing strain, dissonance, counterpoint with an occasional ascending line of resolution that becomes transporting. Only where the ambiguities of existence are seen in juxtaposition with an order of transcendent good, offering redemptive moments, will such a symphonic portrayal of existence appear convincing or even acceptable.

Where human powers and human values are idealized, being identified directly with the divine life, there follows a minimizing of tensions in the encounter between man and God, or even between individual persons. Tension is then located between man and nature, between spirit and material existence. But this permits of no tension in the realm of spirit, for spirit is then subsumed under human value. Where tension is assumed to exist only between man and nature it can issue only in the moral struggle. Under such circumstances the moral struggle is conceived to be simply a battle between acknowledged human values and what is less than human good.

The encounter with spirit is something other than this. In the language of the ontology which affirms a transcendent good, it is the struggle between value humanly conceived, and a depth of sensitivity in which all life is cast, yet which is only partially apprehended in these intermittent moments of experienced relationship, when the self and the not-self are brought into vital rapport, as in the I-Thou, or in other instances of the working of grace. Human value in this perspective is always under the judgment of grace, though it intermittently participates in what Tillich speaks of as "Gestalts of grace." That is to say, grace or the work of spirit is not to be conceived of simply as an inchoate realm of transcendent occurrences or of a supervening nothingness, giving airiness to our higher thinking. It is, in my judgment, a structure of sensitivity or a matrix of sensitivity which we have only limited powers as human beings to apprehend. We nevertheless participate in its transcendent structure, for, in decisive ways, we live by reason of it; our lives are cast in its matrix of relationships. We are concretions of this communal ground, actualizing its intent under certain limited circumstances.

But we know this transcendent life of spirit vividly in "Gestalts of grace"; or, to state it differently, in instances of sensitive encounter, where subject apprehends subject appreciatively (I-Thou); or in acts of forgiveness where the I-Thou is involved somewhat differently, more in a situation of strain and resolution, than in the act of being appreciatively aware of another; or in the moment of heightening, where one can respond in faith to the communal witness, attesting to the goodness of God in Christ;

225

or in times of sobering despair when worlds crumble through realization of the actuality of the Cross in the deeps of experience and the truth of the Gospel proclaiming the Suffering Servant. In all these instances, something more than a rising of consciousness to a sensitive perception occurs. In these instances, the structure of our personality that is definitely ours, by reason of its own individuation and freedom, has concourse with other centers of freedom, and with a matrix of sensitive relations that is in God, in terms of which all individual life is cast.

The imagery best calculated to present the implications of such an ontology is that of ascending structures, with the dimension of man reaching a ceiling which marks his own structural limitations. Within his own human structure man is dominantly personal in the ways that are made possible by his psychical nature and by his rational consciousness, and is thus capable of exercising moral vision and judgment along with imaginative and intellectual achievement. But these limited structures rise out of and exist within a dimension of sensitive relations which can best be designated by the term spirit. Spatially one is tempted to think of this dimension as being at the boundary of our personal existence, but spatial imagery is probably misleading in this instance, for we are involved in this dimension of spirit through internal as well as through external relations. Our acquaintance with such a sensitive order of being is more extensive than our knowledge of it. For in bearing creatural relations with it we are in concourse with it, having been born of its processes, and in our very existence we are daily being sustained and nurtured by its activities of grace and judgment. We do not know this to be true; we infer it from what we discern of the creative act of God as metaphysically defined. What we can know of this dimension of spirit, I hold, is what we can empirically grasp in these intermittent occasions of sensitive encounter, when our lives are actually summoned to express, through human acts or human responses, the qualities of freedom and grace imparted by this sensitive, communal ground. In the language of conventional Christian thought, there come times of immediate access to the Holy Spirit in the lives of individual persons and groups; or times of being grasped by this order of sensitivity which is in God as a communal ground of our existence. We actually transcend our rational and moral structures in these instances of encounter, though we do so in a way which involves us simultaneously with what is given to us as a human structure.

And although these occasions of encounter are intermittent, the interrelationship between creature and this sensitive order of spirit is continuous. We are borne forth as on a tide by its creative passage through participation in the New Creation, which came into history as a social energy of grace through Jesus Christ. We are continually chastened, judged, and offered new life in Christ through this redemptive good.

Now so far I have stated an implied ontology of spirit in terms of a metaphysics of internal relations. The formula here is the individual in community, not only in the sociological sense that each person has relations with the group, but in the ontological sense that all individuated existence arises from a communal ground and derives its meaning from its continual, dramatic encounter with the activities of judgment and grace issuing from that communal ground. But this ontology of spirit, based upon a metaphysics of internal relations, is but an abstract way of speaking of the drama of creation and Redemption as we meet it in the Hebraic-Christian myth. Or perhaps one should say it is but one way of giving intelligibility to a mythical witness to the depth of our culture, and with variations, to the depth of other cultures, the full meaning of which, in the very nature of the case, cannot reach our limited structures as minds or even as experiencing organisms. The metaphysics of internal relations, I am

227

suggesting, is one further confirmation and exposition of the notion of the Covenant and its theological derivative, the *Imago Dei,* which sees man's meaning in its immediate and ultimate aspects as being expressed relationally. He is made for God, he is made for other men, and he is made for himself. Which is to say that man's life is in God, it is in the community of other men, and it is in the individually defined structure of a given organism.

The limits of our own structures as human beings would leave us impotent to partake of this higher order of sensitivity were there not given to us as an act of grace—out of the creative ground and the redemptive life working simultaneously to impart to us a new freedom—a freedom to partake of the freedom of God. Thus faith takes on a transcendent aspect, coming into our human situation as a renewed condition of trust and of openness to the sensitive order of spirit. Following as it does upon our awakened state in which we have become self-conscious as to our limits as creatures, the transcendent aspect of faith would seem to have no continuity with faith as primordial trust, given in creation. The imagery of serial events may be an obstacle here. The fact that these two levels of faith are separated by an interim of maturing life in which the human spirit falls away from its creative ground gives them the appearance of being distinct and dissociated. The answer here must be that they are distinct in the sense that creation and Redemption are distinguishable as separate events. Yet Redemption is, in effect, the renewal of a relation with God known in creation. Biblically, as we know, the Hebraic-Christian doctrine of creation followed from apprehensions of redemptive acts in history. The acts of God primordially are seen in the light of Redemption. In a similar way, one must see that the whole of redemptive history and creation is re-envisaged and conceived in the light of the New Creation, once this work of Christ becomes known and received as a social energy in history reclaiming men from themselves and creating within the stream of history a witnessing community of faith.

God is known anew through the New Creation; but what is thus known as a redemptive good, was and is creative act, giving to each creature out of His sensitive ground the primordial gift of trust, essential to the very act of actualizing existence. The continuity between Redemption and creation cannot be thought of simply as temporal or sequential; in fact this tends to be misleading. It is, one might say, an ontological continuity, in the sense that the one involves the other as expressions of the communal ground.

There are problems to be explored here. This I do not deny. All that is implied in the figure of the broken image is involved in a discussion of such problems. But a further question must be raised having to do with the nature of relationships that form the creative nexus. Are all relationships to be conceived as being of this communal and redemptive ground? I must answer this with an emphatic "no!" One cannot say simply that all relations partaking of the communal and redemptive ground are internal relations, and all others are external. I do not choose to make this arbitrary distinction. Only, one must say that there are various grades of external relations operative in existence which have their origin in purposes motivated by self-interest. All the power structures of society designed for various ends are of this order of relations. They must be conceived of as the mechanisms of human imagination and effort, and no more. They serve various practical functions, and these are of various grades. All the ambiguities of human nature and action enter into these relationships to qualify their character and worth. It must be recognized too that this very capacity in man to organize his ideas and energies into vast mechanisms and power structures amplifies his capacity for evil as well as for good. And it remains to be determined which outweighs the other.

There are also various grades of internal relations expressing themselves through sentimental, even sexual attachments: dependence, anxiety, fear, hate, guilt, remorse, all of which yield their share of pathology in the human character or in some way confound human personality and human association. There are, as well, relationships growing out of normal and responsible actions between people, eliciting respect, appreciation, good will, and camaraderie, all of which involve responses carrying some degree of internal relations. Yet none of these as such may normally be considered more than the interplay of human beings within the sphere of human intercourse. Some of these internal relations, to be sure, partake of a deeper dimension and, provisionally, may be considered possible participants in the nexus of relationships which we have identified with the realm of spirit. All such relations stand under the judgment of the creative ground and its redemptive life, but they may not necessarily be subsumed under it or associated with it in any organic or ontological sense.

The relationships which rise out of the creative nexus are twofold: those which form the nonconceptual, bodily awareness at the level of creature-feeling, where prehension is experienced as a living nexus; those which arise as highly conscious instances of encounter between persons as subjects, in appreciative acts such as in love and friendship—sacrificial, kind, or beneficent acts in which another person's good is contemplated and served as a subject; or acts of guilt or repentance, and forgiveness where, again, there is an I-Thou encounter. Among these I would include all negotiable acts, looking toward the triumph of the reconciling act among men, or the healing of men's brokenness through a witness to the life of love in Christ. Whether Christ is known and acknowledged or not, their acts partake of the goodness of spirit, and bear silent witness to his New Creation.

X The Reality of Spirit

"No man is an island," wrote the poet-churchman, John Donne. Might he not better have said, Every man is an island, but islands are not what they appear to be: isolated bodies of land. For if one presses beneath the surface of the water one will come upon a land base that unites these individual bodies of land with all land.

I

This claim that a social reality defines our ultimate ground as human beings is the insistent insight with which we have to deal in attempting to understand the reality of spirit. The significance of Buber's imagery of the I-Thou relationship is that it offers some insight into the kind of encounter that can awaken human beings to this depth of sensitivity that cradles their human spirit. Buber's analysis of the I-Thou relationship at times seems to suggest that when two people meet one another at this level of the I-Thou encounter, they themselves create a spontaneous occasion of spirit. The subtleties of this occurrence are such that one has difficulty trying to speak accurately of them. My own view is that the mystery of this occasion is more complex than such an analysis seems to imply. Man's own acts certainly do bring something of importance to the occasion. The kind of sensitivity to which each individual is able to rise provides a human situation in which the innovation of spirit can occur. The question is: "Must we view this occurrence under the imagery of a flame that spontaneously bursts forth as two substances ignite? Or must we think of it, rather, under the imagery of a door opening, a gate swinging wide, through which two sensitive individuals pass into a freer range of relationship, because the barriers of individuality have momentarily been lifted—and, having transcended these barriers of individuality, have felt the power of spirit to grasp them and to empower them with its greater dimension of goodness?

The point at issue here is, whether spirit is a rare flowering of our distinctly human occasions, or a dimension of sensitivity, a kingdom of mystery and meaning into which we are released, enabling us to participate more freely and consciously in the mysterious depths which hold us in existence. I am of the opinion that the latter is the truer imagery for this situation. Existence, itself, is a greater mystery than we know or acknowledge it to be. We but touch the fringes of its meaning in our day-to-day transactions. Our utilitarian existence is far removed from the depth of sensitivity in quality and meaning which forms the communal ground. Often its objectives, in fact, tend to go counter to this sensitive ground. And insofar as it leans upon coercion or upon external force for achieving its coveted ends, it rears formidable resources of power that increasingly become a vast surd in the community of men. Yet even as these power structures mount in magnitude and force, the negotiable life persists among men and nations as a quiet prodding of these deeper veins at the level of spirit. These gentle emissaries of human relations, often unpretentious, always appearing in the garb of the informal, unofficial spokesman, carry an enormous weight or significance within our human encounters, despite their seeming humility. It is one of the ironies of human history that vast power structures have acquired the connotation of strength; yet they rest precariously upon the delicate balancing of relationships for their very survival. The durable bonds which bring assurances beyond the dubious securities which power structures provide are in these ne-gotiable relationships wherein the deeper resources of spirit become available and creative of decisions.

Spirit connotes a depth of sensitivity that forms the matrix of relations in which all life is cast. This depth of sensitivity is not so much known as lived in. It is a kind of womb or matrix out of which the waking life of in-dividual persons emerges and in which individuals partici-pate, knowingly or unknowingly, as living creatures. We may say that spirit is a quality of being which arises out of a particular depth of sensitivity in relations. It is, in other words, a goodness in relationships.

In saying this I am not suggesting that all sociality, to-getherness, communalism, group membership, or concern with solidarity in the sense of the greatest good for the greatest number leads to such an encounter with spirit. These, in fact, may have nothing to do with the sensitive ground of the human dimension about which I am speak-ing. Much of this kind of sociality or solidarity is util-itarian in basis, bent on such practical ends as well-being, economy of effort, or the distribution of the tangible goods of production. These humanitarian impulses and ideals have their legitimate claims; but they are not to be confused with the communal ground of being to which the term spirit applies.

Communalism in this utilitarian sense is generally in-different to the ultimate ground of communal being that is defined by our life in God. For on the one hand it tends to dissolve the claims and authenticity of the individual person, except as they are given a "corporate signifi-cance." On the other hand, every instance of utilitarian communalism tends to be a mass effort in the interest of a privileged or underprivileged group against some im-agined opposition. What is dominant in the reality of spirit, namely, selfhood as an objective good, is virtually nonexistent in such corporate movements toward com-mon ends. And since this is absent both as an immediate concern and as an ultimate end, communalism as a utilitarian drive toward security, dominance, or well-being implies the disregard of, if not the destruction of, the objective good of vast numbers of people. Man as a human being, or as a creature before God, is not what is in focus, but man as a member of a self-conscious community seeking common ends. Even the community of democracy that exists by a strategy of achieving the greatest good for the greatest number tends to disregard the life interests and standards of minority groups and to impose the will of a majority upon them, though it must be recognized that concern for the protection of minority opinion is a distinctive sensibility in the democratic experience; and procedures to safeguard against such disregard of its interests have generally been instituted. The one aspect of democracy which approximates the objective good of selfhood is the equality of justice before the law. Where this is made actual, it exemplifies the structure of spirit, which is objective concern with individual selfhood in a context of the communal ground. Where it is only an ideal, it points to this reality of spirit, even as the actualities of fraud, tyranny, or injustice profane this holy ground of being.

Spirit then is a given structure of being and sensitivity which awaits our participation in the creative ground of each actual self, imparting to it relationships which at once qualify and enhance its individuated self-experience and bringing to each self a visitation of judgment and grace. These observations may be sufficient to differentiate the communal ground of being as a reality of spirit from sociality in general.

II

The goodness of spirit that comes into the human situation is as a gift of the relationships we sustain at this deeper and sensitive level of communal being. But the point of first importance is that this goodness in relation-

234

ships is not just a human thing. It is not just a product of human association which we can produce at will, or manipulate and direct. Although this goodness of spirit inheres in the communal ground of our existence as a matrix of sensitivity, and as such is a durable ground of grace, our conscious encounter with it is spontaneous, intermittent, and of short duration. These are occasions when the ultimate dimension of our existence breaks upon our waking world as a vivid, experienceable goodness. Such occasions of encounter are always in a situation of extremity, that is, situations which bring us to a vivid awareness of our limits of selfhood, either through a sense of defeat, depletion, or despair, requiring the healing of forgiveness and a redemptive good; or through a heightening experience of appreciative awareness in which that which is not-self can be apprehended as in the I-Thou relationship. I am saying here that experiences of extremity may be either experiences of defeat when, as it were, we are laid low, and the limits of selfhood impress us with a sense of dependence and of need; or they may be times of great joy, when the fullness of grace, of life's goodness, overwhelms us. Our cup runs over. These moments do come to individuals in whom the ego is sufficiently humble to be capable of joy. The Christian faith has always put a premium upon this capacity to be joyous, even in affliction; for only in this way does one rise above the demands of the ego to recognize the reality of goodness in our very midst when it does not happen to meet the demands of the self at that very moment. The demands of the self, in the form of anxiety and fear, along with untempered desire, can generate an aura of distrust and insecurity which tends to drive one in upon oneself and to equate goodness with oneself or with whatever the self demands. What does not serve oneself is thus accounted evil. Relationships then lose the connotation of grace, and become, instead, a threat. Fortunately, one is not always made the victim of one's illusions. The grace of relationships, which is a good not our own, is not wholly dissolved by such egoistic withdrawal, though of course it is hampered, and to some extent dissipated. But the goodness of relationship may save one, despite one's distrust and withdrawal. For the actualities of grace go deeper than the conscious response. They are real energies of spirit, and thus an objective resource of goodness that endures and acts upon us even as we distrust or defy relationships.

There are moments in an individual life, however, when the self is peculiarly grasped by a goodness not one's own, and is able to respond in freedom to the gift of the relationship that provides these occasions of grace. The freedom with which we are able to avail ourselves of these occasions of grace is what makes possible moments of joy. In the last analysis, then, the capacity for joy, or the capacity to live with a sense of joy, even as one is experiencing defeat or frustration, depends upon relaxing or restraining egoistic demands. But this, of course, is not as simple as it may sound.

The Christian view of man has generally taken the position that all men and women, all human beings, are more or less caught in this condition of egoism, and, consequently, in a situation of alienation from the goodness of God. Thus it requires Divine Initiative to save us from ourselves. This doctrine has sometimes been employed arbitrarily to discount all human effort or capacity to respond to the resources of grace. In its extreme form it amounts simply to a formalism, a matter of carrying out the logic of an imagery or of a system of theology. The situation is much too complex and subtle to be dealt with in this one-sided way. Yet it is true that, ultimately, we depend more upon the movement of grace as a good not our own, than we do upon our own effort. Whenever we act as if the responsibility is wholly our own, or as if we could manage the affairs of our ego in response to the grace of God, say, simply as an act of will, we fall into a moralism that is just as fallacious on the side of exaggerating human initiative as theologies which can speak only of the Divine Initiative.

This is an exceedingly perplexing problem to which there is no simple answer. But one may be helped in one's thinking upon it by distinguishing between two levels of freedom which are at work in human personality. Freedom as we discern it at the first level of creaturehood comes into the human structure as a feature of personality, i.e., as a concomitance of individuation in the person, releasing certain of its functions from the automatic responses of organic life. Through imagination, reverie, and critical thought as well as through decisions of the will, man employs this freedom to express and to assert the powers of this particular human structure. This freedom, implicit in the human personality, is the source of much of its creative, rational, and moral experience. Freedom at a second level appears under different circumstances and with different qualitative consequences, where the human personality participates in the spontaneous and transcending acts of spirit. Here the person is not so much asserting his structure as responding to the lure of the sensitivity that inheres in the relations that form its creative context.

The freedom that turns the human mind and imagination to self-assertion can be said to be the structural condition that opens the way for tendencies of dissociation leading to autonomous action. This possibility has been perceived Biblically as the fallen nature of man.

To speak of this tendency as the transition from *essence to existence,* as Tillich has done, overstates the matter to the point of seeming to depreciate existence unduly. Existence and the Fall then tend to be equated, which is to imply that all concrete structures by definition are depraved. Tillich avoids this extreme implication by saying that something of man's essential nature, if only as a dreaming innocence, persists despite the alienation, and

237

precludes complete separation and a consequent loss of communion with God. The net effect of this line of reasoning, however, is to resist applying any concrete or actual relation to the reality of God. As a result the only discourse that is found applicable to the reality of God is symbolic language. I am insisting that it is not the transition from an ideal state to actuality that marks man's fallen nature, but a transition within individuated existence from the creative nexus that forms the complexity and depth of man's nature to a state of individuation that presumes to disregard this creative nexus. Individuation in itself, however, is not "the Fall"; for it is a consequence of the creative act forming the sensory structure of the creature. It is the freedom within the structure to move toward self-assertion, building toward autonomy of functions, that generates the condition within individuation leading to "the Fall."

Existence then may be said to be possessed of a two-fold freedom, pressing in opposing directions: the one toward possible autonomous self-assertion, the other toward participation in the creative realm of spirit. The true condition of man is best described as being involved in the Fall simultaneously with being involved in the lure of spirit arising from relationships. This describes the ambivalence of existence. It is, as it were, a counterpoint of freedoms within the human creature, the freedom of the individuated self countering the freedom of spirit, or, more accurately, the freedom to respond to the level of spirit. Are these two levels of freedom related? This is an awkward question to answer, but it can be answered in part. And the consequence of its answer is far-reaching in its implications for saving human reason and volition from complete rejection as agencies of self-autonomy.

The question will have to be answered in this way: Where man is reached by the work of grace through the freedom to respond to spirit, the total personality is affected by the lure of sensitivity. The functions of the human personality, including the bodily feelings, the mind, and the volitional responses, are, as it were, brought within the orbit of this freedom which is of spirit. One may say that, under these circumstances, the freedom of the mind, of the imagination, and of the will, concurs with the freedom of the spirit. Intellect, imagination, and will, in other words, are summoned up to the sensitive level of spirit. Reason, imagination, and volition function with a responsible regard for the relations which hold them within the creative nexus.

Whether or not this rapport between the human personality structure and this margin of sensitivity opening into the creative matrix can be sustained is not a question that one can answer. The evidence reveals that it is not sustained. The redemption of intellect, imagination, and will comes intermittently and repeatedly, overcoming the alienation, and invariably persists as individuation and its assertiveness continue.

But one will see from this statement that sufficient interplay exists between the level of freedom defining our distinctly human functions, and the freedom at the level of spirit, to indicate that one cannot set reason, imagination, and will aside as being wholly destined to contributing to autonomous self-assertion. Under certain circumstances, which do occur intermittently, reason, imagination, and will operate within the orbit of spirit as redeemed functions of the human person, participating in the powers of grace.

I would point out here that the margin of sensitivity that persists in the human structure as a form of freedom at the level of spirit is not to be equated with religious experience in the usual liberal sense of that term. The liberals made of this sensitivity a capacity in man which man, himself, initiated and more or less regulated. Thus man could take the initiative or not, as he chose, to pursue the religious life. The freedom in man to be sensitive and responsive to spirit is not a capacity in man to manage. It is, as it were, the depth in his nature that relates him to the sensitive ground of all actuality, including his own, and enables him to participate in relations which form the creative nexus.

Now the differences among human beings in regard to their sensitive natures, their degrees of empathy, their degrees of responsiveness and yearning toward the things of the spirit, as we say, are illumined by this recognition of a second level of freedom. All men sin within the sphere of their individuation in the sense that the freedom within their rational, imaginative, and moral capacities impels them to self-assertion and to the tyrannies, corruptions, and perversions inherent in such assertiveness. But men vary in their responses at the second level of freedom, or in availing themselves of this freedom of spirit. And this makes for real differences in human beings. Make no mistake about that. Let us be done with this bludgeoning theology that takes the true and sobering confession of the Biblical witness that "all have sinned and come short of the glory of God" to mean a leveling down of the human creation where no distinctions in character and quality of the human spirit are possible. This quality of goodness that comes into the human spirit at this second level of freedom is a creation not our own. There are no grounds here for pride and self-righteousness. The inclination of the saint to be over-zealous in confessing his failings has been a sound intuition. He has been aware of the fact that a proneness to evil, however restrained, has persisted in him along with the joy and intimations of goodness that he bore within his being. He has been aware, too, of the uneasiness with which he found himself bearing this treasure of good; thus he has frankly asserted that such elation of spirit was not of his own character or making, but a gift, a visitation of the Holy One in the house of his body. The studies of the saints and mystics which have isolated this quality of goodness in human beings as being a charismatic power or capacity in especially gifted individuals [1] have, in my judgment, done a disservice to the Christian understanding of man. In so doing they have obscured the gift of grace that is latent or meagerly present in every human being by reason of this second level of freedom. The flowering of spirit in the human personality, in the saint as in more common instances of grace in the human structure, is not a charismatic power or capacity which the individual himself possesses or controls. It is, I am persuaded, a consummation of what occurs or can occur when, out of this margin of sensitivity that is our freedom to respond to the spontaneity of spirit, the gift of God's grace actually reaches the human structure to transform or heighten its every power and response. But the point is, there is goodness that comes into the human structure and situation, not of its own making, but as a gift of spirit affording it opportunity to be the bearer of goodness that awakens in man a profound and expressive joy. These occasions, I admit, are intermittent, though they are recurrent; and they may persist for extended periods of time.

The realm of spirit, then, is no mere figure of speech, or symbolic doctrine; nor is it a remote or esoteric sphere which a few rare souls encounter. It is a reality of grace that presses upon our common experience, a depth of sensitivity and power awaiting our response and our participation. We apprehend it in moments of tender relationships, and in times of extremity which throw us back upon the help of sustaining relationships; for then we are made aware of the communal ground in which our lives are cast.

The gentle might that occurs in acts of love, in forgiveness, in the exploration of one another's good, in the care of one human being for another, in the negotiable life

[1] I have in mind here particularly Bergson's *Two Sources of Morality and Religion,* Henry Holt, 1935; and Rudolf Otto's *The Kingdom of God and the Son of Man* (new and revised ed.). Lutterworth Press, 1943. See also his *Mysticism East and West.* Macmillan, 1932.

among sensitive human beings, is not just one man or woman dealing with another; not just a variation of moral or ethical good. It is the wonder of the realm of spirit made manifest again and again in human relations, in human history. It is the mystery of the Kingdom made luminous in common events.

III

When the reality of spirit is understood in this way, conveying the community of being underlying and defining the nature of man's existence, one begins to grasp the full significance of the Christian doctrine of forgiveness. As creatures before God human beings not only encounter one another, they prehend one another; and in common they prehend the Creator of their being. This is a depth of concreteness which we can hardly envisage or even perceive in its most meager dimension. It is a burden we carry: a burden of opportunity and a burden of risk. The opportunity is that of giving actuality to God's intent within the range of one subjective experience, the opportunity of feeling and communicating with the joy and anguish, the hope and despair of one's fellow creatures in manifold experiences. The significance of our concrete existence and its meaning lies in adding to our subjective aim, in correlating with it this depth of being which our capacity for prehension as creatures opens up to us.

But this is a burden we may not be able to bear. In any event, the burden is great. Significance of attainment lays upon us a demand for humility, for love, for the enduring of suffering, and for composure in faith in the face of continual defeat which these poor bodies of our human spirit cannot sustain. The best of men fail, therefore, to be what they were made to be. All fall short of the glory of God and of the creative work of his hand.

The sins of omission are implied in thus falling short of our creatural intent, failing to do what we ought to have done. Only a perception of the depth of our meaning as creatures can convey to us this vision of our deficiencies. Yet this great omission that gathers in the whole of the human family may not be regarded simply as a negative reminder of what might have been, a lost opportunity, a failure of God's creative act to find full fruition in our one structure of existence. For while it appears simply as the defeat of any one man's ideal possibilities, this deficiency operates with unrelenting consequences upon every structured event. The good that might have been actualized as sensitivity, feeling, rapport, and understanding is by default metamorphized into a surd of insensitivity that works on as an invisible barrier between creatures, effecting their mutual estrangement. What is given in community is thus rendered impotent to commune. This contradiction at the base of our creatural connections has its own dynamics of evil. We may not fathom the depth or scope of it. Some intimation of its tragedy may be conveyed through painful experiences of broken relationships; or through occasions in which one actually experiences the bond of humankind in some rare instance of companionship or solidarity, and against this experienced fact, is able to ponder the brokenness of life. Some intimation of it may come to one more abstractly and impersonally as one thinks about world community. But for the most part men and women remain relatively oblivious to this basic condition of prehension implied in the Imago Dei, relating men to God and men to other men. This surd of insensitivity thus looms as an invisible empire of uncalculated evil, countering what is given in our inescapable oneness of life in God and in one another.

From the sins of omission that issue daily from this basic contradiction in our concrete existence there is no release, save through forgiveness. One might even say we are born into a state of forgiveness, else the freedom of our possibilities would be too vast a burden to bear. Were this not so, the risk of concreteness, apart from utter determinism, would entail too much anguish within the experiences of the human being. Thus one may say that our sanity rests precariously upon this initial premise that we begin our lives as forgiven persons.

For many individuals, in fact for most, this ground of sanity is never brought to consciousness. It persists as an unencountered resource of the human spirit pending an awakened sensitivity. But once the human consciousness awakens to its depth of being in the face of its creaturely limitations, once one becomes aware of oneself as prehended and as prehending the whole drama of creative life, the need for this resource of forgiveness becomes acute. For the disparity between what is and what ought to be would lay upon the creature so great a burden of guilt that one's sanity would be imperiled. Actually the loss of sanity frequently reveals that this kind of sense of guilt has been present throughout as a festering wound of the human psyche.

The complexity of human existence within any individual experience is compounded by its sins of commission. The source of this kind of human evil is in the subjective ego, though not in the ego taken by itself. For sin, as we have implied, is a breach and betrayal of relationships. The complexity of the human creature arises from the paradox of its existence in being an individual in community. The individuation of self is no less a fact of creation and of creatureliness than prehension and the community of being. They who have sought to simplify the problem of man by absorbing the individual into the community, thus dealing with him as mass man, have seriously oversimplified the human problem and, as a result, have radically depreciated his meaning and stature. One may even say that to elevate relationships or the community of existence to the point of disregarding or demolishing the center of dignity which defines the individuality of human beings is to betray the order of relationships which defines the community of being that is in God. It is, in fact, to show contempt for the creative act of God, which creates individuated events of existence in community. Man without community of being is deficient in depth; but man without an authentic subjective experience is deficient in concretion and in centered existence. The burden of actuality rests in the last analysis upon individual concretion even though the ground of communal being forms the indispensable matrix of every instance of actuality. The self, therefore, has ontological significance no less than the community of being. The powers of the self are unique. Its opportunities for fulfillment are distinctive. Its destiny is a route of occasions that has no parallel either in its immediate historical existence, or in its ultimate outcome. Thus individuality lays upon man a demand to fulfill himself that is no less unyielding than the demand to live in community.

Yet it must be clear also that attentiveness to self carries implications of peril as well. It is here, in fact, that the most explicit sins of commission arise, the total complex of which is often described as egocentricity. If by egocentricity one means simply the restrictive orientation of the human psyche, due to its sensory facilities and its circumscribed vision, equating sin and egocentricity is hardly accurate. Rather, it is the perverse assertiveness of this centered existence, disregarding or betraying its communal ground which initiates the complex of human responses and behaviors which may rightfully be termed sin. The details of this complex of perverse acts have often been enumerated under the caption of the defects of sense, or sins of the natural man, or of the animal in man. Such characterizations betray an oversimplified view of human nature, as in the case of the Gnostic view of man which associated flesh with evil, and of evolutionary idealism which represented man's animal impulses as vestigial remains of a lower ancestry blocking man's spiritual progress. One of the real contributions of our contemporary theological period has been its insistence that sin

245

in its virulent form applies to the higher reaches of the human spirit, motivating and directing this centered existence of the individual, rather than to the evident physical side of man's nature.[2]

While the judgment of a higher righteousness, inhering in man's life in God, offers the corrective of this human perverseness, actually serving to restrain, even to put to rout, human evil, one is not justified in assuming that a balancing of the moral scales is inevitable within historical existence. Here again something beyond what can be righted by moral effort or by the corrective of judgment persists. Man is destined to remain unrelieved under judgment, except as a goodness not his own intervenes as a resource of grace. In this sense forgiveness neutralizes the peril of individuation.

But forgiveness does more than that. It enables the individual person to receive the grace that is given in relationships. Thus we can speak of forgiveness as the threshold to the realm of spirit. It is what gives man access to what we have called the second level of freedom. And this means that it affords man the capacity to participate concretely in the depth of his relational ground.

Now it is here that Christology enters into the Christian understanding of man and of the reality of spirit. For it is the New Creation in Christ that proclaims and exemplifies the good news of forgiveness as an ultimate fact, and thus foretells man's Redemption from the fallen state implicit in his individuation. Through participation in the New Creation man is reclaimed from the isola-

---

[2] This note was sounded simultaneously by a number of contemporary theologians speaking out of various theological and philosophical traditions in reaction against modern idealism. Cf. Karl Barth, *Commentary on the Epistle to the Romans* and *The Word of God and the Word of Man,* Pilgrim Press, 1928; H. N. Wieman, *Religious Experience and Scientific Method,* Macmillan, 1926; Anders Nygren, *Agape and Eros,* S.P.C.K. 1932; Emil Brunner, *Man in Revolt,* Westminster Press, 1937; Reinhold Niebuhr, *The Nature and Destiny of Man.* Scribners, 1941.

tionism and fragmented human existence attendant upon his own individual freedom to the higher level of freedom in relationships.

The assurance of forgiveness in the realm of spirit not only brings release from a sense of guilt; it bequeathes to man a new sense of joy and freedom in the ethical life. Ethics thus ceases to be a matter of principles and imperatives expressing the "oughtness" of responsible existence and becomes an adventure at the second level of freedom in which relational existence is taken seriously. Under the assurance of forgiveness and the judgment of grace, ethics points the way beyond the protective measures of self-interest, beyond fears and intimidations arising out of an overweening self-concern, to the pursuit of one's authentic existence. In this context, authentic existence is the life of the individual in community, the life of the individual free to receive relationships and free to be oneself in one's relationships, thus really free in relationship. Such a life is at once empowered by the goodness of grace in relationships and enhanced in being responsive to the judgment of grace.

The resources of grace, understood as a goodness in relationships, are concrete, social energies that have become released into the human situation under the condition of forgiveness. We may better understand this resource of grace as concrete energies of the spirit when we have considered its meaning in the context of Christology. And here we come upon what is distinctive in the Christian understanding of spirit—its reality as a new creation. To this aspect of the problem we must now turn.

XI The New Creation

More than thirty years ago Charles W. Gilkey, as the Barrows Lecturer to India and Burma, presented a kind of summation of Christian thinking on the historical Jesus as liberal theologians and scholars had come to view him. It was a winsome and arresting interpretation of this interest then current, and the crowds that gathered to hear him at various university centers and churches in India and Burma are still something of a legend in these places, as I discovered when I undertook a similar mission there recently. These lectures were later published under the title, *Jesus and our Generation*.[1] There had been many biographical studies of the life of Jesus, and I recall quite vividly how we reveled in these very human accounts of Jesus' life. Since 1900 a great deal of work had been done also in the social background of the Gospels and in the environmental interpretation of early Christianity.[2] This had followed in part from the stimulus of evolutionary thinking which then loomed so prominently in theology. Troeltsch's work was having considerable influence upon European scholarship, and the effects of it were seeping into American thinking at various stages of interpretation of Christian history. The emergence of the new science of sociology at the turn of the century, and

[1] Published by the University of Chicago Press in 1925.
[2] Samuel Angus, *The Environment of Early Christianity*, Scribners, 1920 and S. J. Case's two works, *Social Origins of Christianity*, University of Chicago Press, 1923, and *The Evolution of Early Christianity*, University of Chicago Press, 1925, were the studies in English being read at this time.

its conjoining with evolutionary thinking and social history, formed a perfect medium for studying early Christian times, and particularly the background of Jesus' life and teaching. Shailer Mathews's *Social Teaching of Jesus,* published in 1898, and a later work, *The History of New Testament Times in Palestine,* were pioneer studies in American scholarship reflecting this interest. Under Mathews at the University of Chicago the sociohistorical method of studying theology developed, projecting on the American scene a mode of inquiry similar to the one which had had considerable vogue in Germany under Harnack and Troeltsch. By the nineteen twenties this approach to the study of Jesus' life and teaching had about reached its peak. A book by Shirley Jackson Case, *Jesus —A New Biography,* could be said to be a summit work, gathering up the salient points of this sociohistorical approach to the life of Jesus, and setting them forth imaginatively, yet with an eye to precise facts, as these had been established during that period of historical study. The genius of the early Chicago School in theology was its capacity to make critical scholarship in religious study vivid and exciting. Since the founding of the University of Chicago under President William Rainey Harper, this community of scholars had considered itself to be a university on the frontier with responsibility for interpreting the critical findings of scholarship to lay people. Thus many of their major works appeared in the form of handbooks, designed to communicate the findings of critical study even as they conveyed their own judgments concerning them. Professor Shirley Jackson Case was a master at this art of giving serious scholarship an imaginative interpretation. He had a gift for narration. He could take the smallest detail and, with the skill of a Sherlock Holmes, weave a fascinating web of conceivable circumstances which became more and more plausible as his story continued.

I am sobered as I reflect upon the contrast between that

lighthearted period of storytelling in relating the life of the historical Jesus and the grim, earnest efforts of theologians today in their efforts to probe the meaning of Jesus Christ. Christology today is serious business. For this task, the gift of storytelling and of imaginative portrayals is hardly enough.

But the contrast between those earlier years of the liberal interpretation of the historical Jesus and the current concern with Christology is more than a difference in mood or intent. It represents a radical reconception of the problem, and a wholly different level of inquiry into the mystery of Jesus Christ. The critical literature in New Testament study was already laying the ground for this shift in theological interest at the time that Doctor Gilkey was giving his Barrows Lectures, and when Professor Case was writing his biography of Jesus. In fact a decisive blow had been struck against such portrayals of the historical Jesus several years earlier when Albert Schweitzer, then a young theologian, published *The Quest of the Historical Jesus*. This work was well known to both Gilkey and Case, but at the time New Testament scholarship was not wholly persuaded of the cogency of this line of analysis. In this work, Schweitzer took issue with the liberal interpretation of the historical Jesus on the grounds that the mysterious references to the end of time, which appear frequently throughout the New Testament, what Schweitzer called "the mystery of the Kingdom," had been wholly ignored, or consciously deleted, in the zeal to present a relevant picture of Jesus for today, based on his ethical teaching. These references to the mystery of the Kingdom, the eschatological teaching, said Schweitzer, are inseparable from the life and teachings of Jesus, and thus may not be set aside or ignored in any faithful interpretation of Him. For Schweitzer this made of the historical Jesus an impressive man of destiny who belonged peculiarly to his own time and generation and was therefore alien to our own. Later New Testament scholarship was to find Schweitzer's view extreme because of his error in ascribing to Jesus radical eschatological utterances which have since been identified as coming from a later Palestinian community. Nevertheless, his essential thesis concerning the vulnerability of the modernized portrait of the historical Jesus has persisted. The necessity of acknowledging these references to the mystery of the Kingdom in the New Testament, and their decisiveness in interpreting the meaning of Jesus Christ, has been well established. It has been this recovery of the eschatological dimension of Jesus' teaching that has brought Christological discussion once again to the fore in theological study.

Liberal theologians since Ritschl and Harnack had sought to dissociate the problem of the essence of Christianity from Christology on the grounds that theories about Christ, which theologians and church councils formulated subsequently to the historical appearance of Jesus Christ, tended, in their judgment, to focus attention, not upon the good news of the Christian Gospel, but upon the problems men have experienced in believing and understanding the good news. The Gospel teaching and the direct experience of the person of Jesus, they argued, has thus been wrenched from its simple and forthright historical setting and been artificially reset in a mosaic of ontological themes and motifs, the choice of which has been determined, not by the actualities of Gospel history or teaching, but by the ideological preferences or biases of those who raised such questions in the first place.

The problem here has since been more sharply focused as an issue between centering attention upon Christianity as an ethical gospel, and seeing the whole of the Gospel in the light of its eschatological claims. For the most part, liberal theologians, influenced by the demand to make Christianity reasonable, which was a way of accommodating it to the demands of the modern consciousness, seized upon this distinction between an ethical and an eschato-

251

logical gospel as a way of separating the kernel from the husk. Eschatology was seen to have been a particular mind-set of first-century Christians which caused them to confuse these incisive and radical ethical insights of Jesus' teaching with an otherworldliness which obscured the essential thrust of their meaning. The liberal felt obligated to rescue these precious Gospel insights from their obscure and dated setting and to let them shine forth with clarity and relevance upon the modern situation. This meant for him eliminating the eschatological dimension and accentuating the ethical aspect.

This mode of establishing the essence of Christianity for the modern mind should not be confused with Bultmann's method of demythologizing the Gospel. Bultmann has come to his method by way of taking eschatology seriously within the modern idiom, not as a means of eliminating it. The liberal theologian explicitly sought to eliminate this dimension on the grounds that it implied a world view and an imagery which he believed could have no relevance for the modern consciousness. Bultmann, too, speaks of myth in the New Testament as being a mode of thought that is alien to the modern man, but he is speaking here of the Biblical mode of expression, not of eschatology as a dimension of ultimacy in the immediacies of experience. Bultmann, in keeping with a prevailing judgment of current New Testament scholarship, is convinced that one can do justice to the witness of the Christian community in the Gospels only as one takes seriously "the mystery of the Kingdom" as being a dimension of existence which simultaneously inheres in and transcends historical experience. It is this depth in experience, pointing existence toward its ultimate end, that impels the man of faith to live with openness to the future.

The point at which New Testament study, and subsequently theology, took a fresh look at the eschatological dimension as it relates to the gospel witness was, as we have said, the publication of Schweitzer's *The Quest of the Historical Jesus.*[3] Whether or not concern with the eschatological aspect of Jesus' teaching would have persisted to reactivate the Christological problem apart from developments in form-criticism is not an easy question to answer. Rudolf Otto in *The Kingdom of God and Son of Man,* which was published in 1937, was to re-examine the eschatological issue within the perspective of his own special interest in numinous experience. From his study of the numinous in religious history he had developed analogies with which to apprehend the idea of the holy within a liberal ethos. Otto's contribution had the effect of reaffirming Schweitzer's stress upon the importance of eschatology in Jesus' teaching, but of countering its negative import for liberal theology. Set in the wider context of the history of religions, Otto saw this quality of Jesus' personality and teaching to be a more familiar element in religious experience than Schweitzer had acknowledged. Nevertheless, he argued, it is peculiar to relatively few religious personalities in religious history, and marked Jesus as being in the lineage of charismatic individuals. In this way the eschatological problem was gathered into the study of mysticism and, for Otto, it was thereby resolved.

For those who had taken form-criticism seriously, however, establishing the historical Jesus as a charismatic personality offered no resolution to the problem of eschatology. For, on the one hand, form-critics became less and less confident of the capacity of historical study to deal directly with the historical personality of Jesus. For what is apprehended in the Gospels and in other New Testament writings as being most elemental in origin, these critics claimed, is not a direct recording of Jesus' teaching and preaching, but a community's witness to what was

---

[3] Von Reimarus *Zu Wrede,* 1906. English trans., London, A. & C. Black, 1910. His *The Mystery of the Kingdom* appeared earlier (1901), but did not reach a wide critical audience until *The Quest of the Historical Jesus* attracted attention.

seen and heard and what was apprehended in Him. In short, we confront a community's portrait of Christ. The more radical of the form-critics have insisted that we cannot go behind the picture, that such historical data with which we must deal are a community's response of faith, of which the person of Jesus is the presupposition.

We are dealing here, not with the denial of the historical existence of the person of Jesus in the form, for example, in which this question appeared among certain skeptical philosophers and historians of a generation or more ago. Nor are we necessarily seeing here a dismissal of the significance of His historical existence. In fact, when a theologian like Paul Althaus counters Bultmann's thesis by protesting his disregard for the historical existence of the person of Jesus, one feels that his argument slides off and away from what Bultmann is saying. The historical existence that gave rise to the Christ event and that formed its existential center is assumed in Bultmann's position without hesitation; but the evidence for this assumption, it is claimed, is made known to us through a witnessing community. Thus the historical reality that looms as the focal point of the Revelatory event is the new life made vivid and transforming of human existence in the early Christian community. This, one will see, alters the nature of the Christological discussion. The focus of inquiry shifts from a concern with the nature of the person of Jesus who was called the Christ to the appearance of a saving reality experienced as the New Creation in an entire community within history following his death and the Resurrection experience. The reality discerned, then, is a depth within historical experience which loomed as a resource of new freedom and power in individual lives and in the group response as these transformed individuals intermingled with one another.

The problem of interpreting this Revelatory event thus broadens to include the eschatological dimension of history. In its fuller scope it is the problem of understanding the interplay of ultimacy and immediacy in the events of existence. It is this that was being pointed to in the phrase, "the mystery of the Kingdom," which, as Rudolf Otto stated it, "is a paradoxical notion." Logically, he said, eschatology and ethics are inconsistent with one another. Religiously, however, he argued, they go together. Jesus was aware of the brevity of time, the judgment at hand, and the need for repentance; nevertheless he assumed that the world would go on, and, on occasions, spoke accordingly. These seemingly contradictory moods, Otto said, are not to be dissociated, but must be seen to be concomitant perspectives upon the nature of existence. It is a life of obligation in this world of events which nevertheless fronts an impending mystery that gives overtone and depth to this world of events. In this way Otto related the Christian life as an ethical path to the mystical quest.[4]

One will see then that the Christological question, in the form in which it is presented in contemporary Biblical study and in constructive theology, issues in a problem of understanding history in terms of its qualitative depths where the reality of spirit as a Revelatory and Redemptive resource is taken seriously. This is the burden of many of the current studies in Christology, ranging from ontological analyses of the Christ as *New Being* in Tillich's theology, and the re-examination of the Trinitarian approach to the God-Man in Barth's *Dogmatics,* to the meticulous analysis of New Testament reports on the development of the Christ event in John Knox's several studies.[5] All these studies presuppose one thing which sets them over against earlier studies in the life and teaching

---

[4] *The Kingdom of God and the Son of Man.* Lutterworth Press, 1938. Reprinted in 1951, Book II.
[5] *The Meaning of Christ* is particularly pertinent, but the two earlier works, *The Man Christ Jesus* and *Christ, the Lord,* now gathered together with the first-mentioned book in a trilogy, are relevant to his argument.

of Jesus; that is, that the signal fact about Jesus Christ is the new life, "the New Creation," that came into history through this event of Jesus Christ. The perspectives that have been employed to present and to interpret this New Creation have been various; but all of them draw upon this singular fact that the eschatological references in the New Testament point to a dimension of depth in history which needs to be taken seriously as bearing upon the meaning of Jesus Christ. Any minimizing of this reality or effort to circumvent its disturbing sense of mystery can only result in missing the import of the witness to Christ in the effort to trim it down to modern sensibilities.

The burden of our analysis in the chapter on the formative imagery of our time was to suggest that many currents of thought in our day have converged to enable us to recover genuine awareness of this deeper meaning of the Christ as the New Creation. This has come about, not just through the study of the theological concern in Christology, but through a re-examination of the meaning of nature and of history as they apply to all scholarly disciplines. No area of thought has been more revealing here than that of the new physics and the various metaphysical efforts in process thought to extend this revolutionary inquiry into problems of space-time to the larger issues of historical existence. Serious work in the philosophical analysis of this problem has been progressing under other auspices as well, notably in Existentialist philosophy such as that of Heidegger, Jaspers, and Berdyaev. Theologians have availed themselves of several of these strands of current inquiry, and at the same time have given serious attention to studies in New Testament scholarship bearing upon the nature of the *kerygma,* that core of primal witness to faith in the New Testament which appears to be our nearest approach to the human response to these signal events comprising the New Creation in Christ. With these resources at hand, there has been every reason to suppose that modern theologians might accomplish what theologians historically have, for various reasons, evaded, or failed to accomplish, namely, to express the full Christian evangel within the contemporary idiom. My purpose in this chapter is to contribute further toward that end. And I shall begin that task by enumerating some observations which could lead to that accomplishment.

An important corrective to make of liberal interpretations of the Gospel story, beyond the ones dictated by New Testament criticism, is in this sphere of understanding natural and historical events. Neither Newtonian physics nor Kantian Idealism were able to do justice to the subtle and organic happenings of concrete events. Nor could Darwinian evolution, or any sociological variation of this theory, do justice to events of novelty or mystery, or to any sensitive occurrence in structures in which transcendence and immanent happening intermingle. All that I have been trying to convey in the preceding pages bearing on an ontology of spirit, which is based upon a knowledge of the development of structures through what has lately been called field theory, the dynamic interplay of relations in a situation of emergence, throws a flood of light upon these events of history which the theologian may not ignore.

1. The first point to make, then, in moving toward an explanation of what happened in the situation reported by the Gospel story is that real novelty, real mystery, was encountered in the historical process.

2. The nature of that novelty is in part illumined by its antecedents. That is, the events surrounding the Christ stand in a relation to redemptive and prophetic events in Hebraic history in a way that compares with the relation between any novel event and its antecedent structure. That is to say, they are similar, but not identical. The earlier anticipates the later, but in the context in which the earlier events appeared, one could not make the judgments

and declarations that were evoked by the later, more decisive event of emergence.

3. The ground of sensitivity, from which the Gospel events flared forth, was equally present in the earlier events of Hebrew history, but the structures differed. The time was not at hand. There is a ripeness of time and events when energies of the spirit break forth with novelty, just as surely as there is a ripeness of time and events when physical energies can be released into the actual processes of history.

I would insist that the Christ event was a revelatory moment in history, summoning the motives, the intellectual vision, and imagination of men to a new center of focus as truly as the heralding of atomic energy was a radical disclosure of a new level of physical powers, altering materially the structured experiences of men. We are dealing here with the dynamics of relations. In the one instance, physical structures were altered by man's inventiveness to release into history a power hitherto unknown, except faintly through scientific intuition and imagination, anticipating it as possibility. In the other instance, human structures, already impregnated with the seeds of Redemption through antecedent events, became articulate and responsive with a sensitivity and perceptiveness that literally thrust upon the social community a new level of consciousness, a new center of consciousness and concern. One may speak of this new level of consciousness, in which love (agape) became regulative as the appreciative consciousness, in contrast to the levels of conscious decision characteristic of the human structure of experience, namely, the rational consciousness and the moral consciousness. I think anyone who has the patience and perceptiveness to observe the contrasts noted in the Gospel witness between the appeals to love as over against the law, faith as over against reason, will be moved to ponder this suggestion.

The orders of justice and reason were not set aside.

They were the antecedent structures in which the new emergence, agape, appeared in the relations of men who had become responsive to the Christ. The initiating vehicle of agape, releasing the matrix of sensitivity or creative ground of spirit into full actuality as a historical being, was the person of Jesus. All one can say is that this structure of consciousness became the bearer of sensitivity in which this love was dominant.

Here was a new center of consciousness in which spirit appeared, not as a margin of sensitivity, characteristic of the human structure, but as a full release of the sensitivity of grace which is of God. What may be called the second level of freedom, freedom of the spirit, was in dominance, and thus wholly responsive to the sensitive internal relations uniting this individuated experience with the lives of other men and with God. In the language of the *Imago Dei,* this was the image of God unbroken, the new life in God.

I would not wish to have these remarks on Christ as a new center of consciousness interpreted to mean a non-historical or superhistorical occurrence. What occurred took place within the conflict of two social orders in which the tenuous but creative forces of the new Israel, working through the Christ, engaged in deadly battle with the vested interests of a receding Jewish order. Amos Wilder's depiction of this setting in his *Eschatology and the Ethics of Jesus* seems to me to be highly relevant. In a later volume, *Otherworldliness and the New Testament,* he writes, "Jesus' message was both political and religious at the same time: a call to repentance, a challenge to corrupt institutions and authorities, and a compassionate action directed toward the neglected and the victimized of his day. He was indeed concerned with the eschatological new age to come, but in his context this meant no lack of realism as regards the actual historical situation of his people." [6]

[6] Amos Wilder, *Otherworldliness and the New Testament.* Harper, 1954.

All this I would agree to; only I would insist that this very revolution within the culture of Israel in which Jesus played the crucial role is not wholly understandable within the methodology of the sociohistorical analysis. The mystery of the Kingdom must be taken seriously as a work of spirit issuing from a new center of consciousness, providing a "new center of history," to use Tillich's phrase, a new level of creation.

In speaking this way of the new center of consciousness in Jesus I am overreaching a bit. I am speaking as if we had access to the historical Jesus for direct inquiry. On the contrary, I am persuaded by the judgments of New Testament scholars who say we cannot go back of the picture which the Gospel witness presents to us. Yet the reality of this historical life is acknowledged, in Bultmann's words, as a presupposition of the *kerygma*. I have simply brought to bear upon this presupposition the light of a contemporary imagery and orientation of thought which seems to offer intelligibility to this event of novelty, this revelation of grace and spirit, without detracting from the mystery that attends it.

The historical datum that we have is a vivid account of the transformation of human lives, individually and corporately, in response to this new life in Christ. And this, we are earnestly advised by New Testament scholars, we must take seriously as being of a piece with the reality that was in Christ. This is the leaven of spirit at work in history as a communal event. This is "new being" assuming structured form. This is the meaning of Christ, agape embodied in the structures of human experience as redemptive energy, the work of grace reconciling the world to Him in whose infinite judgment and grace we have our ultimate ground.

Jesus Christ, then, as an innovation of sensitivity in human form, appears as the summit of a working of grace within a Middle Eastern culture. This antecedent aspect of the revelatory event should never be minimized. But to treat it simply as a cultural evolution is to miss the radical and revolutionary character of this innovation of spirit. The Christian assertion in speaking of Christ that "this is very God" points up the objective fact that a new level of conscious spirit had broken upon the structures of history. This is the force of the Pauline assertion that Christ is the New Creation, the New Man, who, in the familiar language of Christianity, is the God-Man. Present-day theology is at pains to reassert this transcendent truth of the Incarnation, yet to see it in juxtaposition with the dynamic events of a cultural history. Thus if we speak of this event as a new emergence, we point up the radical innovation of spirit within the structures of man. When we speak of this event as the New Creation, we point up the work of God in history as grace transcending the moral and rational consciousness, as love transcending the law.

Important as the person of Jesus Christ is in the story of the Gospel, the magnitude of the event of revelation is obscured if one does not see that a significant dimension of that event was the energy of spirit that broke afresh from the community of people into which this new life had come. They were transformed, the Gospels say—yes, but not just individually; relationally as well. Centers of an innovating righteousness appeared within the culture, in which the New Creation became flesh again and again. The Christian witness becomes vivid and impressive when it is seen in its corporate context. The new life becomes a cultural force. It becomes an enduring depth of grace within the relationships that body forth the living Christ and his reconciling Word, in the decisions, acts, negotiations, and responses of men and women working at pertinent issues in society. Here we see the goodness of grace assuming the force of a new level of social energy. Here we have the seminal beginnings of the Church as a witnessing community becoming the body of Christ.

But what was the nature of this new social energy? This is another way of pressing for an understanding of the nature of the New Creation which proved redemptive again and again. We have already intimated that it was a decisive expression of mind and of personal response that stood in judgment of the rigid structures of law and rational decisions. It was not amoral, or irrational; yet it transcended these codes and categories in a way that brought greater vision to each critical human situation. Moral law and reason were not routed, but summoned up to a higher order of goodness and righteousness. God's love as a judging yet redemptive power was made manifest to the dismay of legalist and rationalist. Love, issuing in justice, bearing grace and forgiveness, triumphed as a saving and healing force amidst the brokenness of men and women. This new kind of goodness, or you might say this new kind of justice motivated by love and forgiveness, releasing men and women from guilt and failure, from despair and anxiety, from the unrelenting actualities of history, opened up the life of hope in the face of defeat. This was the new life that looked to the future, leaving the dead to bury their dead, the antiquarian to cherish his tradition, the rigid moralist to nurture his offended sensibilities.

In recent writings in Christology it has become common to employ the symbol of the Suffering Servant as being expressive of the quality of new life disclosed in this work of grace, a quality of life that stands in sharp contrast to the strutting power structures of modern life. The force of this symbol is to say that this new life of God released into history as a work of grace and Redemption is no easy way out for whomsoever might try to possess it. The love of God incarnate in Jesus Christ is a suffering love. And this is the heart of the matter.

Enough attention has not been paid to the symbol of the Suffering Servant which runs through the whole of the Biblical story, coming to a climax in the Cross and the Resurrection. Yet the clue to God's nature as seen in Jesus Christ is given here. It acknowledges that the way

262

of love and forgiveness is at a price—to one who loves and who forgives, whether God or man; yet that suffering, when it is incurred through acts of love and forgiveness, is the way to a significance which transcends all other forms of satisfaction or good, both in the common events of history and in the life of the spirit as an ultimate goal.

Let us see how significance in this new form follows from a life that is free to have relationships, that is free to love, to forgive, and thereby to accept the role of the Suffering Servant. Concern with the security of the self turns life in an opposite direction. The aversion to suffering, or the fear of it, will lead in the direction of disciplines that still the sensibilities, that restrain relationships, that hold in check the flow of fellow feeling; for in these investments of self, the risks of well-being, to serenity of mind and spirit, are great. One may not necessarily come to the conclusion, as did the Buddha, that all existence is suffering, and thereby seek to insulate the self from the actualities of human existence through a studied practice of world denial. He may, instead, rear a citadel of selfhood that remains impregnable in the face of life's demands and responsibilities. In one's self-assurance, bolstered by indifference to humankind, and by a studied effort not to become involved in their sensibilities and needs, one may escape the anguish of relationships, though one will hardly escape the hell of isolation and of alienation, for these are of a piece with the life of security in its egoistic extremes.

Egoism, or hedonism, which is the denial of relationships, and a clinging to the sensibilities of the self, must mean the forfeiting of the goodness of life that can come through relationships and through the New Creation of spirit that is made manifest in such relationships. Asceticism, whether it takes a middle path, as in Buddhism, or a more extreme form of denial, forfeits the significance of the New Creation as a final goal as well as a present reality in its quest for equanimity which must eventuate in the dissolution of consciousness. These are choices which hedonistic egoism and asceticism make respectively, setting them apart from the Christian path of grace and forgiveness which steadily sets its face toward Jerusalem.

Now it must be recognized that, indispensable as the concerns for the moral and reasonable life are in themselves, their bent of interest, when exclusively pursued, tends to magnify the will to security at the expense of the life of the spirit. This is no easy problem, and we should not deal lightly with it. But there were ample grounds for Jesus' impatience with the Pharisees; and they are the same grounds that make it imperative that we do not allow Christian faith to lapse into an ethical legalism or a rigid moralism. The work of the spirit is a creative movement of life beyond these fixities; and in the end, it must triumph over them, else an inversion of good must follow.

Lest we lose sight of the essential thrust of the symbol of the Suffering Servant as it is being employed in modern Christological thinking we would do well at this point to state its meaning more explicitly. Professor Daniel Day Williams's words will help us here. He writes:

We miss what is involved in the question about God's suffering if we think primarily of physical pain, mental torment, or death. These are forms of human suffering, to be sure. In Christ, God has in some way experienced them. But "suffering" has a broader meaning. It signifies to undergo, to be acted upon, to live in a give and take with others. To say that God suffers means that he is actively engaged in dealing with a history which is real to him. What happens makes a difference to him. He wins an actual victory over the world through a love which endures and forgives. It means that the world's sorrow and agony are real to God, indeed in one way more real to him than to us, for only an infinite love can enter completely into sympathetic union with all life.[7]

[7] Daniel D. Williams, *What Present-Day Theologians Are Thinking.* Harper, 1952.

In pointing up this symbol of the Suffering Servant as meaning a God who participates in His world in the relationships that form it, modern Christology parts company with that kind of thinking about God which makes of Him an impassive sovereign or the Absolute, devoid of relationships. The essence of God's meaning, and this is the essence of the meaning of Christ as a revelation of God, is that God is related to men, that He is concerned, that He is involved in the travail of our critical circumstances. This is not to say that He is involved as we are in the turmoil and indecision of this troubled existence; but He is intimately concerned. In our agony, our arrogance, our stupidity, our willfulness, our blindness, God suffers, as He suffered in Jesus Christ who died on the Cross.

To say that God suffers, then, is to assert the ultimacy of relationships, and to affirm their significance, both as the bearers of good and as the creative ground of the new life which spirit alone can generate. There is a way by which a goodness in life beyond all cherished goods may be apprehended, known, and enjoyed. It is participation in the New Creation, which is to live in Christ.

I am troubled a bit about what may seem to be implied in what I have said in this analysis, namely, that the Christian life must emulate the divine life of suffering. In a sense this is what must be affirmed; but it must be affirmed with a realistic recognition of our human limits and frailties. We are human beings, not God. We may participate in the New Creation and be judged by it; we may not hope to be Christ himself.

One of the most persisting obstacles to understanding the force of the Christian interpretation of life is the perfectionism which assumes that we have only to define the nature of God and Christ, and thereby live out that divine nature. This is clearly to think more highly of ourselves than we ought to think. The life of the spirit is strong medicine when it is taken seriously. It may not be undertaken as a romantic venture. In our human and finite existence we could not bear the life of the Cross in its fullness as a daily demand. We participate in the New Creation that is born of the life of the Cross. As human beings, seeking to do the will of God, our human spirits will be bent toward this ultimate demand. But our lives are ambiguous. Our dedications are ambiguous. Though our faces are turned toward the light, we of necessity grope through the darkness of daily events. We participate in the demands of self-experience, even as we participate in the New Creation. We cannot escape this ambiguity of human existence, so long as we are in existence, though we may rise to moments of genuine encounter with the life of spirit. To be self-accepting, yet fully aware that we are under the judgment of the love that is in Christ, is to assure, not only our sanity, but our capacity to receive the grace that is given, which can do exceedingly abundantly above all that we can ask or think.

The symbol of the Suffering Servant points to the way of the Cross as the life of significance beyond every other good. It is, however, a way, not the goal nor the end of the Christian life. For the Christian faith points beyond tragedy to a life of triumph, even in defeat; to hope, even as we despair; to a capacity for joy, even in days of sorrow; to life, even in death. Thus in the last analysis the New Creation, which is a dimension of spirit beyond every structure of existence, is a resurrection experience which comes to us again and again, bringing perennial renewal amidst moments of decay and defeat. To know this is to know the depths of our existence when we say that our life is in God.

XII Christ and the Problem of Power

The distinctive message of the Christian faith, we have said, is that a New Creation has occurred in human history, releasing into its processes and relationships a new kind of social energy that is both redemptive and fulfilling. This is to involve the Christian witness in the problem of power, which brings its message to the heart of our human situation today. Power itself has become malignant in our time; and whoever aspires to attain it, or succeeds in attaining it, acquires its malignancy as well. The fact that every nation feels the demand to accelerate its acquisition of power in one way or another, and that resources are at hand for extending the range and intensity of power with ever-increasing magnitude and efficiency, literally confronts us with the most visible facilities of demonry that our modern age has known. The age-old phantasy of God and the devil has now assumed startling concreteness. It is no fairy tale with which we are dealing. It is the issue between power and goodness at its gravest.

I

This issue is at the heart of the doctrine of Christology. And in the last analysis, the effectiveness of the Christian Gospel in dealing with the problems of faith and culture turns upon the sharpness with which Christology illumines the difficult interplay of power and goodness in the affairs of men. It will be my concern in this chapter to show that we are peculiarly fortified with insight and imagery in theology today to enable us to grasp the Christian witness with fuller scope as it bears upon this problem.

267

The power motif played a significant role in establishing the logic of the Christian faith. The late Alfred North Whitehead was pointing to this fact as a symptom of our pathology when he wrote:

When the Western world accepted Christianity, Caesar conquered; and the received text of Western theology was edited by his lawyers. The code of Justinian and the theology of Justinian are two volumes expressing one movement of the human spirit. The brief Galilean vision of humility flickered throughout the ages, uncertainly. In the official formulation of religion it has assumed the trivial form of a mere attribution to the Jews that they cherished a misconception about their Messiah. But the deeper idolatry, of the fashioning of God in the image of the Egyptian, Persian, and Roman imperial rulers, was retained. The church gave unto God the attributes which belonged exclusively to Caesar.[1]

Whitehead then adds this telling observation, almost in a mood of nostalgia:

There is, however, in the Galilean origin of Christianity, yet another suggestion. . . . It does not emphasize the ruling Caesar, or the ruthless moralist, or the unmoved mover. It dwells upon the tender elements in the world, which slowly and in quietness operate by love; and it finds purpose in the present immediacy of a kingdom not of this world.[2]

In these terse strictures upon Christian theology Whitehead has put his finger upon the central issue which tugs at our depths in this age of deified power. Yet his way of stating the matter, pitting the tender elements of the Gospel story over against the power-ridden enterprises of "the emerging great church," comes close to sentimentalizing the Christian imagery. The fact is that the process of giving form and visible structure to the Christian witness during this early period of its history was even

[1] *Process and Reality*. Macmillan, 1929, pp. 519-20.
[2] Ibid. p. 520.

more disastrous than Whitehead's words suggest; for it translated the power of the creative act and of the work of grace, of forgiveness and love, which had transcendent meaning in the Gospels, into power consonant with physical and political force. It is not so much that tenderness, simply as sentiment or social feeling, was set aside as irrelevant in this ancient power age, but that "the power of God unto salvation," as a creative and redemptive work of grace revealed in Jesus Christ, appeared to be lost to the imagery of the Church as the omnipotence and absoluteness of a righteous God and his judging Son took on the character of a Roman ruler. God and the Kingdom which Christ had established became a sovereign power above an earthly sovereign. The power of heaven (visibly operating through a visible church) was set over against the powers of earth.

This separation between the realm appropriate to man's rule and the realm appropriate to God's rule as rival power zones, comparable to political blocs in a power struggle, set the stage for changing the imagery of the drama of Redemption from that of the just, yet gracious Father, forgiving His children, to the imagery of an absolute ruler standing in judgment of His offending subjects.

The "tender elements" of which Whitehead speaks were not wholly lost to this earlier age of power; only they were identified with the agencies of intercession, rather than with the Godhead. Although the cult of the Virgin Mary emerged among Christian congregations as early as the second century, it was not until the eleventh century that Mariolatry loomed as a significant and indispensable expression of medieval piety, probably in direct response to the insecurity which Christian worshipers experienced in the presence of a wrathful God and an avenging Christ, as these were met in the ceremonies of the Church and in the emboldened art exemplifying this ultimate austerity. The "tender elements" could well have been lost from the formal practices of the medieval Church and from its message had it not been for the fact that its "good news of damnation" was moderated by the intercession of the Virgin Mary and by the company of the saints, in heaven as well as in monastery gardens, who served as a buffer between wrathful Heaven and the community of men. One is not able to assess the import of this interceding grace conveyed by good and trusted men and women, living or in memory only, or the warmth of the feminine symbol expressed in the image of a mother with child, except as one has felt the fierceness of an ultimate judgment shorn of the promise of grace. But the sculptured façades of the Gothic cathedrals and the thirteenth-century illuminations, as well as the art of fourteenth-century wood carvings, attest to the reality of this perception of grace in an age when God, as imperial ruler, and the judging Christ were the dominant themes of doctrines; while the Holy Spirit was virtually absent, except as it broke forth vicariously through these concrete evidences of intercession. If it is true that in Catholic practice, following St. Augustine's close correlation of the work of grace with the visible church, the mediation of the Holy Spirit was seen to occur through the visible Church itself, then these acts of intercession provided by the saints and the Virgin Mary must be understood to be the medieval counterpart of the Comforter, generally ascribed to the Holy Spirit. Apart from these provisions of grace, there seems to have been no explicit doctrine of the Holy Spirit at work in the medieval Church. Yet in being strands of concession, moderating the authority of the Godhead, these concrete expressions of grace could only assume the status of minor motifs, representing a concession to the frailties of man, rather than of intimations of a transcendent power of goodness, expressive of the love of God Himself. In the drama of Redemption, both in antecedent form as a general revelation, and in the Gospel stories, grace as a tender element of the spirit had been a major motif. The balancing of power and goodness in this later reinterpretation of doctrine was thus greatly altered, judgment assuming an ascendancy which all but put to rout the tender elements of faith.

The contribution of Reformation thinking takes on greater significance when viewed in relation to this issue. For in this matter of which Whitehead was speaking, "the tender elements as seen in the suffering love of God" revealed in Christ, the Reformers made considerable advance upon earlier periods of classical Christianity. This applies particularly to Luther's contribution in restating the doctrine of justification by grace through faith. The insight of Luther in grasping afresh the redemptive significance of the righteousness of God as revealed in Jesus Christ was precisely a transcending of the purely censorious ground implied in the doctrine following from the analogy of the penal code. It is true, as Shailer Mathews pointed out in his *Atonement and the Social Process*,[3] that Luther's conception of God's grace and forgiveness carried implications of the forensic doctrine derived from the persisting notion of penal justice; but I would suggest that it is a mistake to carry Mathews's caution so far as to obscure the Reformation insight into God's righteousness, and hence lose what light it sheds on the problem of power and goodness through its doctrine of forgiveness. Despite this intermingling of imagery, or perhaps we need to say, in the context of it, in which forensic elements along with ethically defensive intuitions of grace and righteousness appear interchangeably, a genuine emergence of new meaning was occurring in this Reformation thought. The impersonalism and the mechanistic determinism of punitive justice were broken through, even though something of their logic remained if only as a tag end of the argument. Some would argue today that this retention of what may appear to be an impersonalism

[3] Shailer Mathews, *Atonement and the Social Process.* Macmillan, 1933.

in this context was itself a sound act, preventing the moral sensitivity which motivated this Reformation change in doctrine from acquiescing wholly to human sensibility. Something of a tension between what was apprehended as a divine structure of righteousness and the demands of the moral sense was maintained. However this may be, a new alignment between the two was being attained. In this brief moment of insight, born of desperation, man the creature became a child again and assumed the attitude of faith as explicit act in response to "goodness," not to power deified. This is the point to emphasize here. Luther had actually recovered what the logic of penal justice in Christian theology had obscured in forensic doctrines. He had, in fact, broken through the egoistic barrier of his own consciousness and spirit to look at God's righteousness for what it is: an abundantly gracious and forgiving love, which in its own structure of goodness and justice stands in judgment of every man and of all that man tries to be. It is the goodness of God that is the prior fact, Luther discovered. The judgment proceeds as a perception of oneself because of what the encounter with such goodness evokes. The judgment is no less real because it is so elicited. We still stand as unworthy before this holiness of God's goodness, and the judgment is an ontological fact. But in this situation of being judged by a good not our own, by a goodness infinitely greater than our own, we encounter, along with judgment, the grace of God which offers forgiveness and acceptance. This is the resource of great moment, the resource which enables man to accept himself as forgiven and thus to live for God and for other men in repentance and trust.[4]

[4] I am not overlooking the fact that Luther himself vacillated between this sure vision of the righteous God as a God of grace, and the melancholy of anxiety when the wrath of God appeared to assume demonic initiative. Wilhelm Pauck has depicted this ambivalence graphically in describing Luther's faith in his book, *The Heritage of the Reformation*. I have meant to focus upon this summit vision as being the decisive discovery in Luther's faith, however vacillating or intermittent it might be.

If the mind of Roman Christendom intruded a tendency toward idolatry in fashioning God in the image of an imperial ruler, the mind of Reformation Protestantism may tentatively be credited with an attempt to counter this perversion in pressing forward the doctrine of grace. What is implicit in this effort is a concern to lift the tender elements of God's nature to dominance and to redefine His sovereignty in terms of forgiving love. The note of judgment and selectiveness, however, everywhere attends the divine act, and by this means, the power element was maintained as a condition of control in the divine act of forgiving love. This was more explicit in Calvin, but it was never really absent from the thought of Luther.

II

But now we need to look more critically at what has been insinuated in the discussion so far, first in the quotation from Whitehead, and then in my own remarks on medieval piety and the discovery of Luther. The question can be put this way: Is it not misleading, if not erroneous, to identify coercive and judging tendencies in doctrine with the power motif, and the "tender elements" with the motif of goodness? Certainly we would have to acknowledge that, in some instances of Christian history, the reverse has been more true. Overconcern with the "tender elements" in Christian thinking has led to a sentimentalizing of faith and of the Christian conception of God which has all but degraded Christian piety. There has then followed a reassertion of the objective and judging dimension of God's righteousness as a way of restoring proportion and dignity appropriate to the sense of the holy, or of simply restoring moral fiber to the act of faith. This is precisely what is occurring in the New Protestantism today in reaction against what is deemed an exaggeration of sentiment in evangelical Protestantism and in theologies shaped by a romantic liberalism. We even hear men like Paul Tillich reasserting the claims of forensic doctrine as a means of preserving the objective quality essential to a dimension of justice in the act of love, and of justice, in turn, being an indispensable dimension of the Christian conception of love.[5]

What must be added, however, is that, in practice, concern with the coercive aspect of doctrine has generally led to specific provisions of censorship in which power without grace has more frequently been exemplified. Men embodying the authority to effect such censorship have thus given to the Christian understanding of jurisdiction or authority the connotation of sheer power, unqualified by goodness; in short, as being simply sovereign and censorious. Religion as bare power, or as absolute power, will always assume an impersonal character which tends to become indifferent to goodness in which the "tender elements" might have their claim.

The issue, then, comes down to a consideration, not simply of the antithesis or contrast between power and goodness, but of their necessary interrelation; of the contribution that each makes to the other, and of the folly that results when the one is dissociated from the other.

As to the interrelation of power and goodness in Christian doctrine, I would suggest that we get a glimpse of what this can mean in the parables of the Gospels when faith is spoken of first as "a gentle might that can move mountains"; and on other occasions when it is likened to a seed planted in the earth, a grain of mustard seed which, when it has burst through the ground, becomes a tree so large that birds can come and lodge in its branches. In each instance cited here power arises out of an internal ordering of relationships, presupposing sensitivity in relationships. Thus the power so created is itself expressive of a goodness that inheres in the relationship. Power in such instances is never itself autonomous, existent for its

5 Cf. also his *Love, Power, and Justice.* This note appears with frequency in his "Systematic Theology."

own sake. Neither is it aggressive or coercive. It is seen as an ingredient of the relational situation such that what is initially given as sensitivity assumes the magnitude of great force.

Here, it seems to me, we have one clue to resolving this issue of power and goodness. We may, in fact, venture a definition of each of the terms on this basis: To have power is to have effects, to be effective. To exemplify goodness is to have effects which not only express relatedness, but which acknowledge and take into account such relatedness. To have power without goodness is to seek effects without concern for the fact of relatedness, that is, to assert oneself with indifference to this fact of relatedness, or to turn this fact of relatedness to one's own interest and thus to exploit relationships for the sake of one's autonomous ends. Power that is simultaneously goodness and force is the power of sensitivity. Sensitivity as I am employing the term implies a tender regard for relationships, a concern that what is intended in these ordered relations shall be reverently regarded. Power that arises out of a sensitive regard for relationships can never be simply external force; and for that reason it will not be simply coercive. For the one embodying the power or exercising it will at the same time be a participant in the relationships. The exercise of power will thus involve him in the sharing of feelings and responses which the exercise of power elicits. The man of power in this instance cannot remain oblivious to the consequences of his acts of power, for they are of a piece with his own existence and experience. Persons of power, on the other hand, who ignore this fact of relatedness and thus remain impervious to the feelings and responses elicited by their exercise of power, can act externally in exercising their power. There is, as it were, no conscious or responsible participation in these relationships. In such a situation, power and goodness tend to be wholly dissociated. One may not say, of course, that the act of transcending the feelings and responses elicited by the exercise of power is always a denial of the good that inheres in relationships. This would be to invest all meaning of good in the tender regard to the exclusion of objective factors which must always serve as a corrective of indulgent feeling and the weakness it entails. Judgment may then be relinquished and justice routed. Love, under such circumstances, would seem to be reduced simply to a condition of enjoying compatible feelings. The transcendent good, however, may never be wholly transcendent, or simply transcendent, that is, enclosed within itself and impervious to all relational concerns. When it is made so, it ceases to be a source of judgment that can restore structure and balance to the feelings and responses of those who are judged. In other words, it ceases to be judgment in any creative or redemptive sense and becomes simply the negation of what is implied in the feelings and responses of those being judged. Under these conditions the impersonal or objective judgment can be made tyrannous.

III

The relation of this discussion to the problem of power and goodness running through all Christian thinking in defining the reality of God will now become apparent. Formulations of the Christian understanding of the nature of God have swung between conceptions which have lifted the reality of God above and beyond the wretched affairs of men, considering Him the Unmoved Mover or the Absolute Ruler, and conceptions which have immersed God's reality wholly in the affairs and feelings of men, even equating God with man's own higher nature. We cannot do justice here to the nuances of thought reflecting the delicate balancing of judgments in all this historical discussion; but we can point out that this rhythmic alternation of thought between transcendent and immanent excesses, between objective and subjective moods of piety, might well be viewed as a judgment of history, itself, upon man's distortions in conceiving of the Holy God. From this judgment one should distill the obvious insight that both transcendence and immanence are essential even to a limited and tentative formulation of the character of the living God; otherwise power without goodness (i.e. an autonomous center of power that disavows relationships), or goodness without power, degraded to the level of sheer sentimentality, are ascribable to deity.

But something more than this obvious and abstract assertion that both transcendence and immanence are essential in a Christian doctrine of God is needed to guide the Christian's thought. The question of how these two dimensions of reality in juxtaposition or in relationship may be understood demands attention. I shall not undertake here to deal with this problem, except to point out that this is precisely the point of inquiry at which our current thinking of God is most sensitively engaged. There are two routes by which this problem is being pursued in contemporary thinking: the one is metaphysical, the other is Christological.

The first route has been opened up by process thinking in the new metaphysics with which the names Whitehead and Hartshorne [6] have been associated; although it should be pointed out that others, working more consciously within the Kantian heritage, but who, like Berdyaev and Tillich, are impelled to deal more realistically with the problem of relations seen as a depth dimension or a Gestalt of grace, have become alive to the same issue, and, in their own way, deal organismically with it. The new metaphysics sees the problem as one of understanding the meaning of internal relations where the transcendence of the individual event must be seen in the context of its

[6] Two works by Charles Hartshorne, *The Divine Relativity*, Yale University Press, 1948, and *Reality as Social Process*, Free Press, 1953, are particularly pertinent to this problem.

communal ground of being; or, if looking from within the life of the individual, as seeing the community of relations transcending the individual experience as being a dimension of each individuated event. In this mode of thinking, God is free and integrated Being with a destiny beyond all creatures, yet intimately partaking of the destinies of all His creatures. And He is involved in every moment of their existence. In this mode of thinking it is possible to see that supremacy in the transcendent sense as applied to the person of God may very well include relations; in fact that it must do so. This is to set the attributes of potency and excellence in a common context wherein power can be limited by goodness, or affected by it, and where goodness can assume efficacy. The nature of power affected by goodness is likewise altered. It becomes a form of efficacy operating through internal relations in which encounter and response are the creative resources. Power unaffected by goodness would be an efficacy derived from an autonomous center and imposed upon dependent entities or upon entities standing innocently in relation to it. Power in this sense would be wholly the efficacy of external relations. The power of internal relations is sensitivity assuming a constructive and creative role. It thus becomes a creative act, as in the imagery of the parables, which generates a novel condition of goodness out of a concerned and communicative encounter with existent feelings or relations, turning them to a new society of occasions. In this context, sensitivity, itself, becomes a significant form of power; to be sure, subtle, often hidden, but under certain circumstances issuing in a force of such magnitude as to make external power in its assertive form seem trivial by comparison.

Concerning the second route in contemporary thinking by which this problem of relating transcendence and immanence is being pursued, I shall only generalize some impressions which seem to me significant. Current discussions in Christology are remarkably fresh and innovating in certain respects.[7] For one thing, instead of puzzling over hackneyed questions, they have set Christology in the center of the most basic questions about God. The Christ event, as the revelation in Christ is called, is seen to be an act of God in history pointing to a presupposition of all existence which, in our empirical and scientific accounts, we so easily overlook. Christology is thus at the task of illumining God's participation in the concrete events of history, disclosing His life as being immanent as a redemptive and creative power, giving depth and new opportunity to men's lives. The scriptural account of the New Creation leaps out from its pages as being startling in its relevancy to our immediate situation, reordering the whole of existence, the whole of history; yet all this is seen to be occurring against the background of the hiddenness of God. Or, the other way around, "the wholly otherness of God" as expressing His power and His glory is qualified by the imagery of the Suffering Servant who came to seek and to save that which was lost.

In its use of the imagery of the Suffering Servant, as being expressive of the Christ and, through Him, of the nature of God, current Christology is asserting the same point that was noted in process thought, namely, the relational and participating character of God which assures that His power is qualified by His goodness and expressive of it.

IV

Now the force of taking seriously the suffering love of God as transcendent power become immanent (that is, relational and responsive) is that it restores to the Christian message the precise interplay of power and goodness which is implicit in the Gospels, especially in the parables:

[7] Helpful surveys of these discussions are to be found in D. M. Baillie's, *God Was in Christ*, Scribners, 1948; Daniel D. Williams, *What Present-day Theologians are Thinking*, Harper, 1952; and Norman W. Pittenger, *The Word Incarnate*, Nisbet, 1959.

a power arising out of an internal ordering of sensitive relations, a power at once power and goodness. We are not driven to choose between a notion of divine power which stands in its own right in judgment of the powers of this world, and a notion of deity defined by the tender elements of the Gospel story, which stand as a quiet lure to whomsoever may read responsively. On the contrary, we may be helped to see that these tender elements are themselves expressive of power that carries transcendent meaning, revealing a new creation, a depth of sensitivity and concern grounded in the communal character of reality which is in God. Every sensitive act, evidencing a reverent regard for relations and for their communal ground which is in God, carries a potency that is beyond calculation or measure. The gentle emissary of the United Nations, or one of no official status, who goes about patiently and quietly effecting negotiations, is a modern parable of this gentle might as surely as in the Gospel witness itself. In situations of extremity, where the balance between war and peace is delicate, the power of this gentle might seems to mock the strutting power of giant nations which seem to depend upon, yes even to wait upon, the outcome of these delicate negotiations. Existence in most instances is sustained by a perilously slight margin of sensitivity. The salvation of a people has often depended upon a remnant; yet were it not for the meager margin of sensitivity in the mass of mankind, salvation, even in these instances, would not be possible. "And the Lord said, if I find in Sodom fifty righteous within the city, then I will spare all the place for their sakes." As the story goes, God reduced the figure steadily until he declared to Abraham, "If there are ten righteous, I shall not destroy the city."

This, too, is an apt parable of what I have sought to express as the power of sensitivity. If the power of goodness that inheres in sensitivity is so decisive in events of extremity, it must be no less decisive in coping with more commonplace issues of the cultural life. It is indeed a depth of New Creation in existence awaiting our acceptance and response as "children of light," as children of the living God.

This is more than nonresistance. It is more than "soul force," with all due respect to those venerable notions. The power of spirit manifest here is an active and aggressive dealing with issues at a higher level of sensitivity and with a greater concern for internal relations than is possible where self-interest, possessiveness, and their attending fears and mistrust prevail.

The force of re-creativity that is generated in situations where such work of spirit occurs comes, not from any single source itself, but from the resource of relationships wherein people, so participating in the New Creation, are released from their own inhibiting fears and fixations, enabling them to lay hold of the energies of spirit at hand. This is one of the insistent points in the new Christologies interpreting the work of Christ.

Now the full force of these statements may not be apparent apart from a theory of spirit which takes the notion of New Creation seriously as a new depth in existence. My own way of speaking of this is to say that man's life moves at two levels of freedom: the freedom that is integral to his own self-experience as an individuated person, and the freedom of response to the communal ground of relationships in which grace abounds, and out of which the energies of spirit emerge. The response of men in community to the New Creation in Christ is thus actual participation in a new reality, a new dimension of sensitivity; not simply anticipation of a kingdom that is to come. The mystery of the Kingdom is at hand. The time is now. This participation at the second level of freedom is what transforms the whole of the human psyche and issues in a new level of social energy.

But I must make one final point. Although we may credit Reformation Protestantism with having repossessed the vitality of the Christian message as a gospel of judgment and grace, it must be said, in all candor, that Protestantism, as a whole, has dissipated whatever contribution it made at its inception by individualizing, and at times, almost trivializing this doctrine of grace. God, in the image of Caesar, was the Lord of Western culture, Who operated through specific institutions, ceremonies, mores, and instruments of social control to affect the whole of Western society. The God of grace in the Protestant faith has been, at best, Lord of the individual conscience. Culturally speaking, one might say that both the power and the goodness of God have been reduced to the proportions of the individual attitude and response. That is to say, the recognized province of God's power and goodness has been considered to be the individual heart; and the moral external expression of God's working within this province was, internally, religious feeling; externally, religious sentiment publicly expressed.

The beginning of Secularism in Western culture, in the sense of an order of life conceived to be indifferent to the judgment and grace of God, may be seen in this transition within evangelical Protestantism wherein the processes and structures of society, by default, fell away from any control of sensibility or direction offered by such judgment or grace. This situation of Secularism has been further complicated and made doubly ominous in the West by its focusing upon physical power, or natural energies, as independent force, with principles and laws peculiar to itself. Here the sciences, in combination with industry, have created a giant leviathan, the magnitude and menace of which we have yet to see.

Now the tendency of our Protestant faith, when it is confronted with such a cultural threat, is to flex its muscles and to break forth with a reforming zeal. I do not deny the need for such prophetic occasions; but I am inclined to believe that often this is a short cut to a sense of justification which may be illusory, and which at best is short-lived. To have the feeling of power in fighting evil gives no assurance that one is witnessing to the power of goodness as a cultural force. The soundest course would be to seize upon contemporary insights, from whatever source, which may help us to elevate this Gospel of grace and judgment to a corporate witness.

Thus the problem of power and goodness is upon us in this generation with a vengeance. Our efforts in dealing with this problem will be greatly helped if we are able to see that the idolatry of power, and the threat it imposes upon us, is not a simple matter of secularization. It is not simply that Christian faith has lost status in the modern world and that the false gods of science and industry have taken over. In a measure that does describe our plight; but it does not describe it fully. The further and important fact to note is that this preoccupation with power, emulating the secular mind, runs through the whole of the history of dogma and comes to focus in the Christian understanding of God. Part of our task is to become aware of this idolatrous strain in Christian thinking, and to become more vividly aware of the kind of power that is peculiar and appropriate to the life of the spirit, lifting up the doctrine of grace and judgment, not solely as a working of the Holy Spirit in the individual heart, but as a redemptive energy of faith within the power structures of man through negotiation and nurture which actually participates in the New Creation as a living force.

Part Three

THE WITNESS OF FAITH

XIII The Church as the
Witnessing Community

The clarity with which we are able to grasp the import
of the Christian Gospel as a witness to the New Creation,
opening up to us a depth of our existence that is at once
an energy of grace and a resource of judgment, will turn
in part upon our understanding of the nature of the
church. Here again we have been helped in recent years
by the new imagery of thought in re-examining and reassessing the meaning and role of the church as a witnessing community.

I

One of the most insistent judgments that has come
from New Testament criticism in recent years is that
there was a body of oral tradition attesting to the
Resurrection that took form during the years immediately following the death of Jesus on the Cross, fragments of which appear as Proclamations in the written
Gospels.[1] Scholars, eager to do justice to this testament

[1] A brief survey of the literature on this problem is to be found in Vincent
Taylor's *The Formation of the Gospel Tradition*. Macmillan, 1933 (re-
printed 1957). See also B. S. Easton, *The Gospel Before the Gospels*.
Scribners, 1928. The pioneer studies in form criticism are Martin Di-
belius, *Die Formgeschichte des Evangeliums*. J. C. B. Mohr, 1919. English
translation, *From Tradition to Gospel*, Scribners, 1935; K. L. Schmidt,
Der Rahmen der Geschichte Jesu, Trowitzsch & Sohn, 1919; Rudolf
Bultmann, *Die Geschichte der synoptischen Tradition*, Vanderhoeck &
Ruprecht, 1921. English Translation (F. C. Grant), *Form Criticism*,
Willett, Clark Co., 1934; and Martin Albertz, *Die synoptischen Streit-
gespräche*. Trowitzsch & Sohn, 1921.

of faith, yet concerned also to retain the judiciousness which their discipline demands, have been put to it to present a forthright statement of what, in their judgment, actually occurred at this momentous time of Christian beginnings. The advantage that the conventionally Christian interpretation of this event has is its daring simplicity. Jesus, so this account runs, literally rose from the dead, sought out His wayward disciples, convinced them that He was alive again, and thus rallied them to a new affirmation of faith and discipleship. Before ascending into heaven Jesus saw to it that this nucleus of devoted followers was welded into a durable witness which was to become the firm foundation upon which he was to build his church.

This is so audacious an account that many have not dared to disbelieve it. Others, plagued with the integrity of their own rationality, have simply not been able to accept it as true. The story so related demands a lapse of rationality, if not its utter rejection, if one is to acknowledge the miracle of the supernatural act to have actually and historically happened.

The problem ceased to be a problem to liberal Christians, once they had diverted attention from "the mystery of the Kingdom." The conviction that miracle could have no place in a world of order and law led them to set aside all such references as fantasies of the age into which Christianity was born, and to appropriate from their own age the presupposition which was normal and persuasive beyond all else, namely, moral faith. Thus the Gospel in the liberals' faith became a selective witness centering in the ethical teaching of Jesus and having its antecedents in the prophetic writings of the Old Testament.

Between this liberal interpretation of a moral gospel centering in a New Testament ethic, and the current, restive efforts of New Testament scholars to repossess the Gospel tradition, there lie the stubborn efforts of men like Albert Schweitzer, Rudolf Otto, and more recently, Karl Barth and Rudolf Bultmann, to reassess the mystery of the Kingdom and, in fact, to reinterpret the element of mystery that supervenes the events of New Testament history. What is being broken through here is the bland supernaturalism of both Catholicism and orthodox Protestantism on the one hand, and the rigid rationalism of the modernist era on the other.

What we have discussed in previous chapters, both as to the dimension of reality over reason and the dynamic and creative character of events in time, hints of the new factor in New Testament criticism as well as in constructive theology which enables scholars to reconceive these crucial happenings to which the Christian witness points. To say that it was miracle, putting to rout law and rationality is, they are suggesting, oversimplified. To say on the other hand, however, that no innovation, no mystery, was at work here in the structure of history, is to be arbitrarily imperceptive and blind. The difference here, as compared with the thinking of nineteenth-century liberal scholarship and earlier, is due to a whole range of happenings in the imagery of thought itself. Continental theologians and New Testament scholars come to this new imagery in a way different from certain British and American scholars. But by whatever path they travel, their revision of imagery takes the form of repudiating the moralistic and rationalistic bent of modern Idealism and of affirming a freedom of spirit that will not be contained within moral or rational categories, since it is a reality of grace that transcends both of them.[2] The British and

---

[2] This point is argued in a neo-Kantian way in the writings of Kierkegaard, R. Otto, Berdyaev, Barth, Brunner, Tillich, Niebuhr, Bultmann, and others; it is developed in a different way by followers of Bergson and James, in the writings of S. Alexander, Lloyd Morgan, William Temple, L. Thornton, John Oman, Whitehead, Dorothy Emmet, Susanne Langer, C. C. Morrison, John Knox, *et al.* Wieman's thought partakes of this new imagery as do John Dewey's writings, such as *Experience and Nature* and *Quest for Certainty,* but in both Wieman and Dewey an

American critics of Idealism go a step further than the Continental writers in that they replace the mechanistic notion of Newtonian physics with the imagery of the new physics and its implications for field theory. In this way they are able to correlate a concern with natural structures as being incipiently responsive to the dynamic of spirit in the way that emergent theory conceives of the concomitance of psychophysical life. Continental writers and those American theologians who follow in the tradition of Kierkegaard's revolt against Idealism hold to an ontology of freedom that assumes the imagery of Newtonian physics in dealing with natural structures. As a result the notions of freedom and transcendence tend to have a Kantian meaning as being necessary ideas that can carry no content of meaning other than being dissociated from contingency and the automatism of mechanism. There is some hint of Bergson's influence in both Tillich and Reinhold Niebuhr, but this becomes formative only as an expression of the dynamic quality of existence as seen in Existentialism.

It will be noted, however, that both groups of modern scholars, whether they are dealing with such notions as "communal witness," "the mystery of the Kingdom," "proclamation of the Word," "the Christ event," "the living Christ," "the body of Christ," "the new life in Christ," or "New Being," "the New Creation," or attempting to point up the import of "myth," of "spirit," "self-transcendence," etc., strive to convey the dynamic and holistic quality of events in history carrying these intimations, as contrasted with measurable and predictable events to which moral and rational categories apply. The language is often different, but on closer scrutiny,

---

insistent instrumentalism, looking to verification, causes them to turn aside from the perceptive field of meaning which the newer imagery provides. In this respect they are more inclined to share the modernists' sensibilities concerning the demands of rationality than to follow the lead of the new imagery in its concern with perceptual meaning.

the intent of meaning appears to be at least comparable if not always the same.

Now I take it that the conviction of both groups of contemporary scholars is that the New Testament bears witness to an occurrence in history in which a new depth of spirit became manifest and regulative. It was more than a single occurrence; it became a sequence of events, not only gathering accumulative power as a communal memory and witness, but assuming a corporate character as a living, structured experience.

What specifically happened in the initial resurrective experience appears not to be explained in this new critical literature. The ground on which specificity has had to be deferred is a technical one, namely, that the actual words and historical person of Jesus are not available to us except through "the picture" that is given us by the witnessing community. This we have already noted in discussing the meaning of Jesus Christ.

The living reality that forms the initial nucleus and organizing center of the emerging church, then, is this primordial group, they who had been brought alive, as it were, to the new life that was among them as vivid and as compelling as when He walked with them in Galilee.

The important fact to see here is that, in the judgment of modern New Testament scholarship and of theologians who take their critical findings seriously, this witness rests upon an innovation of experience, the mystery of which they are not ready or willing to explain away. The *kerygma* without this mystery, they argue, would be a half-truth—a denatured witness. For it was a witness not simply to a man who once lived, or to a man who taught remarkable truths in parables, or to a way of life; it was a witness to a depth of existence that came into man's experience as a New Creation out of the remembered love that met with tragic death and then rose again as a living reality among men. It was the saving and renewing experience of this New Creation as it gathered people together, first in modest groups, then increasingly in mounting proportions of a community, in this place and that throughout the extensive Roman Empire. The meaning of the Church is to be found in relation to this dynamic innovation within Western history wherein a new depth of grace in existence was disclosed, giving assurance of God's redemptive love.

The problem that concerns New Testament scholars and theologians alike is not only that the Church shall be seen to be a witnessing community, but that it shall have historical continuity with the One to Whom witness is borne, namely, Jesus Christ, and through Him, with the people of Israel among whom the eschatological hope of the coming Messiah was born. Thus care is taken to state that, though "one may not go back of the picture," the witness itself is organic to the life, death, and resurrection of Jesus Christ. There was a complex of events that formed a whole, which in its entirety as concrete event is to be understood as the New Creation in Christ. The Church, so envisaged, was not just a communal response that took organizational form, but a living organum that participated in the depth of spirit incarnate.

This point is important. For to conceive of it simply within the imagery of stimulus and response is to lapse back into an environmental theory of the church. This is to lose sight of the innovating mystery to which the new imagery is at pains to do full justice within its disciplined speech.

Thus John Knox writes,

The Church came into existence, not *after* the event, but *along with* the event, and is really inseparable from it at every stage, just as the event is inseparable from the Church.... The Church is thus not so much the consequence of the event as its culmination.[3]

The event, here, is of course "the Christ event," the fact of revelation.

[3] *The Meaning of Christ*. Harper, 1947, p. 97.

Bultmann states it this way:

> The kerygma of Jesus as Messiah is the basic and primary thing which gives everything else—the ancient tradition and Jesus' message—its special character. All that went before appears in a new light—new since the *Easter faith* in Jesus' *resurrection* and founded upon this faith. But if Jesus' person and *work* appear to them in the light of the Easter faith, that means that his significance lay neither in the content of what he has taught nor in some modification of the Messiah idea. It does mean, though, that *Jesus' having come was itself the decisive event* through which God called his Congregation (Church).[4]

Here is the familiar distinction between the historical life of Jesus as a person of Jewish parentage and the bearer of "New Being" or the New Creation. In other words, it was not the man Jesus as a sayer of wise sayings that created the Church, but "Jesus as the Christ," to use Tillich's words, the innovating, revelatory event.

One needs to be sensitive here to the distinction between religion as an ethic that roots in a historical life, and Revelation as an innovating event that compels the reconception of all historical life, even the historical life of the Man Jesus.

Now the next point to note in this new imagery of the Church is that, even though "the mystery of the Kingdom," the New Being in Christ appeared and "dwelt among them," the depth of this Revelatory event was not apprehended by the little group that gathered until after the resurrection experience. It was under the heightening of that event that the disciples, and they who gathered with them, employed their hindsight and the grace of vision then afforded them to "proclaim the Word" that had been given to them in this decisive experience. The "proclamation" then became the kerygmatic occurrence,

---

[4] *Theology of the New Testament.* Vol. I, Scribners, 1952, p. 43.

the bearing forth of witness to the faith and judgment that was theirs to declare.

Bultmann speaks of this initial community of witness as "the eschatological Congregation." [5] By this he means the group that continued in waiting for the end of time to come when their Lord should return.

This stage of the Church's beginnings persisted through the period of its Hellenization, its break with Judaism, and its formation into a cultus, during which the initial steps toward the development of its sacraments, its organization, and its ordinances were taken.

The next important step occurred in its development when, as Bultmann puts it, "a transformation of the Church's understanding of itself" [6] occurred. This transformation in self-understanding involved, in part, a relinquishment of its mood of waiting, or at least its recognition that the eschatological fulfillment, long expected, would not be immediate.

Our concern here is not to trace the historical development of the church. This has been done with great care by a number of scholars.[7] We have been attentive to these initial developments, flowing from the Revelatory event, with one purpose in mind: to make vivid the meaning of the church as a witnessing community.

As a witnessing community, however, the church was proclaiming, not only knowledge about, but knowledge of,

[5] Ibid. p. 53.
[6] Ibid. Vol. II, p. 111.
[7] For a careful analysis of developments in the history of the church, see Bultmann's *Theology of the New Testament,* Vols. I and II, Scribners, 1952, 1955; C. H. Dodd, *The Apostolic Preaching and its Developments,* Willett, Clark Co., 1936; F. C. Grant, *The Gospel of the Kingdom,* Macmillan, 1940; Friedrich Hauck, Koinonia, *Theologisches Wörterbuch zum Neuen Testament* (G. Kittel, ed.) Band III, pp. 808-810; John Knox, *The Meaning of Christ,* Harper, 1947; *The Early Church and the Coming Great Church,* Abington, 1955; E. F. Scott, *The Nature of the Early Church,* Scribners, 1941; L. Thornton, *The Common Life in the Body of Christ,* Dacre Press, 1942; T. O. Wedel, *The Coming Great Church,* Macmillan, 1945.

knowledge by acquaintance. It was a community participating in the "New Being" as a new creation within culture. This realization itself was heightened in the transition from a congregation in waiting to a community in which Christ became known as a living presence. Charles Clayton Morrison has summarized this point incisively, saying,

The initial preaching of the Pentecostal period placed the Risen Jesus at the right hand of God, from whence he would imminently return with power, as Messiah, to judge Israel and to create a new world in whose glory the Church, the new Israel, would enjoy the fulfilment of Israel's age-long Messianic hope. But the Lord did not return. Gradually in the development of Paul's thought, and through him in the thinking of the whole Church, a new conviction took hold. It was the conviction that the Lord had already returned, that what the Church had been calling the Holy Spirit was the living presence of Christ himself.[8]

However it is stated, the insight into the meaning of the Church as a witnessing community, participating in the new life which is Christ, is so important that one can be grateful to the new imagery which has made its revivification possible. I am convinced that, apart from an ontology of freedom with its particular concept of transcendent mystery, or an ontology of spirit made possible through emergent theory of creativity, there is no way to seize upon this insight except as one resorts to supernaturalism. And then one invariably mythologizes its meaning.

The environmental interpretation of Christianity could not take hold of it; for it was not in its methodology to be attentive to such a perceptual meaning. The very notion itself—a holistic reality transcending, yet pervading the events of history as a work of grace and ground of judgment upon all historical events—could not take form

[8] Charles Clayton Morrison, *What Is Christianity?* Harper, 1940, p. 149.

within the vocabulary and discourse of meaning which this sociological method imposed.

II

The readiness with which this insight was obscured in the organizational growth of the Church appears as an appalling and tragic fact of history. One wonders if it could ever have been as vividly held as New Testament scholars lead us to believe. Was the will to idolatry so strong that the power of salvation, experienceable only through participation in the New Creation, the living Christ, could be imagined transferred to a priestly hierarchy, making men, in God's name, the indispensable benefactors of other men?

Some hint of the logic of events is given in Bultmann's explanation of what happened in the eschatological Congregation during this time of waiting. He writes:

> In consequence of the delay of the expected parousia, *"the transcendent character* of the Church gradually came to be seen not so much in its reference to the future as *in its present possession of institutions* which are already mediating transcending powers in the present: a sacramental cultus and finally a priestly office." [9]

In this transition, Bultmann observes, a further development occurs in the outlook of the church: The reference to the future, instead of being the communal longing of an eschatological congregation, becomes the individual concern for future salvation. "The Lord's Supper becomes the medicine of immortality." [10] With the administration of this all-important sacrament depending so exclusively upon the priestly office, the way was opened for another transition in imagery whereby the power of the Holy Spirit, having become vivid as the living Christ within the eschatological Community, appears to be assumed by the priestly office.

[9] *Theology of the New Testament,* Vol. II, p. 112.
[10] Ibid.

One feels that one's insight is not sufficiently sensitive to interpret or to assess this situation of a rising, official priesthood, wherein salvation is mediated through human hands, however set apart. That there is the power of grace in relationships, one need not deny. The spirit selects its structures; of this, even, one can be persuaded. But this is done unwittingly, not through men's calculations and assumption of power. Thus the interim of church history seems to rise as a giant apostasy from which there appears to be no escape. For the very demands of structure, duration, and disciplining impel men of conscientiousness and purpose to impress themselves with authority and usurpation of power upon the sensitive life of a community witness. Calvin no more escaped it than did Gregory the Great and Hildebrand or Augustine and Cyprian before them.

One must say, I think, that every rash judgment of this evident idolatry is bound to be a caricature. It accentuates the bold lines of priestly audacity without sketching in the subtle shades of protest within the usurpers themselves against this grand pretension; without giving intimation of the vast wealth of genuine sentiment and devotion that acknowledges this poor, fraudulent gesture of divine power in human form to be but sinful man's participation in the broken body of Christ.

The impulse today among theologians, who have caught this insight into the Church's meaning as the bodying forth of the historical witness to the Revelation of God in Jesus Christ, to turn with fury upon all religion, classical, Christian, or modern, as a corrupted work of man to be "thrown upon the ash heap" [11] is at once understandable and regrettable. It is understandable because the very fashioning of this New Creation into the image of man's power and possessive spirit is an offense

[11] Cf. Karl Barth, *The Word of God and the Word of Man,* Pilgrim Press, 1928; also Kraemer, *The Christian Message in a Non-Christian World.* 1938. James Clark & Co., Ltd., 3rd ed., 1956.

so great that one cannot bear to confront it with utter candor. Yet it is regrettable, too, because in repudiating the institutionalizing of faith as sheer idolatry one dissociates himself from the responsible art of giving structure and communicable form to this act of witness.

Some distinctions, however, are necessary. The making of God into man's image is, in one sense, unavoidable if there is to be any articulate meaning expressed in the worship or praise of the Almighty. For every symbol that is employed, every liturgical act or gesture that is assumed to be appropriate to the encounter with the Most High, attributes to Him a characteristic of man's own making. The Hebrew people, who were meticulous in their avoidance of the act of idolatry, did not escape the pathology of form and symbol. They kept free of the most obvious caricature of the Holy in their taboo of the visual arts; yet not altogether. For they, too, had their temples and the prescribed furnishings of the altar. But whether this be so or not, can one say that the pathology of form and symbol is evaded when the righteousness of God is molded after the pattern of the Law? Our very speaking in praise or protest presumes to give form to the Holy One. Yet our silence, too, is a symbol when it is made a propriety of the encounter with God.

Now the distinction that is needed in order to exercise judgment in dealing with this inescapable act of idolatry in the worship of God, or in whatever communication with Spirit we undertake through our own creative expression, is that of differentiating the spontaneous act of praise and the more calculated act of simulating divine power through human acts or objects. The one is surely an innocent and transparent offering of one's creative gifts before the Lord. The other can be a brazen usurpation of power that no human hand has the right to possess, involving deceptive and demonic intentions as well.

The innocent act of praise or creative expression will still be implicitly idolatrous. Without the sensibility appropriate to the encounter with the Spirit of the Most High, it may very well degenerate into a formalism or a sentimentalism bent on domesticating the Holy. Even so, the corrective, I am sure, is not to disavow all form and symbol, or all structured meaning expressive of the life of Spirit, of the Holy One; it is rather to be everlastingly vigilant that in our acts of worship as in our acts of service we acknowledge that his ways are not to be equated with our ways, even though our ways are the best we can offer in the service of our God. The clarity of this distinction need not preclude participation in the life of Spirit within the structures that are available to us as human spirits.

III

Professor Tillich, in his delineation of the dynamics of the Protestant principle, has tried to point to a way to live with this dilemma. Tillich sees in the theological movement centering in Karl Barth a striking instance of prophetic protest in our age against the corruptions of the Christian witness in the churches through its multiple forms of religion. And yet, Tillich continues, "the question of the Protestant Gestalt cannot longer be neglected. The fact that it has been overlooked by the 'theology of crisis' has already produced some unfortunate effects." [12]

These unfortunate effects, Tillich adds, are consequences of the failure of the theology of crisis to raise the question of the Protestant Gestalt in its relation to the Protestant protest. In other words, it is a failure of this prophetic movement in modern Protestantism to confront seriously the counter question of form and structure in the living faith.

Then Tillich follows with a constructive suggestion which seems to me both sound and insistent. He writes:

There is in the center of Protestant doctrine a point at which it presupposes what we call a "divine structure of reality," namely,

[12] *The Protestant Era.* University of Chicago Press, 1948, p. 207.

faith. The divine judgment, in spite of its transcendence and independence, has meaning and power only if it is appropriated by faith, in the church and in the Christian faith. Faith is the faith of man. It does not come *from* man, but it is effective *in* man. And in so far as faith is in a community or personality, they are embodiments of grace. Faith is created by the hearing of the "Word." The Word is said from *beyond* us, *to* us. But, if it is received, it is no longer only transcendent. It is also immanent, creating a divine structure of reality. Thus it creates faith as the formative power of a personal life and of a community. The Word is said from beyond man, but it is said through men. Men must be able to say it, they must be grasped and transformed by it, and this must have happened ever since the Word became manifest *in* history—though they do not derive *from* history—if in any moment of history the Word is to be pronounced.[13]

The Protestant protest, Tillich argues, is possible, and he might have added, appropriate, only because "it is rooted in a Gestalt in which grace is embodied."[14] Thus "the presupposition of the formative power of Protestantism," he concludes, "is *the unity of protest and form in a Gestalt* of grace."[15]

"The Gestalt of grace" is one of those perceptive phrases which could only occur within the newer imagery. It seizes with vivid awareness that movement of spirit in relations that have been formed out of a common witness to the Christ. It is a holistic instance of New Being wherein the structure of spirit has become luminous in historic events. It is, as we may say, a concrete structure that has become "transparent," to use Tillich's term, thus enabling the reality of New Being to "shine through." Its transparency is due precisely to its being a "union of protest and creation." It is a structure which exists under the judgment of grace.

[13] Ibid. p. 210.
[14] Ibid. p. 209.
[15] Ibid. p. 210.

This notion of structure under the judgment of grace would seem to be the creative imagery essential to envisaging the constructive route of the contemporary Christian church. With this imagery it becomes possible to perceive the character of relations in church life that could convey to us the church's meaning as the body of Christ: a bodying forth of the work of grace within human structures, both in the sense of pointing beyond its functions as an explicit witness to the New Creation revealed in Christ, and in the sense of bearing the new life, not as its own creation, but as the work of spirit that is made concrete through "the transparency" of those structures. It is indeed a relation of "tension between the holy and the sinful," [16] between the bearer of the New Creation, which the church, as a witnessing community, is, and the church as an organized company of professing Christians. "The moment the church begins to think that it possesses the fullness of divine grace," writes Bishop Newbigin, "it has fallen from that grace." [17] But is not this but half of the story of the church's pathology? Certainly the other important half is that the moment the church forgets that it is the bearer of grace and pursues an independent course simply as people of a common mind, gathered together out of tradition or convenience, it has fallen from grace.

Both forms of pathology lead to an idolatrous situation, either through usurpation of a power of grace not one's own, or through a prodigal choice of going in search of innumerable plans and projects for their own sake as a way of witnessing to the New Creation in Christ.

IV

In our eagerness to lift up the church's role as a witnessing community, have we done an injustice to the many activities that make up the life and program of the mod-

16 Luther's phrase.
17 Lesslie Newbigin, *The Household of God.* S.C.M. Press, Ltd., 1953.

ern church? Can we really reconcile these many activities with the conception of the church as a witnessing community? Must we recognize that the modern church program with its educational and recreational dimensions is an outgrowth of an entirely different conception of the church—a center of religion oriented to the needs of the community, perhaps, rather than to the revelatory event in Christ?

There may very well be an inescapable issue here, once one begins to press for final clarification. Religion and Revelation may not be two different aspects of the church's concern; they may represent wholly different concerns, wholly different orientations of the church's role and mission. This, I take it, is what Barth and Kraemer have tried to tell us in their sharp denunciations of religion in the churches.

The issue here turns upon one's estimate of human creation, of man's work in fulfillment of his response to the grace of God. I think we cannot say that religion is always and wholly man serving simply his ideals or extolling his values. This is a form it seemed to take under liberal Christianity, where man's highest good was taken to be an intimation of God's own goodness. In fairness to the liberal one must see that he was seeking God in these value judgments and idealizations. He was not consciously worshipping or serving his own ends. Even so it becomes relatively easy for Barth or Kraemer, viewing this liberal faith from within a prophetic perspective, to make short work of it as a distortion of Christian faith.

The question persists, however: Does religion, under all auspices, merit the strictures which these men make upon it? To answer this question, we need to ask further: How may we define or describe religion in its characteristic form? Religion is what we inevitably do in expressive and institutional ways in response to our act of faith. It is our way of carrying out the sentiments we feel, the impulses and insights we are led to have, the commands we feel put upon us, and the dedications to which we are able to rise as a result of our vision in faith. One's practicing religion, therefore, be it an individual ritual or pattern of living, simply contrived, or participation in the ceremonial and communal life of the church, is a projection of one's sincerest efforts as a consequence of one's encounter with the Lord of Life. I am stating here the best possible interpretation of the religious life.

There is, to be sure, a more meager, listless, almost indolent level of religion, which amounts simply to hanging onto church membership and to going along with the program of church activities because it is the respectable thing to do, or because one enjoys being convivial. This level of religion is under the judgment of religion itself and merits no further comment.

When we look at religion, then, as the best that we do in response to the act of faith, can we say that it must be cast out; that it has nothing to do with Christian faith? One's response here will tell the tale. Any overeagerness to justify religion will impel one to insist that when man acts in utter sincerity in response to what he has encountered in faith, surely what he does will not be rejected. It may be rejected by Barth or Kraemer, but not by the God of justice and love! But this blurs the point. It is not a question of love or justice; it is a question of how to value our structured efforts, given the ambiguities of man's nature. Are these efforts wholly trustworthy as bearers of the new life? This is really the question. Conversely, any overreadiness to dismiss religion as simply man's acts will cause one not to be impressed by any such notion of religion "as the best that we do" even when done in response to the act of faith. The fact that it is man who does it invites the judgment that it is unacceptable.

Now in confronting these two opposing views, must we not see that it is the best that we do in response to the act of faith which bears at once the transparency of a faithful witness and the marks of our own ambiguities as creatures under God? It is in this sense that religion must always stand in the "crisis" of faith. That is, it requires the chastening of confession and petition. It requires the discipline of a rugged, critical confrontation with the righteousness of God. Accepting less than this becomes an uncritical, undisciplined acquiescence to habit and impulse in carrying out the work of our own hands as the work of the Lord. We then simply pursue our own ends under the assumption that we are doing God's will. The real evil of religion in the churches is this unpremeditated idolatry.

Thus when prophetic minds of our times like Barth and Kraemer cry out in their impatience with the pretension and triviality of the religion of the churches, "throw it on the ash heap, this has nothing to do with Christian faith," one cannot refrain from responding heartily. But as instantly one is impelled to reply, this is an impatience justified, but only in part. For we cannot cast religion upon the ash heap without denying our creatural response, without disowning our creative capacities, through which we celebrate and participate in the New Creation. Religion will and must persist; but it must do so under protest, under the judgment of grace. Any notion that we can behave differently, or should attempt to do so, is to think more highly of ourselves than we ought to think.

The church as a witnessing community, then, will not forsake its expressive and institutional activities in response to the act of faith. But it will pursue these under the judgment of grace. The discipline of protest, chastening the work of the church, will be proportionate to the sharpness of its witness. In the last analysis one cannot escape the conclusion that the witness is central and controlling. It is what determines whether the gathered community is really of the congregation of God, whether the deeps of the Spirit pervade and inspire the work of many hands that fashion the church's program. It is therefore the source of the creative protest by which religion in the churches is disciplined by faith, and at the same time it is what summons the life of the church to a Christian understanding of itself as the body of the living Christ.

We have yet to speak of one more quality of the church's life as a witnessing community before its full character can be perceived. It is the community of the forgiven. The realism with which the Christian criticism of the Gospel lays bare the pretensions and ambiguities of men and women would be unbearable to sensitive persons, and probably would impel the arrogant ones to cynicism, were it not for its assurance of forgiveness. Forgiveness may be taken to mean a kind of divine understanding of our plight and our failings by which we are accepted as persons. In people sensitive to the realism of their situation, the disparity between their intentions and the consequences of their acts, and often between their intentions and their obligations, the sense of guilt and even remorse cannot be wholly obliterated, not even with the assurance of forgiveness. Yet the fact of our ultimate acceptance impels us to a self-acceptance, which really amounts to acceptance of the self-understanding to which we are brought when confronting the judgment of the righteousness of God. Not to be self-accepting is to remain obstinately bound to a false idealization of our good, and of our capacity to fulfill the ideals we envisage. This not only conceals the actualities of our human nature; it borders on being an arrogant spirit, intent upon doing through our own willfulness what is in reality the redemptive work of God's love or judgment through the New Creation in Christ.

The church's realization of itself as a community of the forgiven thus opens up two possibilities of deepening the quality of its life. It brings a resource of grace to alter the situation of tension which invariably arises when people are awakened to their full self-understanding, and to transmute the plaguing anxiety, which could otherwise develop into acrid obsessions of guilt and other pathologies of the spirit, into a realistic and disciplined spirit. The realism follows from our full self-understanding. The discipline of spirit arises when such self-understanding can acknowledge and respond to the resource of grace that is given to a community of people as forgiven persons. It brings to the witnessing community, in the second place, new power of participation in "the Gestalt of grace" under which judgment it lives and upon which resource it depends. Forgiveness acts as a release from the sense of alienation or dissociation, and thus enables a people to give themselves into the keeping of this new life of spirit, into its re-creative and fulfilling power. This is the power of the Holy Spirit to do abundantly more than we are able to ask or think. And in the community of the forgiven, "the more that we are able to do" is discovered to be real and redemptive power that literally reclaims us from the idolatrous pursuit of simply ideal ends to a bodying forth of the living Christ.

XIV Christic and Culture

Throughout these pages I have been using the name Jesus
Christ to convey the new life in God which has come into
history as a New Creation. I have set this forth as a decisive event in history, summoning our human structure of
moral law and reason to a higher order of sensitivity,
impelling the canons of justice to partake of love and
forgiveness; and the logic of the mind to be susceptible
of the transformative powers of grace, which is to impel
the mind to think creatively in relation to the transcendent life of the spirit. Christ as our life in God is inseparable from our life as individual men and women and from
our life in the community of men. What it offers to each
of these facets of our human experience is a new dimension of freedom in grace, enabling us to transcend our
self-imposed limits expressive of our own internal freedom, and opening up resources beyond these given capacities. Thus Christ, as a new level of life, is an ever-present
reality of spirit that supervenes, yet, in decisive ways, in-
terpenetrates our every moment of existence. As we said
in discussing the reality of spirit, we live in a matrix of
sensitivity which is ever present in our structured experience as an impending new creation.

Culture, we have said, is our way of life as individual
men and women in community, in so far as our human
creativity, decisions, and judgments are made manifest in
a group consciousness. One can say that it is our human
flowering, made possible at certain stages of technical development within our structured life. At the level of civi-

lization it may become explicit and articulate in the form of philosophy, art, or literature; in social and political judgments; in scientific inquiry and in the knowledge and decisions that accrue from such inquiry; and together with the consensus of custom and practice which forms the pattern of sensibilities restraining or governing these activities in any given period of time. Culture, in short, is the corporate, qualitative manifestation of the human psyche expressed through a community at any given level of civilization. Here civilization is taken to mean a particular mode or period of social structure based upon technical resources.

Culture is often taken to mean a more restrictive expression of the human spirit, as being confined to the creative and imaginative arts. Thus the Hindu philosopher, Radhakrishnan, will speak of cultural and spiritual values in contrast to the material values of science and industry. My own use of the word culture, as connoting a more inclusive expression of the human spirit, rests upon anthropological characterizations which gather up all psychical and mental responses, individual and corporate alike, as being in some sense expressive of the whole spirit of man, susceptible of nurture and culture. This would mean, then, the realm of human creativity at all levels of human concern and effort, not simply its aesthetic or reflective aspects.

In the broader sense, religion, including the church, must be considered an expression of culture. That is to say, insofar as religious expressions are human creations, they convey the characteristics, along with the limits and capacities, of the culture in which they occur. From the point of view of Christian faith, as we have interpreted it, the church may not be considered wholly or simply a cultural institution. Insofar as it is a witnessing community of faith, in response to the New Creation in Christ, it expresses a new life that has been called into existence by an innovation of spirit that is other than the human spirit. Yet, however much one may press for this transcendent character of the church's life, one may not overlook its cultural dimension, which serves to limit and to qualify both its character and its performance as a structure through which the life of the spirit is conveyed to men.

I

The problem of Christ and culture, as one may see from these preliminary remarks, is indeed a formidable one. We must of necessity limit our discussion of it, focusing, in part, upon aspects which are immediately available to us, and upon others which press upon us because of their urgency. For this purpose, I have chosen to speak of three areas: culture as a bearer of the new life in Christ; some similarities and distinctions between church and culture as bearers of the life of spirit; and the Christian as a member of culture, participating in the new life of the Spirit.

However one may assess what one finds in Christian history, one may not overlook the fact that in cultures where Christian faith has assumed dominance, as in certain parts of the Middle East and in the West, the symbols as well as the sensibilities of Christian faith have become intimately bound up with the cultural forms to such an extent that to remove the Christian influence or conditioning would be to destroy the form itself. This was more particularly true during the periods of Christendom when the Church controlled the culture, as in the years following Constantine through the time of the Protestant Reformation. Here architecture cannot be dissociated from the imagery of the Cross, even to its ground plan. Painting cannot be detached from the themes of the Christian life. Music and music history cannot be described apart from its evolution within the ceremonial of the Mass, or the singing of Christian martyrs during their imprisonment in Roman cells. Political history cannot be told independently of its encounter with the life of the Church. It has even been claimed, by the American philosopher George Herbert Mead in his book, *Main Currents in Nineteenth-Century Philosophy,* as we noted earlier that the scientific conception of order was taken over from Christian theology. And I would go further to say that the Roman concept of law, as well as the philosophical notion of the one and the many as it is used in the West, may be traced to the Hebraic-Christian notion of the Covenant and the concept of relationship that it entails. More basic than these, however, is the shaping of social sensibilities, with its particular conception of right and wrong, love and justice, of human valuations centering in the infinite worth of the individual, and similar qualitative distinctions affecting human aspiration and conduct.

The story of the modern world in the West has been radically altered by the influence of the sciences, which have offered the only serious alternatives to the motifs of Christian faith in the West. Yet no one can say that science itself is devoid of Christian motivation, not to speak of basic imagery in its world view. In certain of its expressions, say in its spirit of inquiry, and in its conception of vocational ends, particularly in certain fields, as in modern medicine, it reveals an implicit if not an explicit dependence upon the Christian conception of life and its valuation of the person. Under the pressure of a defense mentality so acutely forming in Russia and in the United States, a new development in scientific inquiry has occurred in its secret experimentation which introduces a new stage of the scientific consciousness departing from these sensibilities. But one can detect, if one listens to the scientists themselves, how alien this competitive scientific research is to the basic spirit and vocation of the sciences. The genius of its enterprise has somehow presupposed and depended upon more open and inclusive methods, making its discoveries available to all men as a ministry to all men's needs.

In speaking this way of the impact of the Christian witness upon the cultural processes and structures, I perhaps am saying no more than that Hinduism has shaped Indian culture through the years, and that Buddhism has molded the forms and sensibilities of the Burmese people. But this is an important point to acknowledge. Christ and the church have not been able to remain apart from the culture of the Middle East and the West despite the concerted efforts, through the priestly office and church liturgy, through monasticism and the kerygmatic theology of Protestants, to set the church apart from or against the world. Conversely, the culture has not been able to remain impervious to the Christian witness, despite its indifference and, at times, its hostility to this witness of faith. The discerning student of history will see that even in its nonconformity, and in its rejection of the faith, it bears witness to a Christian conditioning which has occurred as an inner working within the human spirit of the West.

The truth of the matter is, as cultural anthropologists have discovered, religion, however transcendent or purist their theologies and liturgies may aspire to be, generate a cultural mythos which works deeply and silently at elemental levels of human sensibility and thought, and thus shapes the culture both wittingly and unwittingly.

One who knows intimately the story of the Christian religion within the cultures of Asia will have another version of this same process by which Christian faith has made its impact upon cultural sensibilities and forms. To be sure, the story is quite different in these instances for the reason that the role and status of Christianity, in contrast to other more dominant faiths of the East, has been that of a minority faith. Furthermore, its influence has been confined largely to selective centers of the cultures. For example, although Christian institutions have themselves been aggressive in providing educational opportunities and resources within the various cultures of the East, they have not attempted, except in rare instances, to encounter the intellectual and aestheic spheres of these cultures in their more mature, self-conscious form. Non-Christian philosophers, whom I met on my tour through India, complained that the Christians more often than not avoided any direct confrontation with the cultural life of India, and thus did not have to contend with Indian culture in its mature and more vigorous form. As a result, they have been able to persist through all these years of missionary activity with a simple apologetic of Christian faith, virtually uncontested. No vigorous critics or contemporaries have arisen among native Christians, they contended, to challenge or to compel Christian interpreters to come to terms with alternative witnesses to faith at their more defensible level. Christian missionaries, they say, have been content simply to counter with their own caricature of the faiths they oppose. For this reason, it is claimed, Christians in India have not been able to present a vigorous and defensible apologetic for Christian faith which Hindu intellectuals could take seriously.

I shall not enter into this problem, simply because I do not have a command of the relevant facts or their history. I cite it simply to suggest that, in the judgment of some, at least, both Christian and non-Christian, the Christian faith may yet have to meet in a vigorous interchange with the cultural mind of India. This may be true of Burma and of other Asian cultures as well.

Even so, I would imagine that few observers of the Christian religion among the cultures of the East over the past fifty years or more would deny that its most decisive impact upon these cultures has been, not necessarily in the area of evangelization, though this had its fruition, but in cultural innovations and reforms which, in some cases, are traceable directly to Christian stimulus or motivations. The Ramakrishna Mission in India frankly acknowledges this to be so, as have other modern reform movements in India. I am not denying the validity of evangelization, nor am I attempting to evaluate it. My impression is that in the main it has been less significant than many had hoped. It has brought to the cultures of the East a level of witness which can hardly be called adequate or impressive. The full stature of the Christian faith does not seem to be in evidence here. But on this point one is hardly entitled to a serious judgment without having had considerable opportunity to experience and to assess its significance.

What I am impressed with, however, is the degree to which basic reforms in the national life of the community seem to be related to, even traceable to, stubborn ventures in community renewal in the areas of medical missions, animal husbandry, agricultural projects, and many similar experiments as adjuncts of or even as explicit forms of the Christian witness. In this respect it would seem that the cultures of the East, through the patient and persistent ministries of dedicated men and women, have become the bearer of this new life, at least at the level of human welfare and human fulfillment. The full force of this new life in Christ has yet to assert itself, and may never be more explicit. But to this degree, and at this level of human livelihood, the evidence is as decisive as it has been in the West, where Christian influence and nurture have been in process for a much longer period of time.

But of course, impressive and important as this witness has been, it has had a relatively slight effect in its total impact on the life of the East. One can say then that, in whatever culture the church has borne its witness, the culture participates in the New Creation under the judgment of grace, whether this be known or not. This is to say at one and the same time that the culture in some sense, perhaps intermittently and on rare occasions, is the bearer of the new life in Christ, if not to the same degree, in much the same way, that the church is, and that it also profanes and perverts that new life.

II

Now if both the church and the culture are the bearers of the new life, and both are under the judgment of grace, how does one distinguish between the church and the culture? At a certain level of the church's life one does not distinguish between them. The church has a cultural dimension in the sense that the people who comprise the witnessing community participate as well in the community of the culture, and bear its markings. In fact, it may very well be argued that much of the activity of the church is cultural, and has little to do with its vocation as a witnessing community.

But there is one important difference: the church is the body of Christ, the living organon, purposively bodying forth and proclaiming the witness to the good news that is redemptive with a degree of vocation and commitment that cannot be found in the culture at large. The church is a self-conscious community or corporate body attesting to a historical fact of innovation and Redemption. The culture, on the other hand, participating as it does in the living Christ and in the life of the spirit, without, in most instances, knowing that it is the living Christ or the life of the spirit in which it is participating, can be said to manifest, to serve, and, in turn, to profane, and to reject what is redemptive in life, without knowing it to be so, without designating it with the symbols of the witnessing faith. But, then, does this not set them apart from one another in a decisive way? The one knows Jesus Christ and declares Him. The other may or may not.

"What's in a name? A rose by any other name would smell as sweet." "Before His name every knee shall bow." The issue is something like this. The cup of cold water given, though not in His name, forgiveness enacted, but not as a response to the forgiving Lord, the love that is tendered, though not as a love remembering that He first loved us; are these of a piece with the grace of the living Christ? Or, to look at it in another way: the sensitive artist, the statesman with integrity and long-suffering devotion to his task, the indispensable agents of reconciliation and peace in the cold war between power structures, the philosopher-physician, these and many others outside the bounds of the church, appear to have perceived the reality of God's grace and judgment as a living word in the routine of work and dedicated service. At times and in certain places they have been as a voice in the wilderness pointing a way—to their Lord? Well, that is the question. They who are committed in fact, but not in name— are they within the circle of faith?

Here is the nub of the matter. You either say yes to this question, or you say no. And a great deal depends upon which answer is given. If the answer is no, there can be no theology of culture, except the Christian critique of culture, or the cultural reflection of the Christian cultus. There is then no revelation of God in Christ beyond the proclamations specifically given in the self-conscious witnessing community of the church. The church is then made a closed communion because it alone conveys the living *kerygma* by which, and in response to which, grace is given.

But if the answer is yes, namely, that this less formalized depth of faith is of a piece with the living Christ, and they who exemplify it are within the circle of faith, one is really saying more than this, for one must see that in being of a piece with the grace of the living Christ, it thereby belongs to His name, and to the explicit witness to His name. The name elicits the intelligible witness of the Christian Church. It elicits a responsible and faithful following, however ambivalent in motive. All that one may say concerning the force of a sharpened focus, of a

315

self-conscious and purposeful effort, can be said of the witnessing community who, in His name, do these things in response to the encounter with Him.

But the deeper truth is that the reality of grace and its judging power is a depth of good and righteousness that will not be contained in a name, not even the name of Jesus Christ, insofar as this is understood to be a symbol ascribed by a particular community or cult; for immediately it leaps beyond the form and symbol to appear incognito in the mode of a suffering servant without a name.

Now I say this, not to minimize the role of the church as a witnessing community with its liturgy and proclamations, certainly not to lessen the name of Jesus Christ. Nor do I say it to idealize or to exaggerate the nameless acts of grace that occur in the culture without knowledge that, in this act, Christ is being lifted up. Rather, I wish merely to underscore the point that the truth of the Cross and the Resurrection, proclaiming the good news that God was in Christ reconciling the world to Himself, is a truth of history that will not be contained within any cultus. And the work of the Holy Spirit is an energy of grace within the whole of culture. The cultus can proclaim and glorify this truth, can point persistently to this redemptive good but it cannot possess it. In fact, there is always the possibility that the church, even as a witnessing community, will itself become an offense to God and to the witness of sensitive men and women inside and outside the church. It has become precisely that in history. In turn, the forms it has created, its signs and symbols, have then become a stumbling block, even a travesty upon the redemptive act of a righteous and just God. The grace of the living God is seriously obstructed and severely tried in such acts of betrayal; but it is not destroyed or dissipated. There have, in fact, been instances in history when the work of grace has found vehicles other than the authorized agencies of the proclaiming church to bear the new creation. By this means, the cultural witness has brought judgment to bear upon the institution of the church. At times it has re-created the life of the church.

Now one may ask, if the work of grace can occur outside the church, what is the point of the church? And why bother to gather these cultural responses to the work of grace into the church? There are two questions here. They need to be taken separately.

What is the point of the church? When it is asked this way, there is generally implied a discrediting of the church in deference to cultural responses to the living Christ which would seem at times to put formal Christianity to shame. The question may well be asked in this mood. The church can be a great offense, as we have said—not only to God, but to sensitive and discerning people of any age. Not only can it be faithless in its role as a witnessing community; it can be faithless in its role as a human community. Under some circumstances, apart from the judgment of grace and the forgiveness it brings, there could be nothing but contempt for an institution when it flaunts its claims with pride and pretension, when it willfully blinds and confirms its people in their own biases and prejudices, when it utilizes its power of numbers to perpetrate bigotry, ignorance, and injustice, or when it sustains the blight of mediocrity through its own unimaginative cultural expression.

But this indictment, true as it may be in certain instances, and however well it may express one's own feelings and resentments regarding the church, actually misses the point. As the institutional witness and vehicle of proclamation, the church is an indispensable means of dramatizing and declaring the Word that has been given to history. At its best, or even at its worst, it contains the community of the faithful, however ambivalent in motive and interest. This dedicated remnant, as community, possesses the dual virtue of being both a nurturing matrix, even a redemptive fellowship, and a self-conscious, articulate witness to the life of the Spirit. This historical community that works through the forms of the tradition, as well as through the devices of the contemporary institution, is the bearer of the precious cargo which the historical witness has transmitted, along with the living Word. They who form this community of the faithful may themselves be nameless. In any given historical church, one may have difficulty designating such a core as individuals. For no one may seem worthy of such a designation. Of course, this is really the point. It is a "Gestalt of grace" that issues from many individuals taken together, who are, in themselves, ambivalent in virtue, yet in their ambiguity participate in the New Creation which is the body of Christ.

This focused, self-conscious act of dedication provides a thrust of spirit and memory within the culture, conveying to it the sensibilities and power of the faith which no other agency can or does enact. In this respect, its witness is vocational and purposeful. It marks its specificity of function, setting it apart from every other social institution.

What then of the second question? Why bother to gather into the church these cultural responses to the Gestalt of grace which presumably have no part in the church's life as such? To this question I can see two answers: one is, don't bother. The other is, do bother.

Don't bother to do so can be said, in part, because the work of grace will always extend beyond the formal bounds of the church. So if one means, by this, the concern to formalize all such acts of grace, the answer is, it cannot or will not be done.

But it must be seen that these cultural responses to the new life are continuous with the depth of the church's witness, whether acknowledged to be so or not. Insofar as one can speak selectively of the Gestalt of grace, or the redemptive community, one would see these inarticulate yet deeply faithful enactments of grace as being of the same spirit, and thus a leavening force out of the same center of witness. The point here is that, however differentiated the human responses to the new life may be, the life of the spirit is one. In this sense, the witnessing community is one, though human frailties divide it.

In saying, do bother, one is expressing two concerns: one must see first that the dedicated remnant or redemptive fellowship of the church would, itself, be greatly reinforced by the inclusion of this cultural sensitivity and discerning devotion within the church's life. The church itself would be made a more effective, historical witness, were this to happen.

But one must also see that such cultural responses to the new life of spirit would benefit from such inclusion, in the way that the vitality of a creative talent can benefit from the tradition of criticism. The cultural response, in isolation from the church, carries all the risks of being independent, individuated, and uninformed by a critical tradition. The folly which can befall such cultural goodness, either in the direction of sentimental spirituality, or misplaced zeal, is well known. And even when it is responsible, it may suffer from loss of proportion. It simply is an evident fact that participation in a nurturing community of faith, and the freedom to do so, releases one from the impulse to overindividualize and to spiritualize what, in the nature of the case, is an act of free grace that will not be so contained, possessed, or domesticated. The church, at its best, is a source of realistic criticism in confronting these amorphous and often mixed-up manifestations of grace.

As a self-conscious witness to the Revelation of God in Christ the church has no peers. To this community of faith it is called, and in being faithful to this calling, it fulfills a mission that no cultural force or agency can emulate. This is why the insistent emphasis today upon the church, centering upon its role as a witnessing community, is both pertinent and imperative. The strength of the church lies in this direction, despite all the peril of

319

formalization that may beset its path in pursuing this purpose.

Furthermore, in responding to this call of faith, the church as a witnessing community actually transcends the barriers of culture in the only way that is open to it. It is in this role that it becomes a witness to the world; for the redemptive love of God is an energy of grace that recognizes no cultural barriers. The actualization of this work of grace in the structures of existence will always occur within the cultural forms and symbols available to the redemptive act; and this must mean that no cultural forms or symbols are to be spurned as possible bearers of the work of spirit, nor is any one culture destined to pre-empt the actualization of this work of grace in its forms and symbols. In this respect, the grace of God's redemptive love transcends all cultures, yet is receptive toward all. "If I be lifted up I will draw all men unto me."

III

But a further question intrudes itself: How far shall any religion that claims to transcend the cultural experience identify itself with cultural change or participate in its efforts? This is no easy problem. There are clear-cut positions that have been arbitrarily affirmed, especially within Christianity.[1] There is the view that religion, particularly the Christian religion, must always stand aloof from cultural involvement; for the authority of faith is in God, while the affairs of culture are administered by powers of this world. This aloof perspective may in time develop into open hostility toward all cultural affairs on the grounds that, being outside of authorized religious controls, they are alien to the will of God. There is also the position that identifies religion wholeheartedly with change and with furthering creativity wherever it appears. The genius of religion, so conceived, is "the break-

[1] Cf. H. Richard Niebuhr, *Christ and Culture.* Harper, 1951.

ing of old molds," as it is put. Insofar as the guiding principle here is that "the living faith of the past shall not become the dead faith of the living," it is certainly justified.

Both these positions, one must say, however, tend toward a kind of irresponsibility with regard to issues of faith and culture. The one is, on principle, indifferent toward cultural responsibilities; the other, identifying itself more and more with the cultural process itself, tends to assume less and less responsibility for its witness to Christian faith. To assume a responsible attitude toward the constructive issue in this matter of religion in a culture in ferment, one must reject both of these positions.

The concern to remain clear of cultural involvement, whether on principle or through inertia, results not only in neglect of cultural problems, but in an impoverishment of the Christian witness as well. For the obvious fact is that no religious group, missionary or otherwise, can isolate itself from the creative currents of a society in ferment without depriving its own witness of relevance; and, what is more serious, without denying to the village or city communities in which it labors the opportunity to enter judiciously into the new life that is being offered them. I must confess that I was disturbed during the few months that I visited in India by a seeming absence of vital concern with what this new order in India can mean to the presentation of the Christian gospel. The fact that the Indian Constitution assures freedom of worship and the propagation of the faith seemed to suggest to many Christians that there need be no further concern.

I should say that the Christian witness must speak to the conditions of men, not simply in bringing judgment upon them, but in lifting up the working of grace in human relationships as a vision of opportunity and of social responsibility where these are implicit in the cultural renewal of any nation or community. It has the obligation, also, to lift up and to encourage whatever in the new policies gives voice or implementation to the freedom of man, to the dignity of man, and to the dignity of his labor, for these are inherent in the Christian understanding of man. Without them there can be no significant witness. It has the obligation, further, of encouraging and, where possible, of providing facilities for realizing these goals of social reclamation within the villages to which its ministries are carried. This is to give moral and practical support to the prophetic vision of a government engaged in the renewal of its people and its cultural life.

But in our concern to co-operate with cultural change, we need to be alert to a counter-emphasis. The witness of faith is to a transcendent good as well as to its immanent working. The uncritical identification of the prophetic spirit of the Christian religion with cultural change or with cultural renewal, however valid, will obviously dissipate its prophetic power, and greatly lessen its strategic role as a minority religion. Where there is no vision, the people perish. Vision in a culture in ferment is difficult to sustain. No cultural agency absorbed in the immediacies of industrialization and in the scientific transformation of its cultural processes is apt to be alert to the far-reaching implications of its reforms. A society on the march toward scientific and industrial goals, for example, can become oblivious of the cultural and spiritual corrosion which these new forces and their demands generate.

I would be the first to defend modernization as a benefactor of any culture where this can mean the lifting of human livelihood and the intelligent attack upon social problems and issues affecting our human relations. Modernization in the sense of employing critical knowledge and improved processes for achieving social and industrial goals is an obvious good that needs no defense. But it is what this can do to the human spirit, and to the culture of the human spirit, that raises all the problems. Science and industry, when left to their own devices and ends, can sweep through a culture like locusts, stripping it of its cultural flowering—its sensitive, reflective, and appreciative dimensions. As a corrective of indulgence in spiritualism to the neglect of bodily needs, as in India, for example, or as a stimulus to enterprise and a foe of decadence, industry and science can be the culture's greatest assets. Their absence in the life of man invariably gives rise to lethargy and acquiescence, to processes of decay. For this reason, modern cultures that have felt the zeal and zest of their transforming power, and that have benefited from their capacity to lift the level of human livelihood, will not disavow them altogether. Like the iron lung that must oppress one at every breath, they are indispensable to survival in the present competition of affairs.

But, though a culture will not disavow science and industry, it need not hesitate to judge their consequences for the life and spirit of man. It should stop short of obeisance, or of aquiescence to their demands. If a culture is to retain depth and expressiveness, not to speak of integrity and vitality, in the arts and literature, in humanistic studies and appreciative interests, in religious faith and imaginative inquiry, it can allow neither science nor industry to play the role of a new messiah or a monarch in its cultural processes and decisions. Science and industry are the technical guides and precursors of progress in any society. As such they are the servants of the cultural good. In any other role they become idolatrous enterprises.

Religion, when it is alert to its witness which transcends all cultural goods, can give vision to a culture in ferment by holding steadfastly to these enduring goods of the spirit, and, if need be, can protest against their corruption or neglect. This is its prophetic task.

Thus, in a culture in ferment, bent on industrialization and the scientific reordering of its life, and this describes most cultures of the world today, I see the role of religion as being both constructive and critical, both priestly and prophetic. It can be worthy only as it participates wholeheartedly, even sacrificially, in bringing forth the new day that is struggling to be born; but it will betray its high calling if, in serving this end, it does not help cultural leaders and the people, particularly its young men and women who will be intimately affected by this transformation, to be alert to the cultural consequences of social change.

Concern with the problem of well-being can be a major goal for the people of the East for some time to come. But must they pursue these ends at the price of secularizing their society? There are those who say today that this is inevitable, and that it is the next stage in social development. Religious forces should resist this conclusion with all their insight and strength, and do their utmost to save these new centers of culture, now emerging, from such a plight.

XV   The Christian Encounter
with the Faiths of Men

Christian faith, we have noted, is a witness to a new dimension of life made known in the historical experience that has shaped the ethos of Western culture. Yet the realities of this faith are in no sense bound to the cultural forms of the West, or confined to the range of meaning which its formulations can convey. In their most sensitive efforts to communicate their witness to Christ, Christian missions have been at pains to speak in these terms. That they have so frequently and imperiously failed to distinguish between forms and realities, thus imposing their limitations of form as an absolute criterion upon others in the name of the Christ, is one of the tragedies of our cultural history. Yet it is a failing that may be readily understood even when it is not condoned.

I

The zest with which Christian people of our own day are coming to a fresh awareness of the realities of Christian faith, at the very time that peoples of other cultures are experiencing a resurgence of their faiths, prompts one to ask: Will this failure be repeated on an even grander scale in our time? Or does the realism of our age and the greater degree of understanding of one another as human beings give assurance that the encounter between peoples of various faiths and cultures can occur with more sensitivity and self-understanding?

However this question may be answered, we face the

325

very real possibility of experiencing within a matter of decades an unprecedented intermingling of peoples of all faiths and nations. This will happen, not simply because concerted plans are afoot within the various religions to make it so, but because the trend of development in world events is such that one can expect more and more exchange between the peoples of various cultures as time goes on. This is so, not only because people in various parts of the globe are becoming aware of one another, but because the very activities that are being brought into play through industrialization and the extension of scientific influence in the new nationalist states require such interchange. The East will be in need of Western facilities for training scientists and skilled technicians for some time to come. This has already given rise to a sizable and steady movement of its young people toward American and European laboratories and industrial centers, though it is reported that, for the present, most of India's prospective technicians are being trained in Australia. More significant still is the movement of life within these cultures themselves, to which we have already referred, as technological facilities develop and as industrialization progresses. The very demands of industry in a technological society draw manpower from all varieties of ethnic and religious groups. The concentration or segregation of such groups in communities is difficult to maintain where these demands are being made. In India, so we are told, village life has been going through such transitions for several years as its young men have found employment in factories and industries, which at present, of course, are located in the cities. Young people on marrying, who normally under Hindu custom would remain under the same roof with the groom's parents and grandparents in the village, are breaking away from the family dwelling to start life on their own in the cities to which their employment draws them.

These social changes in the broader areas of economic

life, stimulating the intermingling of peoples of various ethnic and religious affiliations, have their counterpart in the religious situation of these cultures. The present withdrawal of Western sponsorship of Christian missions, for example, should not be interpreted to mean a decline in the Christian encounter with peoples of other faiths. If anything, it means a more direct and vigorous confrontation with them, as we indicated in discussing one aspect of this problem in Chapter I. Even Western Christians who now go to Asian countries under mission auspices on assignments for limited periods go as participants in churches or projects which are increasingly being administered by indigenous Christian churches or lay organizations. And the circumstances under which they work tend to bring them, in many instances, into daily contact with peoples of other religions. The outlook of Christian churchmen and workers in Asia clearly means to promote this kind of forthright association. This new outlook is reflected in the following statement by a group of Asian Christians who were setting forth their understanding of the unfinished task of Christian missions in Asia:

Most of the churches in East Asia have arisen from the outreach of churches of the West, or of Australia and New Zealand. Foreign missionaries very naturally brought to these eastern shores what they were most acquainted with in the life, thought and polity of their own churches. Since the cultures of Asian countries were impregnated with non-Christian ideas which differed fundamentally from the basic tenets of the Christian faith, they naturally fought shy of any compromise or superficial adaptation of the Church's life to the life-patterns of the countries in which it was established. Therefore, the churches in East Asia have become more or less replicas of the churches of the West, so much so that they have been dubbed "ecclesiastical colonies" of the older churches. During all these centuries they have not produced even one decent heresy. They have even imported their architecture, music, theology and ecclesiastical polity wholesale from the West.

Their foreignness has repelled instead of attracted others to Christ.[1]

They then contrast this mode of approach with that of Islam and Buddhism as they spread into Southeastern cultures:

The swiftness with which Islam flashed from one end of the Indonesian archipelago to the other has few precedents in religious history. Buddhism, ostracized from the land of its birth, swept over Ceylon, Burma, Thailand, China and Japan with much ease. The secret of these successes lies in the fact that these alien faiths interpenetrated the cultures of these countries to such an extent that they shed their foreignness and became domesticated in the lands of their adoption. They were no longer "potted plants" but took root in these countries. Does their experience have any lesson for the Christian Church in East Asia? The Church planted in the East has not been left free, always and in all places, to grow in its new soil under God's guidance and without interference from the planters. That there will be great dangers of compromise, syncretism, etc., if the Churches are left free, it is readily admitted. But is there any other way for real growth?[2]

The conclusion to which these Asian Christians came in charting the course of the future is that, while Christianity compels them to live beyond the claims of their historical cultures, "they must also live in the world and seek to win their fellowmen." These comments by Asian Christians are strikingly in accord with my own observations and experiences, given in Chapter I.

Thus within the enlightened centers of awakened and independent nations of the East, the encounter between Christians and peoples of other faiths appears to be entering a new stage of seriousness. This is occurring, as be-

[1] *Christianity and the Asian Revolution,* edited by Rajah B. Manikam, Madras, The Joint East Asia Secretariat of the International Missionary Council and the World Council of Churches, 1954, distributed in the United States by Friendship Press, New York, pp. 270-71.
[2] Ibid. p. 271.

comes clear from the statements by Asian Christians as quoted, chiefly as a result of the new role which Asian Christians are playing in Christian churches within these new circumstances. More and more they are being brought directly into contact with their countrymen of other faiths.

I had some occasion to encounter non-Christians on my own on some of these issues while in India. I visited several Indian universities, mostly Hindu, with a definite view of engaging Indian educators in conversation on the new situation that was developing in India, as well as on basic questions relating to religion and culture which are of concern to Hindu and Christian alike. As it turned out, the people who were most attentive to such questions were philosophers. Sometimes I found myself confronting an entire philosophy staff of five or six members. I purposely steered the conversation away from points of agreement on the assumption that, as scholars and educators, we should be able to deal with differences in a profitable and exploratory way. And in the main we succeeded remarkably well. The conversation ranged from a cordial and gentlemanly discussion to an excited and rapid-fire exchange of deeply felt convictions and sentiments. The circumstances under which we met may have been especially favorable to such an encounter, and therefore not altogether representative of what can be undertaken. Nevertheless I came away from these visits feeling very much heartened by their possibilities for the future. These Hindu philosophers seemed eager to discuss such problems with Christians. Furthermore I found that one can be quite candid with them, and they, in turn, are usually equally forthright.

On the wider front throughout Asia and beyond, the resurgence of religions portends some significant changes in relationships between the various faiths of the world. Until recent years Christianity has been considered to be the most aggressive religion among world religions in carrying its witness of faith to peoples around the world.

329

Buddhism and the Moslem faith have also been active on the world scene with varying degrees of effectiveness, and since the opening of the present century, Hinduism has had its representatives abroad. Yet nothing comparable to Christian missions in scope and in the focus of energy has occurred among these other faiths. There are signs today suggesting that this situation is changing. The resurgence of Far Eastern religions, partaking of the nationalist renaissance among Asian people, is marked also by an awakening to possibilities for expanding their influence and aid to other parts of the world. There was a story going around in Burma during my visit in Rangoon of a Buddhist monk who called upon a Protestant clergyman in Rangoon and asked to borrow a book on Christianity. The Protestant minister was delighted and said, "Of course! Here are three of them. Take them along and keep them as long as you need them." The Buddhist monk did. After a few weeks had elapsed the monk was back with the three books and asked if he might borrow a few more. The minister was a bit taken aback at this so he ventured to ask, "Tell me, why are you, a Buddhist monk, so eager to read books on Christianity?" "Oh," said the monk, "they tell us the lights are going out in Europe and in America, so we are preparing to send missionaries to these darkened countries." Then he added sardonically, "We feel we should know something about the religion of the natives."

That this story is not pure fiction is borne out by the fact that an advertisement soliciting funds for a Missionary Society in Ceylon is reported to have contained the statement: "For the spread of the Gospel of Buddhism among the heathen of Europe." [3] And in connection with the World Peace Pagoda in Rangoon, erected by the Premier of Burma, a Missionary Training College has been established where monks are being trained for mis-

[3] *Christianity and the Asian Revolution*, pp. 138ff.

sionary work abroad. It is significant that the two languages being taught in the college are Hindi and English. The organizing of The World Fellowship of Buddhists, which held its first congress in Ceylon in 1950, clearly indicates that Buddhism is taking itself seriously as a world religion and has become awakened to its role as a missionary faith.

The zeal to bring Buddhism to the attention of other people of the world seems to be based upon the conviction among Buddhists that the gospel of the Buddha is a message of peace which is sorely needed in the present age of conflict. At the time of the Evanston meeting of the World Council of Churches, a Burmese statesman is reported to have said to an East Asian Christian leader, "What is the meaning of your Evanston theme, 'Christ the Hope of the World?' It is in Buddhism, and only in Buddhism, that there lies any hope for the world's peace." [4] It is significant, too, that certain Buddhist scholars have welcomed the coming of modern science to Asian countries, for they believe it will tend to encourage an attitude of mind that is consistent with the method of the Buddhist religion, and thus enhance appreciation of its rational approach to life's problems. Other Buddhists have been known to say, however, "We don't need science; we have Buddhism."

These anticipations of expansion among Far Eastern religions do not follow the pattern of proselyting among other religions in every instance. They may simply be in response to a widening of horizons among people recently released from foreign domination who are eager to be heard as they find occasion to express themselves in their terms. This is particularly noticeable at the level of religious scholars, where opportunities of exchange between various religious groups in Asia, and between Eastern and Western centers of learning, seem to be on the in-

[4] Ibid. p. 138.

crease. Much of this partakes of a world-mindedness which envisages a growing unity among the various faiths, though in the main it is motivated simply by a concern to give expression abroad to the insight of their own faith and to be in touch with other religious points of view. Insofar as historians of religion and cultural anthropologists contribute to such forms of interchange between the religions of various cultures, they tend to assume a relativistic point of view, eliciting from each of the various forms of faith a full expression of their central affirmations and concerns. It is significant that major foundations in the United States have become aware of the cultural significance of this creative ferment among religions, and are generously sponsoring projects to study its various aspects.

II

In this newly awakened world situation, what are the guidelines to the Christian encounter with the faiths of men? Before setting forth the judgments to which I have come in the course of my own observations, let me review some of the points of view that are now in evidence and that are making themselves felt in this new situation.

Despite the disillusioning turn of events in recent years and the insistent attack upon universalism and idealism, utopian dreams of a world faith seem to be very much alive. I recently had occasion to read many of the speeches and pronouncements that were made at The World Parliament of Religions which met in New Delhi in 1957. The same sanguine expectations that were voiced with such eloquence and fervor at the intitial World Parliament of Religions in Chicago at the turn of the century were being voiced here, and were being given additional motivation by a review of the plight of the world, calling upon all faiths to suppress differences and to join forces in a common attack upon the world's evils. One may not dismiss this concern as being wholly utopian, for in the present mood of affairs, with Communism showing itself more and more aggressive in its intention to outmaneuver all competing cultural forces and if necessary to subdue them, including religious forces wherever resistant, the relevance of such a consolidation of religious protest may not be overlooked. It is reported that the critical situation that was recently created in Tibet caused some Chinese Communists to be apprehensive lest a holy war against their cause might be in the making. This at the moment is but a conjecture and may come to nothing more. If true, it would lend force to the supposition that "religion is a huge potency" in any culture however ambiguous, and a source of final resistance to any attack upon that culture. However, such an uprising could be advanced as justification for a world front in religion only on expedient grounds. And it would bring about unimaginable chaos and tragedy in its wake. Nevertheless it appears to have a formidable common-sense appeal to many who think superficially about the function of religion in culture; and this appeal is heightened under the strain and stimulus of passions in the cold war. There are others outside of religious affiliations, with no particular interest in religion as such, who support the universalizing of faith because they see in such a development a way of civilizing what appears to them to be vestigial remains of an irrational barbarism obstructing the scientific advance of civilization.

This concern with a universal world faith, however, has impressive and substantial support from several scholarly sources as well. For more than thirty years, since the ambitious and sobering undertaking in "rethinking missions," William Ernest Hocking has been a force in this direction. His own summary of that project in a book under that name forcefully stated the case for such a universal outlook. His works since then, especially *Living Religions and a World Faith*,[5] have been more explicit in

[5] London, George Allen & Unwin, 1940.

333

making this argument. Hocking's universal vision is a judicious one. He is not advocating syncretism in the sense of an artificial amalgamation of the many faiths. His view stems from the conviction that an underlying unity of religious faith exists, and that religions, insofar as they achieve self-understanding, will come upon the basic essence that unifies all faiths. His word for this view is "reconception," which he contrasts with that of radical displacement and syncretism.[6]

The concern with a universal faith is stressed by other scholars, notably F. S. C. Northrop,[7] Charles Morris,[8] and Floyd Ross.[9] Recently Professor Arnold Toynbee has brought the vast range of his historical studies to bear upon this problem and in his own way has argued in its behalf. A dramatic action on the part of one religious body in the United States occurred last year when the newly merged Unitarian-Universalist Association took official action to play down their Judaic-Christian heritage and to become more openly receptive and responsive to all religions, looking forward, so it would seem, to a world faith. The work of the Bahai Movement is also influential in this direction, though its form of syncretism follows a pattern of thinking similar to that of certain reform groups in Hinduism, and to that of Roman Catholicism in its way of conceiving of ecumenicity. For while Bahaists are receptive toward all religions, the insights and influences they receive from these many faiths are channeled through and informed by the vision of Bahaullah, who in their faith succeeds all other prophets.

From within any of the major faiths, with the possible exception of Hinduism which is syncretistic by nature, it would seem that this universal hope, as it is commonly

6 A searching analysis of Hocking's position is made by the late Joachim Wach in *Types of Religious Experience*. University of Chicago Press, 1951. pp. 17-22.
7 The Meeting of East and West. Macmillan, 1946.
8 *Paths of Life*, Harper, 1942; *The Open Self*. Prentice-Hall, 1948.
9 *Address to Christians: Isolationism or World Community*. Harper, 1950.

conceived, misses or eludes the central thrust of its witness. For the significance of each witness of faith lies precisely in the area of differences. Where these are ignored or set aside in a concern to accentuate agreements between faiths, the incisive meaning of itself as a faith is obscured by marginal concerns writ large. It is for this reason that they who have been grasped by the essential insight or revelatory word of a religious community see in syncretism the denial, and even the dissipation, of faith itself; while they who are least involved in any specific religious community, and who cherish religion in general as an objective cultural interest, tend to argue most zealously for a universal faith.

It might be well to point out that universalism, as it is conceived and advocated within Western thinking, whether in religion or in other areas of cultural experience, commonly presupposes a certain imagery which took form in the period of the Enlightenment under the stimulus of Newtonian science. World order, which was the cosmic counterpart of natural order as it was then conceived, took on the proportions and sanctions of ultimate truth. That which could be demonstrated to be universally true or universally applicable thereby took on the finality of truth itself. I think it would not be too much to say that the decline of this Newtonian imagery in the face of relativity science has left this form of universalism without the substantial rationale that once gave it ontological support. The hope, if pursued, must rest solely upon the appeal of pragmatic and common-sense grounds.

The thesis which Professor Hocking sets forth on the basis of his Absolute Idealism is only partially countered by the criticisms I have offered. I would assume, however, that even if such a unity as he suggests underlies all faiths, it does so as a primordial ground, or as an abstract vision of their non-cultural and non-historical possibilities. Calling attention to this vision can still serve as a judgment upon each and every faith, but as a faith itself, extricated from the concrete acts of faith within cultural perspectives, it hardly seems available or desirable, given the human condition and the realities which define our concrete existence.

Much as I honor the sensibilities of the men who persist in advocating a universal faith as a solution to the religious problem, I am persuaded that it is essentially an artificial solution, and that it grossly underestimates the distinctive thrust of the religious witness wherever it exists.

In sharp contrast to this universal and syncretistic mode of thought, we are seeing today a vigorous reassertion of the particularistic version of Biblical faith within Christianity. Hendrik Kraemer's two important works, *The Christian Message in a Non-Christian World* and *Religion and the Christian Faith,* present a formidable argument for this interpretation of the Christian approach to non-Christian peoples. Whatever one may think of the conclusions to which Kraemer comes, or of the admonitions he freely gives as a guide to the Christian task among peoples of other faiths, one may not question the integrity and force of this man's utterances. His power of utterance issues from a carefully reasoned intellectual position which presupposes what he understands to be a realistic Biblical faith; yet both utterance and position rest upon a lifetime of genuine encounter with men of other faiths. Kraemer has known how to correlate a vigorous and often uncompromising witness to his own Christian faith with a remarkable acceptance of men of other faiths on their own grounds. What appears to be a dogmatic countering of their cardinal beliefs is, in his view of the matter, a forthright act of encountering them head-on with vigor and purpose, on the assumption that only in such a total and unflinching presentation of self to another self can the truth of God, as embodied in indi-

336

vidual men, be declared. This stance in itself has elemental force and is to be honored as such. With the essential thrust of his effort as a mode of witnessing to the Christian faith, however, I am basically at odds. For his sharp swing away from the contemporary stance of relativity to a reassertion of an absolute stand is bound to issue in arbitrariness or in pretension to that which, in the nature of the case, is not available to man. For if man is "alienated," as Kraemer asserts so confidently, how is it possible to apprehend so decisive an act of truth as God's Revelation with the finality of an absolute? At best this can be a voice of judgment, a shock of reality intermittently overpowering our own assertive minds when we take our finite frames of meaning overseriously, claiming too much for them. But it is not a perspective, or a standpoint which we can presume to possess as an absolute criterion for judging others—other religions, other cultures, other people in the name, and presumably with the authority of Jesus Christ. This would seem to turn what is elemental and vitally existential as a witness of faith, given to men as grace is given, into a dogmatic act.

More recently a younger scholar, Edmund Perry, has put forth this particularistic thesis with even sharper insistence in his book, *The Gospel in Dispute*. In this work, Perry undertakes to trace the lineage of the Gospel faith from the giving of the Covenant to Abraham to the appearance of Jesus Christ as "the Gospel Person" who was promised. What he succeeds in isolating is the particularistic strand that runs through the whole of the Biblical literature, setting Israel apart from every other people, and accentuating the theme of the jealous God as being the criterion for determining the Christian approach to the faiths of other people. This analysis comes into sharpened focus when it undertakes to offer its rationale for the study of religion as a way of preparing for the Christian encounter with other religions. Thus Perry writes:

337

The norm and motive of our study is the Gospel itself; therefore the first step of our method for studying the religions is to acknowledge our involvement in Gospel faith. We believe in the Gospel of Jesus Christ and participate in the community of Gospel faith, the Church. Thus committed we cannot be neutral observers of other religions. In the first place, *the Gospel of Jesus Christ comes to us with a built-in prejudgment of all other faiths so that we know in advance of our study what we must ultimately conclude about them.* They give meanings to life apart from that which God has given in the biblical story culminating in Jesus Christ, and they organize life outside the covenant community of Jesus Christ. Therefore, devoid of this saving knowledge and power of God, these faiths not only are unable to bring men to God, *they actually lead men away from God and hold them captive from God.*[10]

Perry then proceeds to define the motive for studying other religions in preparation for the task of missions, saying:

We undertake the study of religions in order to convert their adherents to faith in the Gospel of Jesus Christ. We are not impelled to this study by anything so casual as our own private and personal intellectual curiosity, nor yet by anything so crucial as our existential concern to find ultimate Truth for ourselves. But because missionary preaching of the Gospel is integral to the Gospel itself, the study of religions is of primary significance for the Gospel cannot be preached to mankind en masse but only to this or that people in the actualities peculiar to their existence as a people. Knowledge of a people's religion is therefore necessary in order to facilitate our communication of the Gospel to them in the realities of their existence. Because as Christians we are under mandate to proclaim the Gospel to and make disciples of all peoples, we readily confess that our motive for studying their religion is ulterior or missionary.[11]

[10] Edmund Perry, *The Gospel in Dispute.* Doubleday, 1958, p. 83. Italics mine.
[11] Ibid. pp. 83-84.

The intention here, one will see, is to distill from the Scriptural account a distinctive Gospel faith in the manner in which Kraemer formulates his Biblical realism. This depiction of Gospel faith within a Biblical realism is, of course, the reverse of the exegetical procedure of a generation ago, when it was the theological fashion to see this particularistic element in Biblical history as the pathology of the Hebraic religion which had persisted through Judaic, and even into New Testament history. The release from this introversion, issuing in a universal outlook, was thus advanced by liberal interpreters as being the enlightened Biblical faith, defining the anticipation of the Christian gospel.

Now I cite this opposing version of Biblical faith, not by way of saying that this idealistic strand rather than the "realistic" one is the Gospel faith, but to argue, on the contrary, that any effort to isolate a Gospel faith as a norm or directive for the Christian encounter with the faiths of men can be a hazardous undertaking, and possibly utterly misleading. For in separating out these strands, one is dealing, not with the Revelatory act itself, but with the human response to it; one might say with a particular cultural response to it. This means centering upon religion, the setting up of human formulations and institutions for expressing or conveying the saving Word of Truth as given. As such, what is delineated as Biblical faith or Gospel faith, whether in the lineage of a universal bent of mind, or of a particularistic tradition, constitutes a human response that is, itself, under the judgment of the saving act of God. Neither of these, in my judgment, may be set forth as being a defining of the Christian encounter with the faiths of men, for each in its own way bears the limiting, even the perverting characteristics of the human situation.

Seeing these two strands in tension with one another, and thus as mutually corrective of the pathology implicit in each of them, would come nearer to a judicious distillation of a guideline within the Biblical witness; but even this procedure could become arbitrary and deceptive in its very will to moderation. For the truth of reality, in which God's ways judge and re-create man's ways, is often in the decisive and radical act, not in the measured judgment. What it comes down to is this: that God's ways and thoughts, not being man's ways and thoughts, are not readily apprehended in any systematic delineation of the Gospel faith where such delineation takes the words of men, even in Scripture, as the definitive Word of God. Such arbitrary efforts to establish a Biblical norm for giving precise injunctions or directives can only result in an oversimplification of the Christian response to the Revelatory act. And the procedure belies the claim that it is God's act in history, not man's finite and often perverse word about God's act, that commands us.

Various attempts have been made, however, to mediate between the universal and the particularistic methods of defining the Christian encounter with the faiths of men on the basis of what the history of religions can teach us. Nathan Söderblom was among the first to attempt this procedure in his book, *The Nature of Revelation*,[12] in which he pointed out that "each religion, inasmuch as it is real, stands under an unconditioned obligation" and thus is expressive of a sense of holiness and obligation. These, he claimed, "are the surest criteria of genuine religion."[13] In this, as Wach observes, Söderblom anticipated Rudolf Otto's "Idea of the Holy." Certainly Rudolf Otto, one may say, moved within this mediating path in his explorative inquiries into Christian and non-Christian forms of mysticism and devotion,[14] as did his faithful student and admirer, Joachim Wach. The following

[12] *The Nature of Revelation.* Oxford University Press, 1903.
[13] Quoted by Joachim Wach, *Types of Religious Experience.* University of Chicago Press, 1951, p. 15.
[14] Cf. his *Mysticism, East and West, India's Religion of Grace and Christianity* and *Kingdom of God and the Son of Man.*

quotation from Wach's *Types of Religious Experience, Christian and Non-Christian,* succinctly expresses this reconciling or mediating view. After setting himself apart from Barth and Kraemer, and indicating his relationship, with distinctions, to Söderblom, Hocking, and Wenger,[15] he writes

The primary concern of the Christian theologian is the hearing, understanding, and promulgating of the gospel of God's redemption of man, the culmination of which he understands to be the work of Christ Jesus. His sources are God's continuous disclosure in nature, in history, in his world, and in the community of those he had drawn to himself. All that proves helpful towards the consummation of this task of interpretation and communication can be judged to belong within the sphere of theology.

The theologian cannot but be aware that, in his infinite love and mercy, God has at no time left himself without witness. It is not in the theologian's competence to delimit for past, present, or future, the self-revealing activity of God. He is deeply aware of the inadequacy and the provisional character of all apprehension of divine revelation, including his own.

To the divine self-disclosure and call through the ages corresponds the seeking and thirsting of man's heart and mind after God and his righteousness, part of which is recorded in the history of the religions of mankind.

The theologian, though conscious of his special task to illuminate the content of the divine message ... cannot but utilize for this purpose, drawing from the sum total of man's religious experience, the insights "revealed" to men of God everywhere ...

It is the task of the theologian to determine the depth of insight into divine truth manifest in non-Christian religious expression, from his awareness of the love and grace of God, revealed in Christ and in the manifestations of his will in nature, in history, in the

---

15 Wach leans heavily upon a view of Christian revelation developed by Professor E. Leslie Wenger of Serampore College, India, in an essay on "The Problem of Truth in Religion; Prolegomenon to an Indian Christian Theology," in *Studies in History and Religion,* edited by E. A. Payne, Lutterworth, 1942.

community, and in the soul of man, while remaining conscious of the limitations of this apprehension.

It is precisely the concept of the Holy Spirit of God, unduly neglected by modern theologians, which should be the guide in all attempts at the determination of the "germs of truth," inasmuch as it represents the only legitimate criterion by which to judge where God speaks and is present." [16]

One will detect in this passage the irenic, yet specifically focused Christian view of Revelation that underlay Professor Wach's approach to this problem, and which characterized his dealings with people of other faiths. Wach's concern to remain faithful to the Christian witness was fully as marked as it was in Kraemer, and his relations with non-Christian scholars and leaders, equally forthright and genuine. The contrast between the two men and their positions stemmed from the different weight that each one gave to the fact of "general revelation" and its claims upon the Christian's understanding of what specifically had been wrought in Jesus Christ.

It has seemed to me that all three of the perspectives which we have noted view the problem of encountering peoples of other faiths and cultures within an imagery of thought that no longer takes full account of the realities and circumstances involved. The revisions in imagery and perspective upon our human situation are so radical, as I have tried to suggest throughout this book, that we would do better to try to extricate ourselves altogether from this dialectic between universal and particularistic emphases, between general and specific revelation,[17] and con-

[16] L. Wach, op. cit. pp. 28-29.
[17] The contradiction implicit in such a term as "general" revelation calls attention to the dilemma in which theologians have found themselves in dealing with the witness of other faiths. As my colleagues Preston Roberts and Charles Long have insisted, there can be no such thing as a "general" revelation. All revelation, if it is really revelatory, is specific. The corrective which relativity theory brings to our thinking enables us to deal with this matter more forthrightly, and to acknowledge all revelatory acts as being concrete and thus specific.

front the problem afresh, if this is possible. In what follows I shall undertake to contribute to such an effort.

III

The notions of depth and complexity, replacing the imagery of clear and distinct ideas, give the clue to changes in our mode of thinking which may enable us to get new leverage in dealing with these issues before us. These notions have plunged our generation into a situation of thought and imagery in which rational and irrational elements traffic together. This simply means that our frames of meaning can account only in part for the realities that we confront or encounter. It means, too, that something has happened to our very processes of perception and cognitive response to enable us to see and to feel realities, or to experience them in more organic ways, such that we have novel instances of feeling the shock of reality, of encountering facts of existence, that reach beyond our self-contained acts of experience or our enclosed mentalism. The whole of our modern discourse, insofar as it partakes of the revolution in fundamental notions, to which the sciences have given the greatest and most concentrated attention, is expressive of this new orientation of human thought and experience.

Now relativity in this context simply takes account of the concrete stance in which all thinking and living is cast. The concretely real means in this instance, not just a fragmentary disclosure of the universal, but a unique and decisive disclosing of reality in all its fullness and glory as event. Depth of being is in God, but His concretions, prehending His creative event with varying degrees of relevance, stand forth, even amidst their perishing, as abiding instances of the reality which is simultaneously of God and of itself, and of some community of men. In their minimum meaning then, creation and Revelation come to the same thing. That is, God gives of Himself in every act of concretion.

343

There can be no denial, therefore, of Revelation as a general mode of actualization. And so long as we hold to any presupposition of the communal ground of being, in which men are made for God, for other men, and for themselves, this general mode of actualization must imply general access to this creative ground, if only at the level of bodily feeling. Men inhere in a life that is in God everywhere. This is the elemental truth of human creation that is derived from the creative act itself.

But the limiting circumstances of each actualized self, together with its freedom as a concretion, opens up another story of its career which is forever in tension with this communal ground. Thus while immanence pervades the deeper ground of our existence, transcendence intrudes at the point of our finite limits as free and individuated selves.

Now what relativity asserts is the reality of the concrete occasion; not that every occasion bears the same weight of meaning, but that each, in its own circumstance, bodies forth its distinctive disclosure as an event of actuality, prehending the creative act of God with its own degree of relevance, and actualizing itself as a specific character and event in a specific space and time.

The configuration of selves that forms what we call communities, which, in turn, can fashion a common culture within a homogeneous level of civilization, introduces a corporate consciousness of meaning and a corporate witness to events. The drama of the self is assimilated into the drama of communal acts and valuations, though never wholly so except at levels where coercion dissolves the freedom of individuation into subconscious acts of conformity; or where common commitments transmute individuated freedom into a creative solidarity.

But the life of a people is everywhere characterized by having access to three dimensions of concrete reality: the primordial ground of each individual person as actualized event; the individuated selfhood of each person, insofar as this can be articulate or expressive; and the cultural history in which the drama of corporate existence is enacted.

The primordial ground, though subliminal, is the one common bond that unites all persons and communities of people. This is their life in God. Universality, then, is itself primordial, having its basis in the act of creation to which all concretion is ultimately due and ultimately beholden. In its ontological aspect it would appear to go beyond cultural form, but actuality, whether in individuated form, or in the communal cultural history, is concrete. Its perceptiveness, its judgments, its formulations, intellectual or institutional, as well as its art, poetry, and religious witness, partake of this concreteness, and in that sense are relative to it. But we must remind ourselves again that the term "relative" in this context means not simply partial or limited, but decisive as well—decisive in the sense that in this time and place reality has spoken. The structures of meaning, equal to a particular level of creative expression, sensitivity, and concern, have bodied forth a particular configuration of living reality as an emergence out of this primordial universal ground.

The universal ground, understood as the act of creation or creative act, is not in itself to be understood as a depth of reality, transcending or supervening each concrete occurrence in the way that the Absolute was understood to complete and fulfill the concrete universal. Creation is an instance of concretion, common to all individuated persons, which defines the base of our humanity. Through this creative act, we participate in a depth of reality which is in God. This primordial act bequeaths to each man as creature the capacity to apprehend both the humanity of another individuated being, and the lure of the creative act, which is, itself, an assertion out of the depth of sensitive reality which is in God. To be human is thus to be expressive, both of an affirming, yet apprehensive, response to the depth of reality, which is our

345

primordial faith, and of an awareness of another man as man. Such universality as we are capable of exemplifying roots in this primordial ground of each man's existence.

Universality, then, is not something we as men can create or bring about through artificial means of negotiation, compromise, or conquest. What we effect through such means are strategies, or devices for curbing and controlling the creativities that arise out of our concreteness. Such strategies and devices are abstractions which we consciously devise, and as such are not of a piece with the concreteness that is expressive of our existence. In this sense they are impersonal structures of meaning or power that serve common ends dissociated from or extending beyond our level of concreteness. The clearest expressions of these impersonal structures of meaning and power in our present world order are science and industry. One might assume that the United Nations would be the most obvious symbol of such universality; but, on the contrary, it is clearly an association of concrete realities, expressing themselves through articulate representatives of those concrete interests and realities. There are efforts afoot to extend this kind of world order in the realm of law and religion. International law and agreement already exist in limited form; but world religion or world faith is as yet but a matter of conjecture. The evolvement of such an impersonal structure in the realm of religion would seem a contradiction in terms; for it is the nature of faith to emerge out of personal existence. As such it can only be a concrete reality.

Universality, then, insofar as it is integral to existence as our primordial faith and our humanity, is a depth of being that must issue forth through our concreteness as a reassertion of our creative ground, or as a redemptive experience re-enacting this sensitive act. It may do so, too, through the personal encounter between human beings when, to use Buber's familiar terms, the I-Thou of two subjective selves meet in awareness of one another as human beings.

The circumstances of this incursion upon the actualities of existence when, as it were, the universal ground breaks through into concrete experience are themselves distinctive of the cultural history in which they occur. In this respect they are relative to that cultural history. However, this is not to say that the incursion itself is limited, or applicable only to that culture. Separating out the Revelatory event and the structural elements of the culture through which the event has occurred is simply not possible as an act of analysis. For structured meaning and occurrences are always embodied events. What is necessary is that kind of attending or listening by which the living Word of the event can speak out of its structured form as event and as disclosure. It is precisely this kind of attending or listening that is intended when one speaks of the Word as issuing from the pages of Scripture, or of the New Creation in Christ being bodied forth in the witness of faith. Something cultural and revelatory is being simultaneously conveyed in this act of communication. Something universal (and thus ultimate in the primordial sense) and concrete is being simultaneously declared.

IV

Now what does this analysis mean in relation to the problem which we are considering, the Christian encounter with the faiths of men? It means first of all that Revelation is itself culturally conditioned; yet it is a Word out of the depth of our reality in God, spoken to all men. We are in no position to judge or to measure the normativeness of this Word for all men. We bear witness to it as such, even declare it to be such; but this bespeaks its decisiveness for us. We proclaim it as the truth of existence which is to be conveyed to all men. The response to this witness is not ours to manage or to assess. Every act or effort, looking toward a self-conscious manipulation of other people to persuade or to compel them to respond, is an overstepping of the role and a profaning of the relationship that exists as a holy bond between ourselves and the depth of our reality in God, on the one hand, and between ourselves and men of other faiths on the other.

The significance of any witness to faith is twofold in that it simultaneously speaks forth out of a primordial ground in which all men share their humanity, and out of a cultural history that bodies forth, not only the commonplaces of its concrete history, but the innovations, the peculiar and distinctive intrusions of judgment and grace which its own structured experience has been able to receive and to make articulate. I am insinuating here that Revelation, in order to be revealing, thus, in fact, "revelation," must be received within some structured experience; and that the receptivity of such structured experience to the shock of God's reality, or the innovations of his grace and judgment, varies from culture to culture, and from one period of history to another, according to whatever generates the probabilities of response. "Just in proportion as an experience is probable will it tend to be directly felt," wrote William James. Cultures or periods of history are prepared through the exigencies of their concrete history for certain innovations to occur. The rhythm of events within their chronological time span builds toward a *kairos,* a time of reckoning, which is at once a time of judgment and discovery. There is a time of ripeness within cultures, as in personal histories, when the Word beyond our rigidly human frames of meaning can be spoken and expect to be received. What is received as a Word beyond our structural experience is, in part, made possible by our own brokenness; that is, by a momentary collapse in the rigidity of meaning and forms of meaning such that innovation and judgment can reach us, and seize us, as with a vision transcending experience. It is made possible also by the heightened degree of sensitivity to which any people is made susceptible in such times of stress or crisis, when the limits of the human structure are laid bare, and their trust in historical forms is made uncertain.

The situation of ripeness within human structures may also be accelerated by leaps of insight or innovating procedures resulting from a sense of failure in customary procedures. These momentary breaks in established forms of intelligibility have the effect of releasing the human psyche from their automatic spell of rationality sufficiently to be receptive to what may be forming beyond its frames of meaning. The initial situation may manifest itself as a pervasive mood of misgiving or disillusionment, even moving toward a despair of attaining meaning. In this mood, what comes to one to restore orientation and a sense of meaning will appear to grasp one holistically. The situation itself seems to speak with judgment and redirection.

Cultural forms, and the structured experience of people within a given period of history, thus rendered pliable and sensitive to the creative passage, give way to openings into history through which a heightened vision of a people's cultural history can intrude, offering a fresh grasp of intimations of depth of meaning hitherto left uncalculated. The deeps of the creative passage are literally opened into concrete history disclosing its eschaton as this particular moment of history can unveil it.

Now the decisiveness of these occurrences is, in part, relative to the circumstances within the culture itself, and, in part, to the level of history or of human emergence at which such innovation occurs. That is to say, every innovation within cultural experiences may not be accounted decisive or revelatory for the whole of history, though the line between what is decisive for a given people and what is revelatory for all mankind may not be readily or sharply drawn. Cultural anthropologists and historians of religion may be of help in giving some appraisal of these occurrences on the basis of their understanding of

349

the structures and levels of human experiences; and they may even attempt some graduation of cultural witnesses. This in fact has been attempted. Thus the emergences of the cultural life within the Tigris and Euphrates Valley and in northern India have been singled out as instances of rare sensitivity in the life of the spirit, while the valley of the Nile and the islands of the Mediterranean, particularly Greece, have been designated as areas in which ethical sensitivity or the "dawn of conscience" first occurred. A hierarchy of cultural witnesses might well be formulated, though this would always be hazardous, and could also become highly arbitrary.

The only point I am concerned to make here is that there is ample ground, speaking out of the context of cultural anthropology and the history of religions, for asserting the decisiveness of the cultural witness of a given period of history within these major centers of human creativity. In this respect the Judaic-Christian witness to the new life in Christ stands alongside of the Hindu-Buddhist witness, and that of ancient Greece, and the Nile, as being of singular importance to world history. If it is true, as has been claimed, that the Indo-Aryan strain of culture stems from Mediterranean origins and beyond, the range of decisive historical witnesses narrows to some extent, though it may be argued that what is distinctive in the Indian cluster of faiths issued from the Indian experience and is in no important sense a derivative of the Mediterranean witness.

However one resolves this complex cultural issue, that which seems to me to be pertinent to the theological problem with which we are grappling, namely, the Christian encounter with the witness of other religious cultures, can be reduced to five observations:

1. That the witness of all faiths, as being expressive both of a primordial experience of ultimacy and of its reality within a concrete history, is to be acknowledged, respected, and to some degree heeded.

2. That the witness of each faith, though acknowledged to have some claim upon all men as being in some
sense expressive of ultimate apprehensions, bears the limitations of its own concrete circumstances. To this extent,
it is culture-bound, even though it may point or reach
beyond this locus.

3. Because of this inescapable conditioning of a limited
cultural experience, each witness, however much it may
bear intimations of ultimate dimensions of man's being,
is ambiguous, and stands under the judgment of the reality
of God to which it bears witness. The decisiveness of
man's language in recorded scriptures, laying claim to
absolute truth, does not alter or lessen the ambiguity that
inheres in such witnessing.

4. Despite this ambiguity, however, one who bears
witness to the reality of God's grace and to the judgment
of His love upon us, is under obligation to speak forth the
truth that is in him, and to do so with the heartiness and
conviction that accords with the intensity and certainty of
his faith. In no other way can the reality of grace which
has come into this historical experience be bodied forth
as articulate meaning. The limitations inherent in the
cultural witness and the ambiguity of what is bodied forth
do not gainsay the fact that a genuine existential witness
has been given, an offering before God and before men of
other faiths and cultures, which can have its own merit
and purpose for what it is, no more and no less. In such
an act, God speaks through men, despite their frailties,
their ambiguities, their sin and inadequacies.

5. What is spoken forth through such a witness may
not be the specific words which men themselves contrive
or intend. In every act of bearing witness, there are at
least four modes of events, other than the actual speaking
forth, which offer greater likelihood of conveying the
Revelatory word of one faith to the people of another
faith and culture. They are (*a*) the simple act of one
human being speaking to another human being out of the

intensity and integrity of his existential witness of faith—
i.e. the act itself, not the symbols employed or the literal
meanings expressed; (*b*) the overt acts of identification,
empathy, or kindliness expressive simultaneously of the
primordial humanity commonly shared with all men, and
the energies of grace now operative in one, speaking out
of the depth of the New Creation; (*c*) the experience of
judgment in confronting another cultural witness to the
Revelatory act of God; (*d*) the situation of grace and
judgment in which all human participants stand in any
such encounter, both the one who bears witness and the
one who receives what another can give, as these human
acts open into the reality of spirit, confronting their humanness with a dimension of sensitivity and goodness that
transcends their existence.

Each of these occurrences follows somewhat indirectly
from the overt act of speaking to a people of another
faith or culture. They are, as it were, nuances of meaning
and energy giving depth to such an act. Much that occurs
here is unintended and cannot be planned or directed. It
is, in large measure, unmanageable; for it follows from
primordial and redemptive aspects of the occasion which
are out of men's hands, even though in imagination or
anticipation they may conceive of it happening.

There may, of course, be released in the direct act of
witness certain offending behaviors or attitudes which
will block off the nuances of meaning, or transmute them
into barriers or feelings of hostility. This is always a possibility. The offense may not be intended or even justified
so far as the direct act itself may be concerned. Something
in the situation, or in the structure of experience of the
one receiving another's witness, may throw up impassable
barriers. This, of course, is precisely what has occurred
in missions at the present time. Designs or strategies calculated to counter such resistance or hostility are fraught
with all sorts of dangers and possible folly. It has become
a growing conviction of mine that nothing less than the

acting out of the integrity of the witness itself is justified here even though this may be the way of the Cross.

One must face up to the fact, therefore, that confronting men of another faith with the Revelation that has come to one out of the circumstance of one's own cultural history is serious business, perhaps the most serious business that we as human being undertake. I would not exaggerate this point, however. In large measure, these nuances of meaning and energy, giving depth to the act of witness, will be present, enabling one to do "exceeding abundantly above all that we can ask or think." But in all such acts there are no assurances beyond the grace that abounds through the integrity of one's witness and one's unfailing trust in God.

V

Thus far we have spoken of certain general conditions bearing upon our problem to which a knowledge of the growth of human structures and the history of religions has contributed. These will seem pertinent to the theological problem insofar as one sees the need of being attentive to the sciences of man and to the study of social structures giving form to men's thoughts and modes of living.

We need now to note certain theological observations which can guide our thinking on this problem.

1. The freedom of God would seem to argue that no human speech or formulation can adequately or even accurately convey the reality of God's saving act in history.

2. Nevertheless, speaking within the language of men, it is the claim of the Christian faith that Jesus Christ, in His person and work, brought the good news of this saving act to a remnant within Judaic history and thereby initiated a new humanity.

3. Now if, in our critical judgment, we accept what New Testament scholarship is at pains to make clear to us, that we cannot go behind the picture of Jesus por-

353

trayed by the witnessing community, what we have in the New Testament Gospels is that which points us to the reality of this New Creation. We have a faithful witnessing to the reality of God that was in Christ, reconciling the world to Himself. But it is an act of witness with which we are dealing here.

4. This witness that is borne to the New Creation in Christ must be taken with utmost seriousness as opening up to us a depth of spirit and saving grace which can reach us and do exceeding abundantly above all that we can ask or think, despite our limitations as human creatures, our sin, and our idolatrous tendencies to fashion this life that is of God into our human image, despite our almost inevitable impulsion to assert this human, Christian image as the authority of God over all men. But the impulsion to take this humanly formed word as the authority, as the defining criterion, is great.

5. The freedom of God would argue that God has to do with all men, all cultures, all stages of human history, in His way, in His time. The depth and scope of this Infinite dealing with men of all ages and all races is a mystery which no one human mind can apprehend, and no one culture may engineer or supervise. God deals with the structures of history, works through them, recreates them, and redeems them as the sensitivity and ripeness of occasions permit and demand.

6. Each culture has its own access to what, in its own history, has been wrought to convey the saving grace of what, in our Christian witness, we know to be the New Creation in Christ. That Christ, the New Creation, is very God would lead us who make this claim to assume that this would be so. At what depth, in what form, and through what media, we cannot be sure. For our cultural forms, our sensibilities and structures of meaning, while they lend intelligibility to our discourse within the context of our history, become barriers between us and the peoples of other histories. And these barriers shut us

out from the depth of sensitive meaning and grace which appears in forms other than our own, and cause us to attribute other meanings to their religious acts, or to judge them in negative ways. That there is gross idolatry, vanity, pretension, pride, and evil in many forms in the religions of these other cultures, we may well assume; for they are human creations. They bear the marks of human depravity. We know this, not by contrasting what they have with what we have as Christians, but by observing that what we have as Christians, our Christian forms and symbols, our categories, doctrines, and practices, all betray our idolatrous ways. God help us, we can do no other as men and women who presume to arrest the freedom and dynamic spirit of God by seeming to capture and to incarnate his reality in our limited form and speech. Thus our very best of human effort, our human creativity, is our idolatry. And we know every other human community to be susceptible to the same human failing and pathology. Thus I say, our very best of human effort, our religion, is our idolatry.

But our very worst presents yet another aspect of our sin and our perversity. And this we share with all men.

7. As between religions, then, Christianity and other faiths, there are grounds for saying that no one of them may stand in judgment of the other, or presume to have the sole criteria by which all other faiths may be condemned. Each may have access to the Source of Judgment, some more explicitly and definitively than others. That is, their very act of witness, what they are able to convey in declaring what God has wrought, what, in the light of their witness, God demands, can serve to evoke in others a sense of being judged. The goodness and greatness incarnate in the Word that is spoken, the proclamation, can be as the rays of the sun that fall upon the just and the unjust, not with the explicit intention of judging, but simply in the act of proclaiming the good news that has been given to a people.

8. The gift that each man of faith may bear as his distinctive witness, this may be offered, though it may not be received. Yet the offering of the gift of grace to people of another faith becomes a command, even a compulsion to one who, in joy and fullness of heart, has the goodness to proclaim.

That men are to be vessels of the Most High, bearing forth the water of life to all men, is a deduction which may be safely made. That any one of them is to be designing and manipulating of other men's lives and circumstances and the judge of their faith is surely a misguided and pretentious claim.

9. I would question whether any one outside of another faith can really trust his own judgments regarding another's faith. Arrogance, bias, ignorance, estrangement, along with confirmed sensibilities inherent in one's own cultural and religious situation, contrive to alienate one from such a faith. Where one has the will to overcome these barriers, there usually follows an overindulgent sense of identification and tolerance that both falsifies and sentimentalizes the factors involved. Any notion that one can bypass or transcend these human barriers in any simple or theoretical way is to ignore a fundamental reality in any such encounter.

10. One could say that the Revelation attested to within any one faith can have specific meaning only to one who has lived within the cultural ethos through which the witness is borne. One does not seek to transmit this ideological or theological aspect beyond the community of witness or the cultural experience to which it is integral.

Yet each revelatory event speaks out of a human situation to a human situation, bearing upon inquiries which men as men recognize and, in their own terms, understand. Self-giving in behalf of another person is a human act. Concern with another person's well-being is also a human act. The expression of joy or sorrow conveys elementally shared emotions. These provide a threshold through which the human community speaks across differences and divisions.

VI

The Christian encounter with the faiths of men is to be guided, not only by what Christian faith, through its own distinctive witness, knows of the Redemptive act of God in its own history, but by what all men can know and experience of the creative act of God through their own humanity. Men have access to one another as human beings in ways that transcend all cultural and historical barriers. To make this point I shall lift out a page from one of Karl Barth's formidable volumes on *Church Dogmatics* (Vol. III, Part 2). The "new Barth," as Emil Brunner has called him, has been saying some surprising things in recent years, as contrasted with what came from his pen during the earliest years of his writing, or with what continues to come forth from the lips of those who call themselves Barthians. And in this third volume Barth has voiced what can only be described as a striking and stirring depiction of our humanity.

Barth starts with the God-Man as depicting the internal relations of God's Own Being made actual within existence, thereby becoming the ground of man's being. Man knows his relation with God as creature through the Man, Jesus Christ, and participates in that relation through Him because Christ is this ground in existence (the New Creation). There is no way by which we understand our full meaning as creatures in relation to God, Barth asserts, except through this vision of Jesus Christ as our creative ground.

There are, however, the phenomena of humanity. This is the vision we each have of ourselves as man in relation to man. Barth insists that the full meaning of this humanity cannot be had apart from Jesus Christ; nevertheless man's humanity is visible apart from a knowledge of

357

Christ. What is our humanity? This Barth tries to explain under three points: First, "The Humanity of each man consists of the determination of his Being as being-together-with the other man." Secondly, "Humanity, as being-together-with the other man is to be distinguished from Jesus' Being-for-man." This is Barth's way of distinguishing man's humanity as a relationship with man from its ontological relationship, the human encounter from the divine ground. Thirdly, Barth stresses that our humanity is to be understood primarily as "our being-together-with *one* other man," not simply in the context of other men. This implies that our humanity is not our communal character as such, but our encounter with another person. At times he speaks of it "as man in relationship to the woman; or woman in relation to the man." "Being with," Barth writes, "means encounter." Hence being with the other man means encounter with him. Our humanity, then, is "the determination of our being in encounter with the other man." [18] The point being emphasized here is that our humanity is in this I-Thou encounter between persons; and that we cannot possess or convey our humanity except as we express ourselves in this way, as a person in relation with a person. Gerhard Spiegler brings this point out sharply when he translates Barth as saying that "man cannot say 'I am human' as if to say he is human out of himself and in terms of himself; but he must say 'I am human in the encounter.' " [19]

Not everything that man does or that can be said about man is to be associated with his humanity. Being born and dying, eating, drinking, and sleeping, developing and maintaining myself, propagating my species, working and playing, acquiring possessions and exercising my powers and thereby fulfilling my aptitudes, "all this as such is

[18] Karl Barth, *Church Dogmatics.* Vol. III, Part 2. T & T Clark, 1960, pp. 247-48.
[19] Gerhard Ernst Spiegler, "Man's Being and Man's Humanity," unpublished paper, p. 4.

not my humanity." [20] In all these activities and functions, Barth observes, man can be either human or inhuman. Barth then proceeds to give four marks of man's humanity, each one presupposing the other:

1. Openness to another as a human being. "Where openness obtains humanity begins to occur. To the extent that we move out of ourselves, not refusing to know others or being afraid to be known by them, our existence is human." [21]

2. Talking and listening to another. "A word spoken by me is my active self-declaration to the Thou, my spontaneous crossing of the necessary frontier of mere visibility in relation to the other. As I take to words I testify that I am not leaving the interpretation of myself to the Thou, but am going to help him by at least adding my self-interpretation." [22] But the I has also to receive the expression of the other. Thus I must listen to another and receive his interpretation of himself. [23]

3. Being there for one another, however limited. Openness to another, talking and listening to another, says Barth, are preliminary steps, expressing the lower level of our humanity. We climb a step higher when we are prepared to "be there for the other, at his disposal within the necessary limits." [24]

4. The fourth mark of our humanity is evident when we do all this joyfully. "We gladly see and are seen, we gladly speak and listen; we gladly receive and offer assistance. This can be called the last and final step of humanity." [25]

When humanity is described in this way, says Barth, it is good unequivocally. Barth then adds this telling statement: "We do not associate ourselves therefore with

20 Karl Barth, *op. cit.,* p. 249.
21 *Ibid.,* p. 251.
22 *Ibid.,* p. 254.
23 *Ibid.,* p. 255.
24 *Ibid.,* p. 260.
25 *Ibid.,* p. 265.

the common theological practice of depreciating human nature as much as possible in order to oppose more effectively what may be made of man by divine grace." [26] Human nature as expressed through our humanity, then, is "good human nature."

Now, says Barth, this humanity which we have thus described is common to all men. And it can be known by men other than Christians. Knowledge of our humanity is not a special privilege of Christians. In fact, non-Christians, he says, can even be more human than Christians. Through sin, of course, this humanity becomes sick. But this is so among Christians as well.

Now this remarkable analysis of the phenomena of humanity gives me the courage to say what, for many years, I have wanted to say, namely, that the Christian's encounter with men of other faiths is not initially, and possibly not ever, in terms of his most distinctive and self-conscious witness; certainly not in terms of theological doctrine, or preaching that conveys such symbolic meaning. Rather, it is initially, and, in many instances continuously, at the level of man's encountering man, people encountering people, at the level of their humanity. Understand how this term is being used now. Barth has expressed it most aptly in his four points: openness to one another as human beings; letting the other person understand me by talking to him, and listening to him; being ready to assist another, being there for another; doing all this joyfully.

Unwittingly, I should say, many valiant souls who have served their Lord on the mission field have taken this path in their encounter with the faiths of men. We have often spoken of this way as being incidental to the main business at hand. If one has emphasized it, one has been inclined to trivialize it through an oversentimental treatment of it. Is it not possible that this is our point of

[26] Ibid., p. 274.

360

encounter; and, at certain stages of our existence, possibly for all of our present history, there is no other point of encounter save through this threshold of creation, which relates us with all men as human beings?

Now there is no assurance that, in being together at the level of our creation (our humanity), we shall come together at the level of our witness to Redemption in Christ. The distinctiveness of our several witnesses may persist. Our differences may persist, probably should persist, and engage us frequently as people of many cultures. There may be no hope of a world faith as a conclusion to such continuous encounter. Yet the barriers that arise from differences at the level of our most serious witness may be transcended through the phenomena of our humanity. In such an encounter we can live together with our differences: yet more than this may follow. For out of this encounter, where we live up to the promise of our creation, where we are open to another as human beings, whatever else may ensue, the miracle of a higher encounter may follow. In this higher encounter, that which has been closed to us as people of our several cultures, may be opened to us; not on any basis that we contrive, but on the basis of a New Creation that can thus occur, disclosing our common ground of being which, in Barth's language, constitutes "the divine Other of every man, even Jesus Christ."

What we do in this humble way of being open to another person, being there for him, may be the human act by which the reality of spirit, conveying the reality of grace as a New Creation, will be made vivid to another man, thereby disclosing to him his "divine Other."

"There is no way," says Barth, "by which we understand our full meaning as creatures in relation to God except through this vision of Jesus Christ as our creative ground in existence." I would add to this that there may be no way by which this vision of Jesus Christ, this New Creation, our creative ground, can be made vivid to one of another faith, except through this threshold of our humanity—being open to another, being there for him.

Now this seems to me to call us back to something quite elemental, yet quite real. There are ways by which Christian and non-Christian people within a common discipline can cut across barriers of culture and religion and engage one another in a most profitable exchange of meaning and mutual criticism. This can have important consequences, even for our understanding of Christian faith. But the encounter between men is not solely an exchange of symbols. In deeper ways it is a confrontation of realities—realities which, at elemental levels of our humanity, speak for themselves, and thereby summon us to what is saving beyond our humanity. These are the realities which speak forth out of the act of faith.

Index

Civilization, distinguishing between culture and, 212f.; relations between Eastern and Western, 3-18, 326-7

Collingwood, R. G., 143f.

Commitment, as a factor in science, 152ff.

Communism, 15, 17, 333

Community, the individual in, 133, 202; the redemptive, 318ff.; the witnessing, 294ff.

Comte, Auguste, 140

Copernicus, 58

Covenant, as the root metaphor of the Christian mythos, 46f., 136, 228

Creation, continuity between Redemption and, 229, 281; the New, 180ff., 217, 230, 246, Ch. XI, 291f., 353f.

Cross, 50, 77, 262, 266, 287, 316

Culture, Christ and, 314-18; Christianity and Western, 44ff., 309-10; the Christian's participation in, 320ff.; Civilization and, 212f., 307f.; the meaning of, 212-14, 307f.

Curie, M. and Mme., 91, 117

Cyprian, 297

Dampier, W. C., 117, 188

Dante, 46

Darwin, Charles, 97, 98, Ch. IV, 145, 187f.

Davidson, Donald, 37

Democracy, Asian attitudes toward, 17-18; minority groups in a, 234

Depth, dimension of, 93f., 343; eschatology and the dimension of, 95f.

Descartes, René, 112, 118, 132, 142, 170, 174, 175, 192, 204

Devananden, Paul, 25

Dewey, John, 61, 105, 129, 174f., 289

Dibelius, Martin, 287

Dodd, C. H., 294

Donne, John, 231

Drummond, Henry, 115

Easton, B. S., 287

Eddington, Sir Arthur, 117, 150, 151

Edison, Thomas, 112

Edwards, Jonathan, 51

Einstein, Albert, 92, 105, 117, 145ff., 150f., 167, 188

Eliade, Mircea, 56-8, 61-3

Eliot, T. S., 46

Emergence, 123f., 126, 130, 134, 181, 258

Emerson, Ralph Waldo, 65

Emmet, Dorothy, 119, 289

Empiricism, 105, 120f., 152, 172, 181, 197, 199, 208ff.; radical, 177f.; rational, 158f., 203

Enlightenment, 134; secularism and the, 5-6, 43-4

Eschatology, 95f.; ethics and, 251f., 289

Ethics, eschatology and, 95-7, 251f., 289

Ethos, the Christian, 44ff.; a threat to the Christian, 86

Euclid, 93

Evil, 236, 242ff.; radical, 131; social, 35ff., 62f., 68f., 199-200

Evolution, Ch. IV; behavioral sciences and Darwinian, 187ff.; creative, 118f.

Existentialism, 51, 52, 71-3, 101f., 121, 175, 202ff., 256, 290

Experience, the meaning of, 208-12; revelation and, 348ff.; the structure of, 193-6; types of, 211

Faith, Biblical, 261f., 287ff., 336-9; the meaning of, 215-21; relativity of, Ch. V; universal, 332-6; the witness of, 350ff.

Fall, the, 87, 237

Faraday, Michael, 188

Ferre, Nels, 50, 53

Feuerbach, Ludwig, 122

Field theory, 133, 147

Fiske, John, 115

Forgiveness, 80; Christian doctrine of, 242ff., 246-7, 263; as a formative notion, 49f.; Luther's conception of, 271

Form-Criticism, 253f.
Freedom, 133; of God, 103, 107; in relationships, 206; two levels of, 237-9, 281
Freud, Sigmund, 122

Galileo, Galilei, 34, 58
Gandhi, 9, 37
Gauss, K. F., 93
Geometry, 147; Euclidean, 93; Riemannian, 93
Gibson, W. R. Boyce, 204
Gilkey, Charles W., 248, 250
God, 79f., 171; Christian doctrine of, 267f., 276ff.; creative act of, 215; freedom of, 103, 107, 353f.; man's life in, 206-7, 215, 221, 246; the meaning of, 265; revelation of, 180ff., 229; the righteousness of, 271
Goodness, the judgment of, 272; the meaning of, 275; power and, 274ff.
Grace, 80, 135, 181, 221, 247, 271; Gestalts of, 225, 300f., 318; under the judgment of, 301f.
Grant, F. C., 287, 294
Gregory the Great, 297

Harnack, Adolf von, 249, 251
Haroutunian, Joseph, 107
Harper, William Rainey, 249
Hartmann, Eduard von, 122
Hartshorne, Charles, 158, 189, 277f.
Hatfield, H. Stafford, 148
Hauck, Friedrich, 294
Hayward, John, 134
Hegel, George Wilhelm Friedrich, 83, 118, 121, 129, 143f., 174, 175, 205
Heidegger, Martin, 72, 203, 256
Heilsgeschichte, 138
Heim, Karl, 149f., 153
Heinemann, F. H., 72, 204
Heisenberg, Werner, 92
Herbart, Johann Friedrich, 122
Hildebrand, 297
Hinduism, 45, 66f., 218, 308, 311, 334; Christianity and, 27-9, 329;

liberalizing tendencies in, 11ff., 39f., 327; resurgence of, 13ff., 29f., 70
Hiroshima, 82, 91, 92
Historical method, 97ff.
History, conceptions of, 98-105
Hocking, William Ernest, 334f., 341
Höffding, Harold, 119
Humanism, 51, 52, 57, 61
Humanity, the nature of our, 358ff.
Hume, David, 189, 198
Hu Shih, 42
Husserl, Edmund, 203-5
Huxley, Julian, 61
Huxley, Thomas, 61

Idealism, 83, 96, 97, 105, 114f., 127ff., 135, 143f., 175, 197, 218, 290
Idolatry, in the Church, 296f.; in Judaism, 298; in religions, 355
Imagery, science and the changing, 85ff.; of thought, Ch. III
Imago-Dei, 136, 182, 207, 228, 243, 259
Immanence, 51; transcendence and, 276f.
Immanuel, Rajappan D., 22
India, Christianity in, 18-30; religious culture of, 29ff.; revival of native art of, 16; secularization in, 10ff.
Individualism, 132f., 200
Industry, cultural significance of, 35f.; secularizing force of, 36-8, 322f.
Infeld, Leopold, 148

James, William, 84, 94, 110, 118-22, 126, 174ff., 183, 188f., 198ff., 289, 348
Janus, 4, 75
Japan, 10; Westernization of, 43
Jaspers, Karl, 72, 203, 256
Jeans, J. H., 150
Jennings, H. S., 124
Jesus Christ, 14, 21-2, 23, 30, 48, 76, 107, 180-4, 225, 227, 228ff., 246, Ch. XI, XII, 290ff., 296, 304f., 307, Ch. XIV, 337f., 342, 353f., 357, 361